L. SARREL

STEPPING OUT

Nine Tours

Through

New York City's

Gay and Lesbian

Past

**DANIEL
HUREWITZ**

An Owl Book

Henry Holt and Company
New York

Henry Holt and Company, Inc.
Publishers since 1866
115 West 18th Street
New York, New York 10011

Henry Holt® is a registered
trademark of Henry Holt and Company, Inc.

Published in Canada by Fitzhenry & Whiteside Ltd.,
195 Allstate Parkway, Markham, Ontario L3R 4T8.

Library of Congress Cataloging-in-Publication Data
Hurewitz, Daniel.
Stepping out: nine tours through New York City's gay and lesbian
past / Daniel Hurewitz.—1st ed.
p.   cm.
Includes index.
1. Gay men—Travel—New York (State)—New York—Guidebooks.
2. Lesbians—Travel—New York (State)—New York—Guidebooks.   3. Gay
men—New York (State)—New York—History—Guidebooks.   4. Lesbians—
New York (State)—New York—History—Guidebooks.   5. Walking—New
York (State)—New York—Guidebooks.   I. Title.
HQ75.26.U6H87   1997   97-1533
306.76'6'09747—dc21   CIP

ISBN 0-8050-4158-3

Henry Holt books are available for special promotions and
premiums. For details contact: Director, Special Markets.

First Edition—1997

Designed by Kate Nichols

Printed in the United States of America
All first editions are printed on acid-free paper.∞

10   9   8   7   6   5   4   3   2   1

For the family

I grew up with

and

for the family I found

in the City

Mannahatta . . .
How fit a name for America's great democratic
    island city!
The word itself, how beautiful! how aboriginal!
how it seems to rise with tall spires, glistening in
    sunshine,
with such New World atmosphere, vista and action!

—WALT WHITMAN

Cherish this city
left you by default
include it in your daydreams.

—AUDRE LORDE

Contents

Acknowledgments

This book has been a long time coming, growing, stretching, and changing shape. As such, it has benefited from the insights and kindness of many of my friends and family, as well as several individuals with whom I had little prior relationship.

Crucial conversations with both Jeffrey Escoffier and Arthur Pinto helped me to imagine doing this work. Sarah Pettit saw that it found an early home at *Out* magazine. Mike Albo, Virginia Heffernan, Alixandra Horowitz, David Kirkpatrick, and L. Shea helped it appear as an eager photocopied pamphlet. Steve Ashkinazy, Paul Cadmus, Avram Finkelstein, Frank Kameny, Ann Northrop, Felice Picano, Rich Wandel, Randy Wicker, and Robert Woodworth all took time to talk with me personally as part of my research. Several librarians offered me patient guidance, especially in the Manuscripts Room of the New York Public Library; and the staff in that library generously allowed me desk space in the Wertheim Study. Liza Landsman, my agent, successfully discovered a publisher. And the staff at Holt—my editor Theresa Burns, her ever-affable assistant Amy Rosenthal, production coordinator Rita Quintas, and generously diligent copy editor Patrick Dillon—all turned the unimaginable possibility of a book into a reality.

Those closest to me made the kindest contributions. Jen and Mark helped in the muckiest of trenches. Stacia and Rebecca inspired with their models of artistry. My Los Angeles friends—JohnO, Laura, Mike, and Ali—buoyed my spirits. My mother, sister, and almost-sister-in-law shared their visual eyes, my brother and brother-in-law their technical aid, and my father his sage counsel and title ideas. Jeanne, often my first and best audience—certainly my best salesperson—encouraged and charmed me unfailingly. Doni held my hand, both in the streets and late at night. And Hermalinda soothed my soul.

They all sustained me long after the deadlines had passed, and they continue to do so. My thanks here is small measure of my abiding feelings.

Daniel Hurewitz
January 1997

Introduction

Stonewall, 1969.

Vito Russo was there. He was twenty-three, working at the Museum of Modern Art, studying film. That Friday night, after having spent much of the day attending Judy Garland's funeral, he was strolling home along Christopher Street. The crowd drew his attention and he walked over to Sheridan Square, climbed into a tree, and watched a movement's embers flash into flame.

Craig Rodwell, Edmund White, Christopher Cox, Sylvia Rivera, Jim Fouratt: they were all there, watching, fighting, changing.

Many of us have learned the Stonewall story—maybe even seen the movie—and transformed it into myth: the evil cops, the Mafia backers, the fearless patrons; the hurled parking meter, the torched garbage, the flying nightsticks; the can-can protesters, the solidarity, the chants—"Pigs!" "Legalize Gay Bars!" "Gay Power!"

For most of us, though, the story and the names are all new, unheard, unlearned, even though that struggle, nearly thirty years ago, made our lives today possible. And, what is more, just beyond the Stonewall story are hundreds of unknown stories—of dinner parties and bathhouses, dive bars and protest marches—each a link in the emergence and transformation of gay and lesbian living.

Gay history—gay culture—is a funny thing. There are no traditional institutions for passing along the lore of the lesbian and gay community: when you're a child, nobody tucks you in

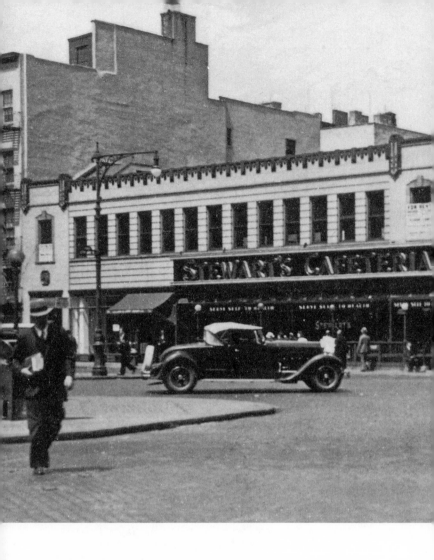

Sheridan Square in the 1930s, with Stewart's Cafeteria in the center and Christopher Street off to the left.

with bedtime stories about famous gay heroes ("*Please* can't I hear the one about **Oscar Wilde** just once more?"); nobody sends you off to gay Sunday school to learn the ancient language of camp ("Repeat after me: 'That's *Miss* Baruch Atah Adonai to you' "). Instead, we find our culture later in life, often on our own: a book or a film suddenly discovered offers up potential lives we had always dreamed of but never imagined possible. And history especially is powerful. It places our lives into a larger, longer story, a broader context. We see ourselves anew, see what is unique about our lives, and indeed, see what is one more step in an ongoing struggle.

New York remains one of the great treasures among the gay
family jewels. It has been the sometime stomping ground of
many an activist, playwright, and screen star, and it has been
one of those magic places where gay liberation has come into
ordinary people's lives. That's a central part of this city's past.
There is power and comfort in knowing that lesbians and gay
men have been forging community in this very city for centuries. And there is excitement in recognizing that it is that
legacy that we carry forward every day.

This book is overflowing with gay lore. But, mind you, this
isn't history the way you learned it in school. First of all, it's a
lot trashier: these *are* gay people we're talking about, and this
is New York. These are stories about whom **Greta Garbo**
squirreled herself away with at the Plaza; where nineteenth-

century drag queens strutted their stuff; how **Tennessee Williams** fared while cruising in Times Square.

What's more, these stories are intimately tied to specific places and locations. New York's buildings and sidewalks and alleyways have been the backdrops for countless crucial events and occasions. That's part of the city's vibrancy and drama. This book, whether you diligently walk each walk or kick back in the La-Z-Boy recliner and just read, will engage you in the very geography of the city.

My hope is that when you read this book, whether you're a visitor to New York or a resident, these stories will change the city for you. They'll remind you that at whatever street corner or stoop or storefront you find yourself, thousands of gay and lesbian people have been there before you—sweaty, impatient, excited, in love, what have you. And as you walk down the street, go to a rally, go to a bar, you walk, quite literally, in their footsteps.

I'm buoyed by that knowledge; I hope you will be too.

Here slept **Walt Whitman,** here drank **Audre Lorde,** here sang **Michael Callen,** and here am I. . . .

As for what lies ahead: nine neighborhood tours that cut across a wide swath of gay living. The tours are limited to Manhattan (I'm only human), but believe me—there's as much to say about every borough. That's the wonderful discovery when you pursue New York's gay past: gay life has touched literally every corner of this city.

The **West Village** tour starts you off at the Stonewall Inn, the mythic birthplace of Gay Liberation, and tracks the path of that revolution as it unfolded across the city, meeting up along the way with gay cultural icons like **James Baldwin, Berenice Abbott,** and **Djuna Barnes.** The **East Village** tour pursues, with earnestness, the path of contemporary bo-hunk living, tracing the lives of **Keith Haring, Janis Joplin,** and **Robert Mapplethorpe,** as well as introducing you to legendary scribes like **W. H. Auden, Walt Whitman,** and even **Oscar Wilde.** Nestled between the two, the **Washington Square** tour covers little physical distance, but takes you all the way from **Henry James** and **Willa Cather** to **Eleanor Roosevelt** and **Larry Kramer.**

For drama, the **Chelsea** tour travels the political cutting edge as well as the shadowy cruisy frontier of New York's gay past. And for true drama queens, the **Midtown** tour drags you—kicking and screaming, no doubt—from the tender clutches of Times Square hustlers and up into the bright lights and theaters of Broadway, mingling with Sir **Ian McKellen, Michael Bennett,** and **Liberace** as you go. Uptown, be it **Upper West** or **Upper East,** you'll dive into pure, unadulterated celebrity celebration, truly the Lives of the Homo Rich and Famous, from **Montgomery Clift, Truman Capote,** and **Greta Garbo** on the east side of the park to **James Dean, Isadora Duncan,** and **Rock Hudson** across town.

At the island's top, the **Harlem** tour explores a handful of years in the 1920s and '30s when much of the world moved to the words and music of gay men and women like **Langston Hughes, Bessie Smith,** and **Ma Rainey,** not to mention some fabulous drag queens. And finally, at the bottom of the island, in the **Battery,** you'll wander in the most distant past of the city, pursuing how we might stretch our notion of what gay history—and even a gay future—might be.

OK, for those of you just itching to step out, which I wholeheartedly and unabashedly urge that you do, let's cover a few practical items:

1. Each tour is loaded with gossip, trivia, mindless chatter, heartfelt sentiment, fascinating recollections—you name it. If you like, bring a friend or two along to banter. Better still, memorize the tour beforehand and then bring a date with you, just telling him or her the stories casually, as you go along: nothing's sexier than a smarty, right? Then again, if you rather go solo, be my guest: more chances for flirting, and, remember, I'll be there with you every step of the way.

2. The walks take roughly two to three hours, depending on how fast you go, how often you need to pull over for a rest stop, and whether you move your lips when you read. If you want something longer, you could easily combine the West Village and Chelsea. If you want something shorter, try Washington Square. Or for that matter, you could do practically all of the Battery while sitting on a bench looking out at the harbor.

3. All the walks come with maps, but should you get lost, remember this: anyone going topless, wearing very short shorts, or sporting a winning smile would be happy to get you back on track. Should that fail, however, begin loudly singing show tunes at the nearest street corner (anything from *Gypsy* will do). You will be promptly identified by the gay security patrol and escorted to your next destination.

4. Bring a snack (my grandmother always favored a homemade cheese sandwich), and don't forget that swell little water bottle you lug around at the gym.

5. Remember every so often to look up—way up—from that cute tush ahead of you. Life at street level always looks fairly contemporary (not to mention kind of sexy), but it's often in the details on buildings, their window patterns and roof shapes, that you'll discover their history.

6. Safety tip: Each of these neighborhoods is different. Some, like the West Village, feel busy all the time. Some, like the Battery or parts of Midtown, empty out at night. Additionally, New York, like most cities, is constantly changing, and usually it's happening one block at a time. So remember some old common sense: If you're going somewhere you've never been before, go in the daytime. (It's certainly easier to read when it's light out.) And if you don't feel safe somewhere, don't stay there.

7. Fashion tip: Wear sun block and comfortable shoes, but don't sacrifice style.

8. No pushing or shoving on the bus.

One last note for you: Everyone in here who I can safely say was a **member of the club, member of the church, on the bowling team, on the softball team, on the bus,** or in any way, you know, **happy,** as well as everyone that I, for one, consider a **gay icon,** I've put their names in **bold** type. Look for them. But don't be fooled: if I've left a name in plain type, that only means I've got nothing official to declare and I live in dread of lawsuits. You, however, may know better. (We can write the next edition together.)

So, what do you say we step on out? These boots were made for walking. . . .

The Dream Come to Life:
The West Village

Picture your dream: your home on the beach; your top-down, radio-blasting, high-speed convertible; your multi-terraced, sleekly decorated penthouse apartment; your minions of carefully attentive assistants and secretaries; your worshipful, massage-giving, ever-sexy lover; your quiet joy.

Somewhere in there, I bet you, be it a vacation spot or a local neighborhood, there is a place like the West Village: where the boyfriends walk, holding hands, down Christopher Street to the pier and the girlfriends make coy snuggled smiles at the Cubbyhole; where the tightest skirts are worn by the men and the toughest poses are struck by the women; where the rainbow flag flies at every newsstand and the sun seems to shine in every face.

Today, the West Village, and especially Christopher Street, is that dream come to life. Sometimes it is hidden, obscured by layers of commercialism or clouds of boozy beer busts. But beneath all that, the dream continues. The wonder of the West Village is that the dream has been present here for more than a century. Not always on Christopher Street—that happened only in the last thirty years. Before that, it lay elsewhere, tucked away in the neighborhood's hidden winding streets, or further east, out along Washington Square. But for decades it has been here somewhere.

Now, long ago, the Village *was* simply a village. The city proper lay way downtown, below Wall Street (the wall was what shut off the city mouse from the country mouse), and Greenwich Village was where you had your country home, where you

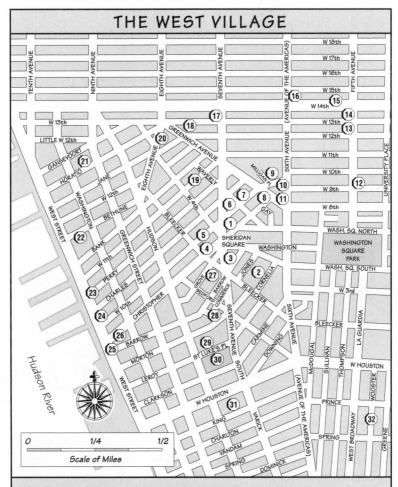

THE WEST VILLAGE

W 18th
W 17th
W 16th
W 15th
W 14th
W 13th
W 12th
W 11th
W 10th
W 9th
W 8th

TENTH AVENUE
NINTH AVENUE
EIGHTH AVENUE
SEVENTH AVENUE
(AVENUE OF THE AMERICAS)
SIXTH AVENUE
FIFTH AVENUE
UNIVERSITY PLACE

W 13th
LITTLE W 12th
GANSEVOORT
HORATIO
JANE
W 12th
BETHUNE
BANK
W 11th
PERRY
CHARLES
W 10th
CHRISTOPHER
BARROW
MORTON
LEROY
CLARKSON
W HOUSTON
KING
CHARLTON
VANDAM
SPRING
DOMINICK

WEST STREET
WASHINGTON
GREENWICH STREET
HUDSON
BLEECKER
8TH AVENUE
W 4TH
GREENWICH AVENUE
WAVERLY
MILLIGAN PL
GAY
GAY PL

SHERIDAN SQUARE
WASHINGTON
WASH. SQ. NORTH
WASHINGTON SQUARE PARK
WASH. SQ. SOUTH
W 3rd

JONES
CORNELIA
BLEECKER
GROVE
BEDFORD
COMMERCE
CARMINE
DOWNING
SIXTH AVENUE
BLEECKER
LA GUARDIA
ST LUKE'S PL
VARICK
SEVENTH AVENUE SOUTH
MACDOUGAL
SULLIVAN
THOMPSON
W HOUSTON
PRINCE
(AVENUE OF THE AMERICAS)
WEST BROADWAY
WOOSTER
GREENE
SPRING

Hudson River

0   1/4   1/2
Scale of Miles

Jeffrey L. Ward 1997

(1) The Stonewall Inn
(2) Caffe Cino
(3) Circle Repertory Company and the Duchess
(4) Lorraine Hansberry's Home
(5) The Snake Pit
(6) Julius'
(7) The Ninth Circle
(8) Greenwich Avenue
(9) Djuna Barnes's and Marlon Brando's Homes
(10) First Gay Pride Parade
(11) Women's House of Detention

(12) Mabel Dodge Luhan's Home and Salon
(13) Malcolm Forbes's Office (a.k.a. Forbes Magazine)
(14) National Gay Task Force
(15) The Little Review
(16) Gay Liberation Front
(17) Parents and Friends of Lesbians and Gays
(18) Lesbian and Gay Community Services Center
(19) Liberation House and the Gay Switchboard
(20) The Sea Colony
(21) James Baldwin's Home

(22) John Cage and Merce Cunningham's Studio
(23) Cruising Protests
(24) The Ramrod
(25) Keller's
(26) Christopher's End
(27) Hart Crane's Home
(28) The Cherry Lane Theatre and Berenice Abbott's Studio
(29) Paul Cadmus's Home
(30) James Walker Park
(31) Paradise Garage
(32) Gay Activists Alliance Firehouse

went to get out of town and escape your neighbors. Around the turn of the century, though, New York high society began heading uptown, and the Village was turned over to immigrants and artists; it became the denizen of poets and painters, a place where "color" seemed to ooze from every garret and cellar and second-story window. Amid the artistry came excitement, adventure, a spirit of unconventionality, and, of course, gay and lesbian living. There was an atmosphere that H. I. Brock and J. W. Golkin, a couple of struggling bohemians, said, "put the come-hither upon the souls of men and strained the women's corset strings to the breaking point." One painter was convinced that "when you made love then, you weren't just making love, you were striking a blow for freedom. Promiscuity wasn't promiscuity—it was something else, a kind of social and moral crusade."

In the roar of the 1910s and '20s, the Village bustled with speakeasies and tea shops. Some, like the Pirate's Den, marketed the "bohemian" life to tourists and wanna-bes; others, like the Flower Pot, primarily served gay men and women. Even in the 1930s there were places like the Bungalow, written up in the *New York Evening Graphic* under the headline "Greenwich Village Sin Dives Lay Traps for Innocent Girls." The Bungalow's patronage apparently consisted almost entirely "of lisping boys and deep-voiced girls. They eat, drink, and quarrel. They display their jealousies and occasionally claw at each other with their nails. They talk loudly, scream, jibe at each other and order gin continually. Always gin." Queens with taste—gotta like that!

After the Second World War, gay life came increasingly under attack, and hence more hidden. It also began to spread east, toward cheaper neighborhoods, but the West Village always remained ground zero. Here could be found friends, tucked-away bars, and of course, love. As Beebo Brinker, the seen-it-all, done-it-all lesbian, told newcomer Laura in **Ann Bannon**'s classic 1950s novel *I Am a Woman*, "That's all the Village is, honey, just one crazy little soap opera after another. . . . All tangled up with each other, one piled on top of the next, ad infinitum. Mary loves Jane loves Joan loves Jean loves Beebo loves Laura. . . . It goes on forever."

Then, in the wake of the Stonewall Uprising, the soap opera went public with a new wave of visibility and liberation. By the end of the 1960s, as *Gay* magazine would report, we were everywhere. Neither sleet nor snow nor driving rain kept gay men and women from their appointed rounds along Christopher and Grove Streets. The shops became gay shops; the sidewalks, gay highways. And the novelty of that and the extraordinary exuberance of public liberation never diminished for that generation. Activist and writer **Arnie Kantrowitz** believed that Christopher Street, with its endless parade of outfits, flirtations, and seductions, was more than just another city spot. "It's someplace very special," he wrote. "Once, seduced by its magic, I could have sworn that it was an enchanted road to paradise, paved with yellow brick. Now, from the windows of my apartment overlooking it, I can see it for what it is: the most honest street I have ever walked."

The scourge of AIDS has changed the face of Christopher Street, as it has all too much of the gay community. Indeed, there are certain faces painfully absent. For some younger generations, Chelsea and the East Village have become the new vital gay centers. But, as you'll see, the West Village remains as vibrant and busy as ever.

This tour steps off with the Stonewall Uprising, the event that redirected the path of gay living toward where we are today. It follows that joyful shock wave of liberation to the first Gay Pride Parade, to the founding of a whole generation of gay rights groups, and to sites of on-going protest and confrontation. You will truly walk the liberation trail. Along the way, though, you'll also stop off at **Julius',** one of the oldest gay bars in the city, you'll see the homes of **James Baldwin** and **Djuna Barnes,** as well as where **Edward Albee** got some inspiration and **Merce Cunningham** and **John Cage** crafted their collaborations.

To begin, hoof it, cab it, or train it (take the 1 or the 9 train) to Christopher Street and Sheridan Square. The Stonewall is just a few doors east of Seventh Avenue.

1. THE STONEWALL INN • 53 Christopher Street
between Seventh Avenue and Waverly Place

Welcome to the world of Legendary Landmarks. Yes, Paris may have the Eiffel Tower, and London, good old Big Ben.

But in New York, in *gay* New York, we have the Stonewall Inn. What is it that Maria sings when she has all the little Von Trapps gathered around her? Something about starting from the "very beginning." Well, dear ones, this is *it*.

The summer of 1969. The summer Earl Warren stepped down from the Supreme Court and Nixon announced troop withdrawals from Vietnam. The summer NASA put men on the moon and Ted Kennedy drove his car off a bridge in Chappaquiddick. The summer when concertgoers over-whelmed the tiny upstate New York town of Woodstock and students were preparing for a yearful of sit-ins on campuses like Kent State. And the summer of Stonewall.

If you were living in New York then, you were tuning in for summer reruns of *Bewitched* and *That Girl* or racing out to see Warhol's *Lonesome Cowboys* and Zeffirelli's *Romeo and Juliet.* You were reading *The Godfather* and Jacqueline Susann's *Love Machine* and listening to *Hair* and *Abbey Road.* If you were saving your pennies ($85 a week if you could type thirty words a minute), $2 at Madison Square Garden would get you Joan Baez tickets—$3.50 for James Brown. Or if you really held out, the new Sharp Mini Calculator, all 8½ pounds of it, could be yours for $775.

And if you were a gay man, at some point you went to the Stonewall: it was the most popular gay bar in the Village, one of a handful in the city to allow dancing. Opened in 1966, it never lost its undecorated charm. **Angelo D'Arcangelo,** one of the fabulous scribes of late-sixties gay life, said that there was a certain "hastiness" in the bar's appearance. "It seems to have only recently been converted from a garage into a cabaret; in about eight hours and at the cost of under fifty dollars." Everything, including the windows, was painted black. In the first room, there was a long bar and a large dance floor. The second room, smaller by far, offered less in the way of dancing and more cruisy standing around.

The whole show, apparently, was a Mafia operation, and run as a private club. Names and vital statistics were supposed to be kept in a box by the door. You had to announce yourself to get in, and on weekends pay a cover charge. The patrons, said Angelo, were mostly young and good-looking, and there were skinny go-go boys who, while nothing to drool over, were worth a gander, "especially if you're in the neighborhood."

Everything changed, however, on that much-remembered June night. Picture it as it happened: It's twenty minutes after one A.M. on the night of June 27, 1969, a Friday night, the night after **Judy Garland** was buried. Nine plainclothes policemen decide it's time to raid the Stonewall and close it, if only temporarily, for selling liquor without a license.

The police enter without warning. Quickly, the lights are brought up, and everyone except the bartender, the doorman, and three drag queens is sent out into the streets and told to go home. It's not an unusual raid for the Stonewall or any gay bar, and it's typical for patrons not to be detained. What is unusual is that the people in the street do not go home. A crowd of some four hundred gathers, watching the police complete their arrests. Angry, they begin throwing coins, bricks, and beer bottles. The police retreat back into the building while the crowd begins chanting "Pigs!" and "Faggot Cops!" Someone pulls up a parking meter and tries to ram the door, and one detective shouts out, "We'll shoot the first motherfucker that comes through!" Somebody tosses a trash can through the front window and someone else tries to set the trash on fire. Finally, police reinforcements arrive, the crowd is beaten away—one protester six times in the head—and disperses. The whole of it takes less than an hour.

But the next night, after a day of fervent rehashing, the crowd is back, a good thousand strong. The Stonewall has posted a sign on the door that reads, "This Is A Private Club. Members Only," and is serving soft drinks, but the crowd outside again begins chanting, throwing bottles, setting trash-can fires. The police arrive, and some of the protesters begin singing, to the tune of "It's Howdy Doody Time," "We are the Stonewall Girls,/We wear our hair in curls,/We have no underwear,/We show our pubic hair." One group of men forms a can-can chorus line, dancing down the street, but the cops charge at them with clubs. For two hours that night, the crowd fills the streets around the bar while the police, in flanks and rows, with their arms linked and wearing helmets, charge at them, sweeping back and forth, shoving and clubbing. Even the *New York Times* later reports that at least twice the police broke rank and simply charged the crowd.

And while things quiet down for a few nights, on the following Wednesday, the second of July, five hundred protesters return to march on Christopher Street. Those nights, according to one onlooker, Seventh Avenue "looked like a battlefield in Vietnam: young people, many of them queens, were lying on the sidewalk, bleeding from the head, face, mouth, and even the eyes. Others were nursing bruised and often bleeding arms, legs, backs and necks."

The original Stonewall, which operated in the space that includes the present Stonewall and the clothing store next door, didn't last long after that. It went quickly out of business. (In the 1980s a natural-wood craft shop and a bagel eatery stood here.) But this square became the new central space for New York gay life. Mind you, socially at least, gay life had roots here at least as far back as the 1920s and '30s when Stewart's Cafeteria and Life Cafeteria faced each other across the square and were established gay hangouts. Stewart's, which can be seen in the introduction, had big plate-glass windows and sometimes packed in crowds three and four deep. Artist **Paul Cadmus** remembers that you could get a full meal there for seventy-five cents and that there was room for "all the freaks in the neighborhood." One fellow from the Bronx remembered coming to the Life as a sixteen-year-old in 1939 because "faggots from all over the country would gather there. They'd just sit in the window, drinking coffee and smoking cigarettes and carrying on. . . . It attracted young people coming out, like me." And during the heyday of Stewart's, says Cadmus, people stood outside just to see who was there.

But gay political life now fixed itself here as well. The Mattachine Society—the primary gay rights organization from the 1950s—moved its offices here within a couple of years, just upstairs from what is now and was then the Lion's Head. (For some of the history of Mattachine, which had served as a primary agent for forming an organized gay community through the 1950s and '60s, see the Chelsea and Midtown tours.) When the first Gay Pride Parade gathered to march up Sixth Avenue in 1970, they stepped off here. When the gay community protested Anita Bryant's 1977 Save Our Children campaign, or tried to shut down the filming of *Cruising* two years later, or decided to stop traffic after the *Bowers* v. *Hardwick* Supreme Court decision in 1989, they met here first. (The George Segal sculptures in the tiny park behind you, themselves entitled *Gay Liberation*, serve to commemorate the significance of this place.) Most recently, in 1994, the city and the world came to the Stonewall to pay their respects, celebrating the twenty-fifth anniversary of the Stonewall Uprising.

Christopher Street, the Stonewall Inn, and Sheridan Square were burnished into the gay memory and the nation's memory as the place where gay pride lifted its head, its heart, and its fist and where all three will always remain raised. As Angelo wrote in 1970, "Let's not ever forget the resistance shown at the Stonewall incident. It was beautiful! *Aux barricades!* . . . Gentlemen, citizens, whenever the cops raid your place throw the motherfuckers out. Make it impossible for them to close you. Force them to bring tanks! Remember, there are not paddy-wagons enough, cells, courts, jails or handcuffs enough to imprison every homosexual as defined by law in Metropolitan New York. Remember, when you go where you please, you are using your god-given rights of free assembly. Or in other words, friends, let the city and the world know that Sheridan Square and its environs is free turf."

Pick up West 4th Street across the square and follow it east to Cornelia Street and make a right.

2. CAFFE CINO • 31 Cornelia Street
between Bleecker and West 4th Streets

Before the Stonewall Uprising, though, the roots of public gay culture were taking hold throughout the city. Although this space now houses a different restaurant, **Joe Cino**'s one-room coffeehouse opened here at the end of 1958 and quickly gave birth to what would become New York's gay and Off Off Broadway theater scenes. The names of the young playwrights (and actors) who discovered and debuted their talents here constitute a nearly complete roster of New York's finest gay playwrights of that generation. It began, perhaps, with **Doric Wilson** reading some scenes from **Oscar Wilde**'s *Salome;* but quickly **Lanford Wilson**'s work appeared, followed by that of **Robert Patrick, William Hoffman** (who later wrote *As Is*), **John Guare, Jean-Claude Van Itallie,** and **Tom Eyen** (who made a name for himself with the book for *Dreamgirls*). Not everyone who came into being here was gay, but there was little hiding, little pretense of being anything other than what you were. Cino himself encouraged gay playwrights to be more open, to "get real, Mary!"—and they did.

The place was strung with wind chimes and Christmas-tree lights. Bentwood chairs were set up around tiny tables. There was a jukebox on one side and magazine pages stuck up on the walls. And in the middle, a space was cleared for the performers. The shows came in all varieties, with professional actors presenting scenes from major plays they had toured in and others offering near-pornographic presentations of classic dramas. The only theatrical standard seemed to be keeping Cino happy, and as long as things didn't move too slowly he stayed happy (otherwise he rang a little bell). Doric Wilson insists that when he first came in to show Cino the script for a play he wanted to put on, Cino merely asked him his astrological sign, handed him a cappuccino, and gave him a show date.

Eventually the Warhol gang showed up here, and the drug scene. Speed became Cino's own playmate, and after his lover was electrocuted doing a lighting setup, his life spun out of control. In 1967, he deliberately cut himself up and, despite more than a hundred friends giving blood at the hospital, died; he was thirty-six. The cafe struggled into 1968 and then closed. But in its decade-long existence, it marked a transition point to a new kind of self-expression. It was the rebirth of small theater and pointed the way toward the kind of Off Off Broadway work that would appear at the Judson (in Washington Square) and La Mama (in the East Village). What's more, it marked the return of public, open gay living.

Make a right on Bleecker at the end of the block, head back to Seventh Avenue and up again to Sheridan Square.

3. CIRCLE REPERTORY COMPANY and THE DUCHESS
- **99 Seventh Avenue South**
between Bleecker and Christopher Streets

The Caffe Cino spirit quickly emerged elsewhere. In 1967, **Charles Ludlam** founded his Ridiculous Theatrical Company and began presenting his very gay high-drama high-camp spoofs. In 1969, our own **Lanford Wilson,** among others, founded the **Circle Repertory Company,** which, by 1974, had made a theater for itself here, where the Garage Restaurant now operates. The theater company produced Wilson's *Hot l Baltimore, Fifth of July,* and *Talley's Folly,* which won the Pulitzer Prize. In March 1985, Cino graduate **William Hoffman**'s play about living with AIDS, *As Is,* opened here.

Hoffman recently recalled standing in the back of the theater during an early performance of *As Is* and noticing a middle-aged man and woman fighting about the play. Once Rich, one of the central characters, revealed to his ex-lover that he was HIV-positive, the man said to the woman, "I told you they were fairies. Let's get the hell out of here." The woman, presumably his wife, replied, "I'm not going nowhere. We spent fifty bucks for these seats. I don't care if they're cannibals." When the current lover discovered a lesion on Rich's back, the husband walked out, but the woman remained.

Hoffman, meanwhile, got caught up in the performance and forgot about the couple until the end of the play. Then, just as the lover was about to climb into Rich's bed in the hospital, Hoffman noticed that there, to his left, stood the husband, his eyes riveted to the stage, tears streaming down his face. After the show, Hoffman saw them once more in the lobby as the husband told his wife, "That's the last time I'll let you drag me to one of these. What's wrong with musicals?"

It's simple enough to imagine an ever-expanding wave of liberation, from Caffe Cino to the founding of Circle Rep and the Stonewall Uprising that same year across the Square and on into the present. And how nice to believe that after Stonewall, gay bars had it easy, at least officially. The history of the **Duchess,** a lesbian bar that was one of the principal women's clubs in the city through much of the 1970s and into the 1980s, is a reminder of how false that impression is. The Duchess operated next to the theater in the corner spot where Nuts and Bolts now is, and during its heyday, it was described as a "relaxed" place with a small dance floor and a jukebox, the kind of place where "you'll catch women arguing feminist politics." But in the early 1980s it came under frequent attack by the state's licensing office. Their license was first revoked in 1980 when two men, after goading the bartender with "Come on, girlie, give us a drink," were refused service. The liquor authority charged the management with running a "clip joint" and shut them down. (The men, it turned out, were inspectors from the liquor office.) Two years later, the bar was raided, all the liquor was confiscated, and the bartender and manager were arrested for operating illegally. A two-year court case changed nothing. And while the officials insisted they were acting justly, the bar owners maintained that the attacks were merely discrimination. The bar closed, reopened, then closed again and did not return.

Follow Grove across Seventh Avenue passing the legendary piano bar Marie's Crisis on your right, and turn right on Bleecker Street.

4. LORRAINE HANSBERRY'S HOME • 337 Bleecker Street
between Christopher and West 10th Streets

Lorraine Hansberry lived only thirty-four years, but in that time she seared her words and vision onto the American conscience. Born in Chicago in 1930, she learned determination at the knee of her father: an active member of the NAACP, Hansberry's dad fought all the way to the Supreme Court for the right to move his family into a white, restricted neighborhood—and finally won. Hansberry struggled as a writer in her twenties, writing for Paul Robeson's *Freedom* magazine but also working as a cashier, typist, and clothing labeler to make ends meet. Finally, in 1959, just as Caffe Cino was taking off, her first produced play, *A Raisin in the Sun*, appeared on Broadway. It was the first play by a black woman ever to be produced on Broadway and the first play directed by a black director in over fifty years. And it was embraced as a powerful and harrowing portrait of a black family trapped between the American dream of success and the reality of black suffering. The praises and accolades she received included the New York Drama Critics Circle Award, which she won over established writers like **Tennessee Williams,** Eugene O'Neill, and Archibald MacLeish.

James Baldwin, who became drinking and politicking friends with Hansberry, remembered being with her on the opening night of *Raisin*. Suddenly, out in the alley behind the theater, she was mobbed by autograph seekers. She handed Baldwin her purse and started signing, telling him, "It only happens once." "I watched the people," Baldwin wrote after her death, "who loved Lorraine for what she had brought to them; and watched Lorraine, who loved the people for what they brought to *her*. It was not, for her, a matter of being adored. She was being corroborated and confirmed . . . [as] a witness."

Hansberry married songwriter and music publisher Robert Nemiroff, but they were divorced before she died, and she spent much of her time here alone. She is known to have had lesbian loves, and in 1957 she wrote to *The Ladder*, the newsletter for the lesbian rights organization Daughters of Bilitis. "I'm glad as heck that you exist," she said. "You are obviously serious people and I feel that women, without wishing to foster any strict separatist notions, homo or hetero, indeed have a need for their own publications and organizations." In a later letter, Hansberry drew a connection between homophobia and misogyny and endorsed the possibility that "there may be women to emerge who will be able to formulate a new and possible concept that homosexual persecution and condemnation has at its roots not only social ignorance, but a philosophically active anti-feminist dogma." Those very connections were indeed explored—and struggled over—by women in the 1970s. Sadly, Hansberry did not live to see that struggle; she died of cancer in 1965. (See the Midtown tour for more about the Daughters of Bilitis.)

Follow Bleecker Street up to West 10th Street and make a right.

5. THE SNAKE PIT • 211 West 10th Street
between Bleecker and West 4th Streets

The police raid of an after-hours bar called the **Snake Pit** in this now bricked-up tenement basement early one morning in March 1970 galvanized many gay people left uninspired by the Stonewall Uprising, more than eight months earlier. The previous night, the police had arrested the management of two gay clubs, the Zodiac and 17 Barrow Street. But this night, not only were the bar employees arrested, all 167 customers were hauled in by the cops. The police claimed that they just had too hard a time separating workers from patrons.

One of the arrested patrons, though, a twenty-three-year-old Argentinean national named **Diego Vinales,** panicked at the prospect of deportation. Once at the station house, Vinales tried to escape by jumping from a second-floor station window. He landed on six prongs of a wrought-iron spiked fence. The fence was cut, and together, Vinales and the fence were taken to St. Vincent's Hospital, where activists immediately began a candlelight vigil.

Vinales survived, but the stakes of unchecked police harassment were clearly raised. One of the leaflets circulated described how Vinales "either fell or jumped out the precinct window, landed and was *impaled* on a metal fence! Any way you look at it, that boy was PUSHED! We are all being pushed!" Eventually, five hundred protesters marched against the police action.

But so many months after Stonewall, the gay community was increasingly divided over how liberation should proceed. Leaders of the 1950s-era Mattachine Society were unconvinced that the police raids were wrong. **Dick Leitsch,** one of Mattachine's influential young leaders, pointed out that since the closing of the Stonewall that building remained empty, largely because it was too rife with safety hazards and structural faults for anyone to try a new business there. "Yet, we were crowded in there every night, risking god-knows-what disasters." Asked Leitsch, "Were the police harassing homosexuals when they put the Stonewall out of business, or were they doing us a favor?" Meanwhile, the newer activist groups, the Gay Liberation Front and the freshly founded Gay Activists Alliance (both of whom you'll hear much more about), squared off over whether to trust the police at all. On the night of the arrests, GLFers gathered with the slightly more conservative GAAers outside the station. While GAA president **Jim Owles** tried to set up a discussion with the police, a GLFer angrily shouted out, "Don't talk to the pigs! We don't talk to the pigs!" (A GAAer cheerily shot back, "Shut up, you leftist dildo!") And while both GLF and GAA eventually agreed to organize a march together, the Mattachine Society refused to do even that.

Follow 10th Street across Seventh Avenue.

6. JULIUS' • 159 West 10th Street
at Waverly Place

One of the longest-running bars of any kind in the Village, **Julius'** dates back well before the gay liberation struggles, even back to before Prohibition, during which time it operated as a speakeasy with a peephole in the door and booze hidden behind sliding panels. Fats Waller even gave an impromptu concert or two here. (Check out the side door: the peephole is still there.) As the century wore on, Julius' became increasingly, if not exclusively, gay, although for a time gay men were let in only through the side door and only if they appeared butch enough. Nevertheless, the place became a favorite of folks like **Tennessee Williams, Truman Capote,** and **Rudolf Nureyev.** According to **Doric Wilson,** this was also the place where playwright **Edward Albee** met a young man who inspired his writing of *Who's Afraid of Virginia Woolf?* The fellow, according to Wilson, was an archaeologist who was married to the daughter of a college president.

In 1966, a few years before the Stonewall Uprising, the Mattachine Society used Julius' as a test site to challenge the state law that prohibited bars and restaurants from selling drinks to homosexuals. Dubbing their action a "sip-in," three gay men (**Dick Leitsch,** future Mattachine leader; **Craig Rodwell,** future founder of the Oscar Wilde Memorial Bookshop; and **John Timmons**) gathered up a group of reporters and moved from Village bar to Village bar, looking to be denied a drink, and eventually ended up here, at Julius'. When they formally told the bartender that they were gay, he told them that he could not, by law, serve them. Over the course of the next year, that much-publicized denial, accompanied by a whirl of gay-positive editorials, led to the state law being overturned. In the future, a bar's license could be revoked only if there was "substantial evidence" of indecent behavior—which did not include same-sex kissing or even touching. And a couple of years later, the bar was used as a setting for the movie of *The Boys in the Band.*

P.S. The bookstore across the street at 154 West 10th, **Three Lives** (as in the **Gertrude Stein** book) was, twenty-odd years back, Djuna Books (as in **Djuna Barnes,** whom you'll encounter soon enough) and specialized in women's

Julius' bar today.

books, records, T-shirts, you name it—even nonsexist children's books. It's still pretty hip.

Head up the street a bit.

7. THE NINTH CIRCLE • 139 West 10th Street
between Waverly Place and Greenwich Avenue

Here, where Caffe Torino now does business, the very gay **Ninth Circle** held sway for several decades, even up until the middle of this one. Part bar and for a time part steak house, the place was also several parts inspiration. Indeed, back in the 1960s, sometime shortly before or after meeting the young archaeologist down the street, **Edward Albee** stumbled upon the title for his masterwork—*Who's Afraid . . .* —here: he says he saw the phrase scrawled on a bathroom mirror. (Who says there's nothing to be gained from tearoom trade?)

Albee had been encouraged to be a playwright by the closeted **Thornton Wilder** (author of the ubiquitously produced *Our Town*, among many other things), and he appeared on the New York scene with a bang in 1960, just as Caffe Cino was coming to life. **Tennessee Williams** had had a couple of very successful one-acts and revivals performed Off Broadway, and Albee's star rose there quickly. That year, the Off Broadway production of Albee's *Zoo Story* won a handful of awards, while two years later when *Who's Afraid . . .* appeared on Broadway proper, it garnered five Tonys. Those rapid successes helped legitimize the notion that real theater could be found as much away from Times Square as in it. Albee's success joined him in people's minds with Williams and **William Inge.** Along with Arthur Miller, the three were considered the greatest American playwrights of the time, and people began talking—and worrying—about the new gay content and subtext of American theater. (For more on Inge and Williams, see the Upper West and Upper East Side tours, respectively.)

Albee has never been viewed, though, as a creator of particularly gay characters. He told the *Advocate* in 1989 that while the presence of gay characters in his plays has often been overlooked, "I have very complex feelings about whether a gay playwright must write about gay subjects on the theory that he or she is incapable of comprehending heterosexual responses to life. I don't think that's true." He added, though, that he'd been in a relationship for twenty years, "which has made me very happy. I've always been given to long relationships."

* *For a scenic circle, head back to Waverly, turn left, then left again on Christopher. As you walk toward Greenwich Avenue, keep your eyes open. The corner of Christopher and Gay (nice location) was where the 1920s tea shop known as the Flower Pot catered exclusively to gay men and women. At the same intersection, 15 Christopher, you'll pass the second (and ongoing) location of the Oscar Wilde Memorial Bookshop. It originally opened on Mercer Street in 1967, as the first gay bookstore in the country; owner **Craig Rodwell** moved it here in 1973. (You'll learn more about both Rodwell and the store in the East Village tour.)*

8. GREENWICH AVENUE
at Christopher Street

Gay life has moved its slinky self all across the face of this city, shifting year by year, block by block. As you pause here, it's worth pointing out that in the 1960s, before Christopher Street blossomed into full gay flower, this stretch of Greenwich Avenue, running a few blocks to your left up to Seventh

Avenue, was what one writer called "the cruisiest street in the Village." There was a late-night lesbian bar and a very gay restaurant called Mama's Chicken Rib. Mama's, according to novelist **Felice Picano,** was much frequented by "slender, no-longer-young men with peroxided hair who flaunted their Broadway dancer legs in tights and Capezio shoes" and flitted about in pastel mohair sweaters. What's more, "they all seemed to possess a genetic inability to recognize the male pronoun or to address anyone except as Mary—or at odd times, Virginia." Until the Stonewall Uprising, anything much farther west of here was what Picano called "homosexual no-man's-land."

Cross Greenwich Avenue and walk around the garden to pick up 10th Street.

9. DJUNA BARNES'S and MARLON BRANDO'S HOMES
- **Patchin Place**
  a gated cul-de-sac on 10th Street between Greenwich and Sixth Avenues

The Greta Garbo of gay literature (author most famously of *Nightwood*), **Djuna Barnes** was living a rather reclusive life in a one-and-a-half-room apartment at 5 Patchin Place the summer of the Stonewall Uprising. Actually, she'd lived here since 1940, having moved back to New York from Paris, where she had been part of the 1920s Lesbians Abroad set—with **Janet Flanner, Gertrude Stein, Alice B. Toklas, H. D.,** and **Sylvia Beach.** (Those of you intrigued by that whole Parisian scene—and who among us isn't just a little bit?—will be eager to know that Flanner once described the regular salons that **Natalie Barney** held as a dance of "introductions, conversations, tea, excellent cucumber sandwiches, divine little cakes Berthe baked, and then the result: a new rendezvous among ladies who had taken a fancy to each other or wished to see each other again." The guests might include Stein, Beach, **Radclyffe Hall, Marguerite Yourcenar, Edna St. Vincent Millay,** and **Vita Sackville-West.)**

Born in 1892, Barnes had written as a reporter for New York City newspapers and had stories published in many local

Djuna Barnes's retreat on secluded Patchin Place.

magazines. One of her delightful fictional works, *Ladies Almanack*, was privately published in France in 1928. Half mock farmer's almanac, half novel, it claimed to show women's "Signs and their Tides; their Moons and their Changes." Each month's chapter updated the travails of Evangeline Musset and her friends but also offered a new take on womanhood. The February chapter, for instance, offered a love letter ("My Love she is an Old Girl, out of Fashion, Bugles at the Bosom,

and theredown a much Thumbed Mystery and a Maze").
March posited a debate about women loving women, and so
forth. In a typically charming exchange, two friends of Evangeline's—Lady Buck-and-Balk and Tilly Tweed-in-Blood—
are sitting around despairing of the need for men. When
milady wishes that men could simply be eliminated, Tilly
sighs: "It cannot be. We need them for carrying of Coals, lift-
ing of Beams, and things of one kind or another." Just at that
moment, Patience Scalpel, another friend, comes bounding in
and, "divesting herself of her furs," asks if there is a man there.
" 'Most certainly not!' cried Lady Buck-and-Balk in one
Breath with Tilly Tweed-in-Blood, as if a large Mouse had run
over their Shins, 'What a thing to say!' "

Barnes lived on Patchin Place until her death in 1981, but
she was so rarely seen that her neighbor for many years at
number 4, the poet e. e. cummings, used to call up from the
street to ask if she was dead yet.

By the way, in 1943 and 1944, sister and brother Frances and
Marlon Brando lived on Patchin Place as well. Brando was
studying acting a few doors away at the New School, where
Tennessee Williams had taken a writing class, and where a
classmate was Brando's future friend **James Baldwin.** Brando
never made a secret of his own occasional homosexual inclina-
tions, and Baldwin later said of him, "I had never met any white
man like Marlon. He was obviously immensely talented—a
real creative force—and totally unconventional and independent, a beautiful cat. Race truly meant nothing to him. . . . He
was contemptuous of anyone who discriminated in any way.
Very attractive to both women and men, he gave me the feeling that reports I was ugly had been much exaggerated."

Follow 10th Street out to Sixth Avenue and make a right.

10. GAY PRIDE PARADE
- **Sixth Avenue at Greenwich Avenue and 9th Street**

On June 28, 1970, carrying signs like "We Are the Dykes Your
Mother Warned You About" and "Free Oscar Wilde," thou-
sands of gay men and lesbians gathered just off Sixth Avenue at
Washington Place, just below where you are now, and prepared

Marchers along Sixth Avenue in New York's first Gay Pride Parade, June 28, 1970.

to march up the avenue. It was one year after the Stonewall Uprising, and marshals from the committee for Christopher Street Liberation Day (that was the name before they discovered "Gay Pride Day" was easier) were wearing orange armbands and handing out fliers that said, "Welcome to the

first-anniversary celebration of the Gay Liberation movement. We are united today to affirm our pride, our life-style, and our commitment to each other. . . . For the first time in history we are together as The Homosexual Community." After a week of workshops on subjects like gays and the law, and a dance at NYU, it was time for the first Gay Pride Parade in New York.

And then they were off. Restricted to the left lane, with traffic hurrying along beside them, they marched uptown all the way to Central Park. They carried their signs—"Hi, Mom!" said one, and "Me Too," said a dachshund's—and chanted—"Out of the closets, into the streets!" and "Two, four, six, eight! Gay is just as good as straight!"—and had their pictures taken, and streamers thrown at them, and occasionally they called out to the many onlookers, "Come on in, the water's fine!"

The number of marchers grew to five thousand and the parade itself stretched twenty blocks long. Shoppers stared at them from the 26th Street flea market, and students waved from a ballet school. In front of Radio City, the men imitated the Rockettes; and a few blocks later, a fellow dressed in a tulle gown, golden crown, and wand appeared at the head of the parade, looking like Glinda, the Good Witch of the North.

Activist and author **Peter Fisher** later wrote about the feeling of that first parade. "I reeled in the glory of it, walked as I had never walked before, soared. I looked up at the walls of glass and stone, at the tiny faces looking down, and laughed and shouted: *I'm gay and I'm proud.* I hadn't shouted since I was a child. . . . The years of hiding and hating myself and putting up with things and hurting and lying and wanting to scream ripped through me and exploded.

"There's no going back after that."

The parade ended with a Gay-In at Sheep Meadow in Central Park where, before settling in for some serious relaxation, the marchers turned and applauded those who followed them. Among the various events taking place in the meadow that day, there were two male couples trying to break the straight record (eight and a half hours) for the longest kiss. One couple, **Cary Yurman** and **Tava Von Will,** had started at 7:45 A.M., and *Gay* magazine kept track of any changes in how Cary felt about Tava's mustache and how Tava felt about Cary's five-o'clock shadow. Cary and Tava made it to nine hours, but when they broke to cheers, applause, ice cream, and cold cream, Cary said he could "hear in the back of my mind just what my mother will say when I tell her. 'So big deal. You're a world's kissing champion. Get a job.' "

But another marcher recalled being in the park at the completion of that first parade: "Wave on wave of gay brothers and sisters, multi-bannered, of all sizes and descriptions were advancing into the meadow, and a spontaneous applause seized the early marchers. . . . For all of us who have been slowly climbing for years toward our freedom, this one last hill which let us look across our dear brothers and sisters was a cup running over. It was as if . . . now at last we had come to the clearing, on the way to the top of the mountain . . . and tho' we knew we still had far to go, we were moving, and knew it."

An idea of how far we've come since then: For the twenty-fifth-anniversary parade in 1994, marchers came from as far away as Taiwan, Russia, and Colombia. Police estimated there were one hundred thousand marchers. Organizers thought more: 1.1 million people.

P.S. Just around the corner here, at 62 West 9th Street, there used to be a club called the Lion. In the summer of 1960, at a Thursday-night talent show (Win a week of dinners and performing!) eighteen-year-old **Barbra Streisand** knocked 'em flat with a rendition of "A Sleeping Bee," and started her career. "In those days," she later said, "I could be had for a baked potato." These days, it seems, you have to know the President.

Study the brick castle you have been circling.

11. WOMEN'S HOUSE OF DETENTION
   at Greenwich and Sixth Avenues

Before leaving this spot, there is more profound outrage to recall. While the stunning structure of the Jefferson Market building now holds a public library, from 1876 until 1945 it housed a courthouse beneath its spires. And from roughly 1929 until 1971, the adjoining plot of land, now a public garden, was the site of the **Women's House of Detention,** or women's prison. Inevitably, in the legally repressive 1950s and 1960s, the prison was a place where many lesbians spent several nights, even years, of their lives. And the streets outside frequently became sites of tragic Romeo-and-Juliet-like balcony scenes as women called up to their lovers in prison.

One night in that same summer of the first Gay Pride Parade, after ongoing police crackdowns in the Village and Times Square, the Gay Liberation Front, the Gay Activists Alliance, and the Radicalesbians organized a march up to 42nd

Street. After hiking back to the Village, they discovered that a Sheridan Square club called the Haven had just been raided, and that the police, while allegedly looking for drugs and liquor, had torn out phones, wrecked couches, and smashed the bar itself, inflicting some $20,000 in damage. (The Haven, mind you, had always been a liquor-free club.)

Several of the activists had already marched here to the prison to continue their protests, but an atmosphere of outrage erupted along Christopher Street and cascaded even through the walls of the prison, where a riot began. By midnight, burning material was visible in the prison windows. The police decided to clear the streets, driving everyone back to 8th Street, but there was little discipline in their technique. A black man was beaten, and a police officer apparently hurled a bottle from a rooftop. Suddenly, people started throwing bottles back. The police attacked another man, and two gay men tried to return the assault. Pandemonium ensued, and the activists lost control. People ran along the street, breaking windows. They stole jewelry and looted a record store. Even cars were overturned.

In three hours of rioting, ten people were arrested, and six police officers and two gay men were seriously injured. Meanwhile, a call-and-response began to echo from street to prison. "Power to the sisters!" was shouted up, and "Power to the gay people!" came screaming back down. Within a year, the prison was closed and the building demolished.

Follow 9th Street east to Fifth Avenue.

12. MABEL DODGE LUHAN'S HOME AND SALON
- **23 Fifth Avenue**
  between 9th and 10th Streets

The drama of **Mabel Dodge Luhan** lay not in protests but in living large. Hailing from Buffalo, New York, via Florence, Italy, Luhan arrived in New York City late in 1912. She was thirty-four years old, had just left her second husband (he's the one who left her a Dodge), and had yet to encounter husbands three and four. But she quickly made herself and her home here, on the second floor, centerpieces of New York life.

Determined to construct her life around art and politics (as well as love and astrology), Mabel recast her apartment as a salon. She bathed the place in white—paint, curtains, chandeliers—and then added dabs of color, with pale-blue sofas and chairs and turquoise paintings. She began to host weekly parties. Wearing a white gown and remaining largely silent, she would greet her guests with an extended hand and a small smile. But each week she invited a new "specialist" to offer his or her views to her guests. The speakers ranged from anarchist **Emma Goldman** and birth-control advocate Margaret Sanger to A. A. Brill, Freud's English translator, who singlehandedly brought psychoanalysis to the United States and wrote essays such as "The Conception of Homosexuality."

Mabel also cultivated great friendships with writer **Gertrude Stein** and critic and fellow saloniste **Carl Van Vechten,** and she had love affairs with John Reed (of *Ten Days That Shook the World* fame—Warren Beatty in the movie *Reds*) and **Violet Shillito.** Dodge was the driving force behind the much-ballyhooed 1913 Armory Show of post-Impressionist art, and it was she who enticed D. H. Lawrence and **Georgia O'Keeffe** to make their ways out to Taos, New Mexico, where she was patron to the artists' colony.

Max Eastman described her once in a poem as "buxom, comely, muscular, / With nerve, and laughter, and a hearty heat / About her, and a way of leaping through / Where other folks sit bold and talk of going." Among Mabel's boldest actions was to detail, in her 1939 four-volume autobiography, *Intimate Memories,* her same-sex attractions, be they her childhood fascination with the housekeeper's breasts or her adolescent gropings with the girl across the street ("When I remember Margaret, everything about her is forgotten except—and they are so vivid still—her two white flowery breasts with their young pointed nipples leaning towards me"). And pages are devoted to her unstinting love of Shillito, who, like Mabel, had studied as a teenager at a private girls' school in New York. They met later in Paris, and Mabel found her one of those rare "marvelous human beings" possessing an "efflorescent soul." One night, they lay down together, and Mabel reached out to touch her friend. Instantly, "there arose all about us, it seemed, a high, sweet singing. This response we made to each other at the contact of our flesh ran from hand and breast along the shining passages of our blood until in every cell we felt each other's presence. This was to awaken from sleep and sing like morning stars." Mabel married four men in her life, but not one, she wrote, approached the profundity of Violet.

Follow Fifth Avenue uptown three blocks.

13. MALCOLM FORBES'S OFFICE (a.k.a. *FORBES* MAGAZINE)
 * **60–62 Fifth Avenue**
    between 12th and 13th Streets

Born in Brooklyn in 1919, **Malcolm Forbes** was another large-liver. Young Malcolm fought in the Second World War, and earned both a Purple Heart and a Bronze Star. After the war, he joined the staff of his father's magazine—Bertie Forbes had founded *Forbes* in 1917—but then went off to test out the political waters: he served as a New Jersey state senator for much of the 1950s but failed in a bid for governor and threw in the towel.

Instead he became editor-in-chief and publisher of the magazine, and in the 1960s focused his energies on diversifying the family company. He had become a bit of a collector as a young man, when he purchased first a note by Abraham Lincoln and, then, later on, the glasses Lincoln had worn on the night of his assassination. Now, though, he started buying up Fabergé art pieces that had been made for the Russian czars, especially those delicate eggs. (Some of the goodies are usually on display in the building lobby if you want to poke around.) Additionally, he made a division of the company a motorcycle dealership. Malcolm's life began to blossom. At forty-eight he took up biking. At fifty-two he started hot-air ballooning (this became a company division also) and in 1973 he became the first person to travel coast to coast in one hot-air balloon.

It is said that he attracted advertisers with lavish entertainment on the company yacht or at the townhouse around the corner at 11 West 12th Street, where a chef remained in residence. It is also said that Malcolm often asked new male employees to dine at the townhouse, an invitation that might include viewing his gay erotic art collection, followed by a visit to the sauna and who knows what else. Himself, he seemed to have a bit of humor about it all, once writing that he got where he is "through sheer ability (spelled i-n-h-e-r-i-t-a-n-c-e)." The homosexual side of Malcolm's private life was made public just after his death by *OutWeek* magazine, which began the ongoing debate over gay publications "outing" famous but closeted gay men and women.

Keep heading uptown.

14. NATIONAL GAY TASK FORCE
 • **80 Fifth Avenue, fifth floor**
  at 14th Street

The founding of the NGTF in 1973 marked the beginning of a new direction in gay liberation, one that has succeeded even to this day. No longer would gay activists simply stand outside the walls of power shouting, as they did in the Gay Liberation Front or the Gay Activists Alliance; now they would attempt to work within the system. The founders ranged from activist to insider, from **Bruce Voeller,** who had been a leader in the GAA, to **Howard Brown,** the first-ever New York City Health Services administrator. (Brown had resigned the post and come out publicly shortly before starting NGTF, an action that garnered him headlines in all the major papers, including the *New York Times.*) In between were folks like journalist **Arthur Bell,** historian **Martin Duberman**, Daughters of Bilitis leader **Barbara Gittings,** and Mattachine lightning rod **Frank Kameny.** These were indeed the cream of the diverse crop of the gay community that had come forward since Stonewall.

The goal of the organization was to "focus on broad national issues" and "to bring gay liberation into the mainstream of the American civil rights movement." To that end, the NGTF worked to help draft local gay rights bills across the country, repeal sodomy laws, and encourage greater gay visibility. In 1974, they fought successfully to get the American Psychiatric Association to stop defining homosexuality as an illness. The following year, they lobbied for a gay rights bill to be introduced in Congress (which Ed Koch and Bella

Abzug did). And in 1977, when Anita Bryant was about to kick off her Save Our Children campaign, they arranged a meeting at the White House with top Carter staff. At one point, NGTF representatives even flew out to L.A. to consult with Hollywood moguls on portraying gays and lesbians in the movies. In 1986, NGTF moved to Washington D.C., where it remains today as the National Gay and Lesbian Task Force.

Cross 14th Street and head left.

15. THE LITTLE REVIEW • 31 West 14th Street
between Fifth and Sixth Avenues

In certain circles (all right, I'll say it: literary ones) the *Little Review* is famous for being the place where James Joyce's *Ulysses* was first published, in installments from 1918 to 1920. What is less discussed is that the inventive and energetic editor, **Margaret Anderson** (who had camped out on the shores of Lake Michigan when she had no home, lived with only a piano when she had no furniture, and continued the *Little Review* when she had no money), and the assistant editor, **Jane Heap,** were lovers. (If you feel like poking around, they lived at 24 West 16th Street, in an apartment they decorated with gold Chinese paper and "a large divan hung from the ceiling by heavy black chains.")

The magazine was founded in 1914 in Chicago, inspired, according to Anderson's autobiography, by a sleepless night. She wrote that she had been depressed all day but awoke in the middle of the night to realize that it was the dearth of inspiring activity that had made her so unhappy. "The only way to guarantee" an engaging life, she wrote, was "to have inspired conversation every moment." But since people's time and energy for cultivating conversation were limited, Anderson decided that "if I had a magazine I could spend my time filling it up with the best conversation the world has to offer." This, she determined, was a "marvelous idea—salvation . . . decision to do it. Deep sleep."

After starting out in Chicago, Heap and Anderson moved to New York in 1917 and, out of a two-room basement office here, they brought the *Review* to life. (They also sold books out of the office to help make ends meet.) Together, Anderson and Heap published not only Joyce's work but that of **Hart Crane, Djuna Barnes, Sherwood Anderson,** various Dadaists, and many others. When Upton Sinclair wrote Anderson, "Please cease sending me the *Little Review*. I no longer understand anything in it, so it no longer interests me," she replied, "Please cease sending me your Socialist paper. I understand everything in it, therefore it no longer interests me."

One note: During the publication of *Ulysses*, which ran for three years in the monthly magazine, the *Review* editors were constantly under attack by the Society for the Suppression of Vice. Four of the issues were confiscated and burned by the Post Office, and eventually the two women were convicted of obscenity and fined $100. Not soon after, they took themselves and their magazine to Paris.

Follow 14th Street west to Sixth Avenue.

16. GAY LIBERATION FRONT • 534 Sixth Avenue
on the northeast corner of 14th Street

The **Gay Liberation Front** was the first activist product of the Stonewall Uprising. It grew out of a Mattachine Society committee that planned the first New York City gay rights march in July 1969 (see the opening of the Washington Square tour). The GLF was in many ways yet another embodiment of the radicalized protest spirit that was taking various shapes across the country that summer: they took their name from the Vietcong's National Liberation Front and identified their politics with nongay groups like the Black Panthers. And in their statements, they described themselves as "revolutionary homosexuals, men and women, fighting together with all oppressed peoples for a new society, free of roles, class, competition, hierarchy."

They met here, in the space of a radical organization called Alternate U, at regular Sunday-night meetings, which, according to one member, were "classic studies in chaos." **Jill Johnston,** who later wrote about these years in *Lesbian Nation,* described one such meeting as "very camp" and "rowdy," with "much hilarity at expense of three straight dudes from prince-ton wanting to set up an 'encounter' situation with straight and gay people." Beneath the camp, though, there was a serious earnestness and sometimes a heated anger as the GLF began to wage public battle on homophobia.

The GLF aimed broadly, organizing protests against polit-ical candidates and the *Village Voice*, discussing guerrilla street-theater tactics and socialist reform; they even had a rifle club. Their spirit was perhaps best captured in their newspaper, subtly entitled *Come Out!* The first issue, in November 1969, showed a group of young men and women almost diving over the masthead and opened with a litany of rallying cries: "Come out for freedom! Come out now! Power to the people! Gay power to gay people! Come out of the closet before the door is nailed shut!" and went on to insist that "through mutual respect, action, and education *Come Out!* hopes to unify both the homosexual community and other oppressed groups into a cohesive body of people who do not find the enemy in each other."

While there had been homophile societies in the past, never before in this country had gay people organized with so explicit a protest passion. The *Village Voice* received GLF wrath early on. The *Voice* had covered the Stonewall Uprising with an arti-cle called "Too Much, My Dear," and had described the pro-testers as "fags," "swishes," and "queers." When the GLF placed an ad with the heading "Gay Power to Gay People," the *Voice* simply deleted the heading, explaining eventually that they considered "gay" as obscene a word as "fuck." In response, the GLF staged an all-day protest on September 12, 1969, in front of the *Voice* offices in Sheridan Square. Near the end of the day, the paper met with three GLFers: they agreed to use both "gay" and "homosexual" in advertising copy but refused to dictate the terms or tone their writers would use.

Importantly, the GLF also attempted the work of generat-ing a coherent gay community. Briefly in 1970 they set up a Gay Community Center down on West 3rd Street (it's in the Washington Square tour), but well before that they also held fabulous dances where beers were fifty cents and sodas twenty-five cents and to which hundreds of gay men and les-bians came as a first alternative to bars in a long time. (There probably hadn't been organized gay dances in the city since the 1930s drag balls.)

The difficulty that GLF faced, though, was that their revolutionary protest spirit didn't just cut outward. The older, conservative Mattachine Society equally came under attack. **Jim Fouratt,** a young gay man who had spent some time in the Caffe Cino scene and would later go on to promote clubs and concerts around the city, wrote in the second issue of *Come Out!* that Mattachine was "about as relevant to me as are the Democratic and Republican parties. All three are concerned with preserving a system which is threatened by everything I stand for. Mattachine wants all homosexuals to somehow nicely fade into the mainstream. I want all people to stand outside and create a new society."

Tensions within the newly emerging gay community grew. A rift began to divide the GLF men and the women, and entirely separate women's organizations began to form. One of the truly explosive conflicts in the group centered on GLF's ties to other radical organizations, specifically its commitment to the Black Panthers. Those who believed in broad coalition organizing increasingly butted heads with those who wanted a gay movement focused exclusively on gay issues and not on some larger revolution, or at least not one led by the likes of Eldridge Cleaver, who had said that "homosexuality is a sickness, just as are baby-rape or wanting to become the head of General Motors."

Ultimately, the GLF agenda splintered. By December of that first year, a dozen GLFers met to start over and formed the Gay Activists Alliance—a single-issue group organized by old-fashioned parliamentary rules. For several months, both groups competed for community attention and called each other various names (as they did outside of the police station the night of the Snake Pit raid). Folks like **Bob Kohler,** an avid GLFer who later worked at the Club Baths in the East Village and opened a clothing store on Christopher Street, struggled to find common links, a shared pride, even while accepting that homosexuality was not "a magic tie that binds us all." Quickly, though, the GAA came to take on the central role in the developing politicized gay community, and the GLF faded away. But in the meantime, the GLF served as an essential angry energizing catalyst that led to the formation of not just the GAA but groups like Radicalesbians, Gay Youth, Transvestites and Transsexuals, and a whole new wave of vibrant and vocal gay activism.

Head down Sixth Avenue and turn right on 13th Street. For a tiny detour, though, you might want to cut over onto 12th Street and check out the pair of townhouses at 167 and 171. The first belonged to master chef **James Beard***, with a special training kitchen designed by his then lover, architect* **Gino Cofacci***. The second was occupied by* **Grace Hutchins** *and* **Anna Rochester***, two labor activists who fell in love as Socialists and matured into firebrand leaders of the Communist Party, living here together from 1924 through the 1960s.*

17. PARENTS AND FRIENDS OF LESBIANS AND GAYS (P-FLAG) • 201 West 13th Street
on the northwest corner of Seventh Avenue

As the GLF and the GAA dueled to lead the new community, the spirit of liberation spread in unexpected directions. In the summer of 1972, for instance, **Jean Manford** decided she would march with her son **Morty** in the third Gay Pride Parade. What's more, Jean later reported, "I thought I should carry a sign, so I did. It read, 'Parents of Gays, Support Your Children.' " Dr. Spock was also marching that year, and when onlookers began to cheer, Jean says she thought they were responding to him, but they weren't. They were responding to her. "Every few steps gay people applauded, kissed me and said things like, 'I wish my parents were here.' I couldn't believe the strong emotional reaction to my marching."

Jean and Morty later discussed the response she had received and decided to start an organization for the parents of gay men and women. By the following year, with the support of the Reverend Ed Egan at the Metropolitan Duane United Methodist Church, they were holding monthly meetings in church and they continued to meet here for nearly two decades. Initially called simply Parents of Gays, they added first "lesbians" and then "friends," not to mention hundreds of chapters throughout the country. In 1975, Jean said about her son that she never regretted his being gay. "I didn't feel guilty because Morty was always the leader type, a wonderful, capable son. We all thought he was going to be a congressman. He still might. He's always organizing something. But I was never a domineering mother. I gave him responsibility and he took it." She also noted that while her husband had a harder time not thinking he had "failed as a father," eventually he came around and began attending meetings as well.

Morty died of AIDS-related illnesses in May 1992; his father had passed away several years before him. The New York chapter of the organization continues, however, presently including several hundred members, and Jean remains active in a chapter.

Head west on 13th Street.

18. LESBIAN AND GAY COMMUNITY SERVICES CENTER
- **208 West 13th Street**
  between Seventh and Greenwich Avenues

This building, which has a long history of making a home for the stranger, is where liberation lives today. Built in 1844 as a city schoolhouse (and with a last incarnation as the Food and Maritime Trades High School), this building has housed a school for orphans as well as a home for sailors. (Try calling out, "Oh, sailor . . ."; I'm sure you'll get a warm response.) In 1983, two mere subtenants—Senior Action in a Gay Environment (SAGE) and the Metropolitan Community Church—joined other groups in pleading with city officials that New York's lesbian and gay community needed a permanent home. Establishing a meeting and organizing center had been an ongoing effort that the GLF, the GAA, and others, as you shall see, struggled to achieve. This time, however, nearly fifteen years after the Stonewall Uprising, they succeeded: they convinced the city of the necessity and then promptly raised $200,000 for a down payment. (The initial organizing board included former GLFer turned club promoter **Jim Fouratt** as well as Flirtations singer and, later, AIDS activist **Michael Callen**.)

Since the spring of 1984, from nine A.M. to eleven P.M., 365 days a year, these doors have been open. The list of organizations that now meet here—groups for gay book-lovers, for advertising professionals, for twelve-steppers who occasionally two-step—is enormous. It was here, in 1987, for instance, that **Larry Kramer** issued a call for a community organization to respond more effectively to the AIDS epidemic, and within a week ACT UP was formed. ACT UP—the AIDS Coalition to Unleash Power—quite literally unleashed the kind of activist energy that the gay community hadn't expressed in over a decade. Gay men and women, as well as other individuals concerned about AIDS, used dramatic acts of civil disobedience—shutting down the Stock Exchange or interrupting a mass at St. Patrick's Cathedral—to wake the city and the nation from its torpid response to the epidemic. Officially, ACT UP continues to meet here. (See the Upper East Side and Battery tours for more about ACT UP.)

It was also at the Center, in the spring of 1990, that Queer Nation first raised its head. Queer Nation grew out of an interest in applying ACT UP passion to broader gay issues, and while that felt new again in the '90s, its rhetoric and tactics echoed the early gay liberation activists. One of their first statement sheets, a page decorated with a pink fist and entitled "I Hate Straights," insisted that "until I can enjoy the same freedom of movement and sexuality as straights their privilege must stop and it must be given over to me and my queer sisters and brothers. Straight people will not do this voluntarily and so they must be forced into it." Following in the footsteps of the Gay Activists Alliance, for instance, Queer Nation organized kiss-ins at McSorley's Old Ale House in the East Village and at the White Horse Tavern in the West. But when a Saturday-night march through the Village entitled "Queers Take Back the Night" provoked some onlookers to yell antigay remarks, some fifty activists chased the hecklers down. This was activism with a new defiance.

There are countless meeting rooms inside, a library, bulletin boards, medical services, an archive, hordes of helpful folks, even a men's room decorated by **Keith Haring.** Poke your nose in. You're always welcome.

Continue west on 13th Street, make a left on Greenwich Avenue, follow it toward Seventh Avenue, and then turn right on 11th Street.

19. LIBERATION HOUSE and the GAY SWITCHBOARD
- **247 West 11th Street**

between Waverly Place and West 4th Street

Throughout the 1970s, prior to the opening of the Center, establishing such a permanent gay community center remained an elusive dream—one gained and then quickly lost over and over again. In the beginning of 1972, this building became home to **Liberation House,** one of the first such efforts. Setting up a basement storefront "gay-care center," they had ambitious plans for a free store, a food co-op, a gay street-theater group, and a "cooperative workshop where gay people can make and sell things." According to their literature, they met with some success. They set up a Men's Coffee House (the flier for which said, "Bring music, instruments, poetry, reading or anything else you'd like to share with other gay brothers"); a Gay Bake Shop that sold, each Saturday, "breads, cakes, pastries, baked fresh & gay"; and in case of "a draft problem or any problem," they offered the chance to "speak with a gay sister or gay brother."

That last project quickly turned into the **Gay Switchboard,** which was staffed by volunteers who took calls for doctor referrals and bar suggestions, for dance schedules and apartment listings, for recommendations for barbers and orgy rooms, and from lonely folks who just wanted to rap. The staff soon received four hundred calls a week, and the early log books have notes like:

> **4:00** 17 year old guy who lives with his parents called— needed a motel or something where he could go for a night with his friend.
>
> **9:25** 14 year old guy. Loves men but not sexually, is he gay? Gave him Liberation House night [info]. Said come down and find out.

And one afternoon on a Gay Pride weekend, a call was taken from a male "masochist ordered by his master to call the switchboard to ask how many lashings he should receive."

The Switchboard remained Liberation House's greatest legacy. By 1980, it was receiving sixty thousand calls a year.

Scoot up West 4th Street to Eighth Avenue. As you do, though, keep an eye out for the Cubbyhole on your right: it's the lesbian bar where **Madonna** *and* **Sandra Bernhard** *made their claim to lesbian identity.*

20. THE SEA COLONY • 52 Eighth Avenue
  between Horatio and West 4th Streets

Now the hipster Art Bar, in the 1950s, '60s, and even '70s this building housed one of the preeminent lesbian hangouts, a bar where the classic ideals of butch and femme identity held sway. Historian and archivist **Joan Nestle** has written passionately about the **Sea Colony,** and of how, especially in the 1950s, "we needed the Lesbian air of the Sea Colony to breathe the life we could not anywhere else, those of us who wanted to see women dance, make love, wear shirts and pants. Here, and in other bars like this one, we found each other." (Throughout the 1950s and 1960s, it was illegal for women in New York to be dressed in men's clothing.)

The bar had a two-room setup, with dancing in the back. When the cops would drop in for their payoffs, the manager flipped on a red light in the back to signal for the dancing to stop. If the cops looked in there, they would simply see women seated at square tables. "But if they had looked closer," according to Nestle, "they would have seen hands clenched under the tables, femmes holding onto the belts of their butches, saying through the touch of fingers: don't let their power, their swagger, their leer, goad you into battle." When the cops decided to raid women's bars, especially in the 1950s, they were frequently abusive, even violent. At the very least, women were pushed up against the walls, and a cop might put his hands in a woman's pants, taunting, "Oh, you think you're a man. Well, let's see what you've got here." But as **Leslie Feinberg** has written in her poignant novel *Stone Butch Blues*, raids could prove much more violent.

And violence wasn't the only fear. At a 1964 raid of one lesbian bar, Mary Angelo's, forty-three women were arrested for allegedly dancing together. One woman, though, was so frightened of being publicly identified as a lesbian that she ate her driver's license while in the paddy wagon. After being strip-searched, jeered at by a gauntlet of cops, and forced to spend the night in jail, all the women were released in the morning when the judge discovered the police officer could not identify exactly which women were dancing. And just that quickly, after only one night of sheer life-altering terror, the case was dismissed.

Cross Eighth Avenue and follow Horatio Street west.

21. JAMES BALDWIN'S HOME • 81 Horatio Street
between Greenwich and Washington Streets

By the time **James Baldwin** moved in here at the beginning of the 1960s, he already had left New York, lived in France, published several important essays and two novels (*Go Tell It on the Mountain* and *Giovanni's Room*), fallen in love, and returned. He was busy working with Elia Kazan to transform *Giovanni's Room* into a stage production, and he was focused on finishing *Another Country,* his third novel, which wove a tale of complicated lives in New York and Europe and was destined to be a best-seller. In spite of all that seemingly resounding success, life was just not easy. And indeed, though he had three large rooms here for $100 a month and remained at this address for several years, when he moved in he had to borrow the $50 security deposit from his brother.

Life was always a challenge for Baldwin. Born in Harlem in 1924—at the birth of the Harlem Renaissance—Jimmy Baldwin was the eldest of nine children. As responsible as he was for his younger siblings, he was also beaten and taunted by his stepfather. He found frequent refuge in books and movies and school. At the age of fourteen, he was transformed by a powerful religious conversion and started a junior ministry. He came, however, to see Christianity as an enslaving faith, not a liberating one, and within a few years he left first the church and then his family. After struggling around the Village for a time (and working over in Washington Square), he left the United States for France, where he remained as a kind of part-time expatriate for much of his life.

Once in Paris, Baldwin said, he had a clear vision of himself. "I could see that I carried myself, which is my home, with me.

James Baldwin, his career well under way in 1964, and his companion cigarette and typewriter.

You can never escape that. I am the grandson of a slave, and I am a writer. I must deal with both." Baldwin wrote and spoke bravely and vividly. His probing essays about America's racial struggles shook the nation's conscience and placed his name and ideas at the forefront of the emerging civil rights struggle. Indeed, when Robert Kennedy, as attorney general in 1963, wanted to gain a black perspective on that effort, he called on Baldwin to assemble a group of black leaders.

In Paris he also fell in love. "I realized, and accepted for the first time," he later wrote, "that love was not merely a general human possibility, nor merely the disaster it had so often, by then, been for me . . . : it was among *my* possibilities, for here it was, breathing and belching beside me, and it was the key to life." Love, of course, would not prove so simple for Baldwin: the man he loved, Lucien Happersberger, who would remain his friend for life, would remain mostly *just* his friend. What's more, when Baldwin introduced homosexual relationships into his fiction, as he did time and time again, he was met with either scathing criticism or utter silence from those eager to embrace him only as a black writer. Only his homosexuality kept him off the speakers' platform at the 1963 March on Washington. And, when he finished the manuscript of *Giovanni's Room*, the powerful and moving tale of a tragic gay affair in Paris, his agent suggested he burn the manuscript, and Knopf, the publisher of his first novel, rejected it as "repugnant." Only later, after a British publisher agreed to publish it, did Dial Press in the United States decide to print it here as well. Its publication was met, ultimately, with significant acclaim.

Giovanni's Room, I must tell you, was one of my most cherished gifts—one of those books that awakened in me a whole world of possibilities—and there was a time when having a copy in your lap was a clear signal to other men (let alone the world) that you were gay. Criticized by some as overly sentimental, it throbs with love and ache and pathos. Moments such as David's contemplation of the litany of days ahead without his lover Giovanni are luminescent: he envisions a future where again and again, "in the glare of the grey morning, sour-mouthed, eye lids raw and red, hair tangled and damp from my stormy sleep, facing, over coffee and cigarette smoke, last night's impenetrable, meaningless boy who will shortly rise and vanish like the smoke, I will see Giovanni again, as he was that night, so vivid, so winning, all of the light of that gloomy tunnel trapped around his head."

As a writer, Baldwin was a night person, beginning writing at eight or ten at night and writing until five or six the next morning. Then, off to bed, up in time for late lunch, and the cycle would begin again. "It's not all writing," he once said. "A lot of it is tearing up paper and tearing your hair." In the later 1960s, Baldwin bought a building on the Upper West Side (71st Street), and there he kept his living quarters upstairs and his writing room downstairs, in what he referred to as the "torture chamber" of his home. New York, and the United States in general, proved a hard place to be creative. "There are too many interruptions in Manhattan," he once noted, "the whole social and political situation. But one has to find a way to do both, to be private and involved in civil rights." Nevertheless, much of his life after 1968 was spent abroad, mostly in France, and it was there, in a farmhouse in Provence, that he died in 1987.

Make a left on Washington Street and head down to Bethune Street.

22. JOHN CAGE and MERCE CUNNINGHAM'S STUDIO
- **55 Bethune Street**
  between Washington and West Streets

One of the great themes of gay history is the preeminence of gay men and women in the arts and the dominating significance of their artistic networks and collaborations. (Let's be honest, there's nothing we can't do with a few pins and some hair spray. Well, some of us, anyway.)

One of the great collaborations of the century, much of it conspired in this massive housing and community building called Westbeth, was between composer **John Cage** and dancer/choreographer **Merce Cunningham.** Cage was born in Los Angeles in 1912, and by the age of twelve, he was hosting a radio program that featured himself on piano. He exuded artistry—studying painting, working for an architect, writing poetry, and composing. In 1937 he met Cunningham in Seattle, and they became collaborators in art and life for the next fifty-five years.

Cunningham, ten years younger than Cage, grew up in a lumber-and-coal town in Washington State. An eager student of dance and drama, he met Cage because he was the piano player for one of his dance classes. Cunningham went off to Bennington College for further study and there was discovered by Martha Graham. He quickly became her protégé and she created several roles for him, including the Revivalist in *Appalachian Spring,* to **Aaron Copland**'s score. Meanwhile, he began to choreograph on his own—his and Cage's first true collaboration was a piece called *Credo in Us,* crafted in 1942, after which they toured the country. In 1952 they set up the Merce

Cunningham Dance Company, with Cunningham in charge of movement and Cage of sound. And while Cage married briefly in the 1940s, he and Merce lived and created here in an apartment and a studio from 1970 until Cage's death in 1992.

The kind of performances they created were not narrative dances; they explored movement and chance. Cunningham once insisted, "Dance is concerned with each single instant as it comes along" and that "sequence and continuity are totally irrelevant." "Anything," he said, "can follow anything." Indeed, the choreography of a given piece was often determined by coin tosses or writing out steps on individual pieces of paper and then shuffling them.

Fascinatingly, the endeavor that came to be the Cunningham Dance Company was created not only by Cage and Cunningham. In 1952, the two men met the painter **Robert Rauschenberg** at the Black Mountain College summer school, a place for experimental arts. In 1954, he became the artistic adviser to the company, and that year he also introduced his beloved friend (and 128 Front Street building neighbor) **Jasper Johns** to working with them. Rauschenberg stayed on until 1964, and then, in 1967, Johns, also a painter, became artistic adviser. The four, like the men who made *West Side Story* or *La Cage aux Folles* (see the Midtown tour), created a gay community of artistry.

Make a left on West Street and head down to Perry.

23. *CRUISING* PROTESTS
corner of Perry and West Streets

Late in the summer of 1979, the production of *Cruising*, the bleak Al Pacino film about a murderer in the gay S&M scene, came to the streets of New York. Pages of the screenplay had been leaked to the public, and they depicted brutal violence against gay men: assaults, attacks in the park, castrations. Much of the community was outraged that so homophobic a fantasy was being brought to life, let alone that it would be distributed across the country. Almost ten years after the filming of the self-loathing *Boys in the Band*, the very same director, William Friedkin, was once again putting a grim spin on gay life. Community members began to demand that city officials shut down the filming. They didn't want to censor the film, protester **Steve Ashkinazy** recently explained, but they felt that "it was inappropriate for the city to be spending money supporting a movie that was so antigay." When the city refused to intervene, a wave of protest began that would mark the last large show of power before the energy of gay rights activism would be funneled toward fighting and surviving AIDS.

Night after night at the end of July and the beginning of August, the gay community, hundreds and sometimes more than a thousand strong, would gather in Sheridan Square, rally, and then head off to block traffic or disrupt the filming with noise and whistles. Leaflets were posted and distributed, some of which were simply xeroxed pages from the most brutal scenes in the working script. On one leaflet, the printer had written, "This printing is paid for by a fag who doesn't want his cock cut off. If you don't want yours cut off—picket & hassle this film crew & actors," and gave the number of the Gay Switchboard for more information.

One night in August, the city had licensed filming along Christopher Street. The local shop owners, though, shut down their stores, blocked their awnings and signs, and put up placards in their windows saying, "Stop the Movie *Cruising*." As a result, the filming had to be relocated, and the production shifted to this intersection, of Perry and West Streets; the demonstrators followed, blowing whistles and horns, even throwing bottles, during the filming. Two men were arrested, and the producer, Jerry Weintraub, was hit in the head with a bottle. "The gay leaders keep asking me why I don't make a nice film about homosexuals," Weintraub noted. "I don't know what that means." Ashkinazy, in attendance that night, was pulled aside by the police and beaten, first against a car and then on the ground, by a gathering of six cops. He later sued the city and won.

As in so many other things, the gay community was hardly unanimous in its condemnation of the film. One local gay paper insisted, "Before you ask for voices to be silenced—ask yourself this: What would you do if someone took away your right to protest this film? You would cry 'Oppression! Discrimination! Fascism!' . . . Look in the mirror. What are you asking for?"

Nevertheless, when the movie opened in New York the following year, demonstrators protested the first screening in Times Square. When a gay man was stabbed in a particular scene, six activists stood up, blew whistles, and chanted, "The murder of gay men is not entertainment!" They unfurled a banner and carried on for a full minute before the film was stopped, the lights brought up, and security took them outside. One theater company, General Cinema, refused to show the movie in its theaters, but the president of Sack Theaters in Boston (also the president of the National Association of Theater Owners) took out a full-page ad in the *New York Times* declaring his support of the film.

Follow West Street downtown.

24. THE RAMROD • 394 West Street
between Charles and West 10th Streets

In the late 1970s, the **Ramrod** was one of the most popular leather and motorcycle bars. Winner of the first bar-league softball season in 1977, Ramrod life captured all the contradictions of gay life. That year, for instance, a typical Wednesday night found the bar commandeered by the FFA (hint: the first word is "Fist"), with "lots of Red Handkerchiefs in Right or Left pockets." Then again, on Sundays, according to one rag, "they serve the best brunch bargain in town . . . Steak n Eggs and a Bloody Mary at an unbelievably low price."

In a wonderful moment in **George Whitmore**'s novel *Confessions of Danny Slocum*, Danny is standing around at a bar like Ramrod wearing none of the appropriate attire. A man with a shaved head, a big mustache, and ensconced in leather "from the tips of his boots to his lean jaw" steps up beside him and gives him a once-over. He shakes Danny's hand (the other one is gloved) and quickly invites him home. "What's, what's expected of me?" Danny stammers, worrying which one of them will be whipped or chained to the wall. The fellow purses his lips, eyes glimmering, and says, "Well, tonight . . . tonight, I just saw *Tosca*, and to tell the truth, I'm feeling mellowed out. You?"

So it goes. Sadly, these are not the only contradictions of gay life. On November 19, 1980, the year that *Cruising* was finally released, a thirty-eight-year-old former transit cop named Ronald Crumpley, armed with a semiautomatic rifle and two pistols, opened fire from his white Cadillac into the Ramrod and at two nearby street corners. He fired more than forty bullets, injuring six men and killing two. Crumpley later told the police, "I'll kill them all, the gays. They ruin everything." Yet when he was brought to trial, Crumpley said he was acting on orders from God and was found not guilty by reason of insanity.

Follow West Street downtown across Christopher.

25. KELLER'S • 384 West Street
between Christopher and Barrow Streets

Keller's has been through several incarnations, but it is certainly one of the oldest and longest-running gay bars in the city: it dates back to the end of the 1950s, at least. And what's more, it was one of the first leather bars, perhaps the first real "specialty bar."

As at the Ramrod, there was always an element of theater here. The posing was perhaps no greater than at any gay bar, but the roles were much more carefully scripted, and the costuming, well . . . Writer **Wallace Hamilton** said that the sadists stood around the edges of the bar, lounging like "lethargic tigers" in their black leather caps, jackets, pants, and boots, set off with chains and key rings and dark glasses. Center stage, at the pool table, posed the pretty boys in black plastic jumpsuits, "fetchingly unzipped." "To watch one of those masochists take a stance with a pool cue," wrote Hamilton, "was to know the full eloquence of body language, right down to the twitch of the buttocks as the shot was made. The tigers would stir languidly."

Interestingly, a 1970s bar columnist, **Beau Moore**, suggested that Keller's gave fruit to some of the earliest stirrings of disco. According to Moore, at one point a group of men just started bopping over by the jukebox. When nobody complained, "the boys went wild and soon the entire clientele were feverishly at it. . . . So it seems that the real urge to dance started where everything starts, the sea. Or in this case, down on the waterfront where all needs seem more urgent."

Speaking of the waterfront, before you head inland, look up the river. You should be able to see some of the piers stretching toward New Jersey. Early in the century, these were the piers where people, produce, and livestock arrived at our fair isle. And while waterfronts the world over have been notorious cruising grounds, when the ships stopped docking here, the gay men got started. The piers became gay nude beaches, nightclubs, pick-up joints. (Keep your eyes open: some still are.) Several of the piers held long-empty warehouses that stretched out over the water and at night were filled with men. In the late 1970s, a nightclub actually opened up on one of the piers farther upriver. Since then, a number of the piers have been allowed to decay and crumble. But for many years, the piers that remain and the waterfront lot down here were the site of the final moments of Gay Pride weekend, with dancing, fireworks, and celebration.

Turn around and head right onto Christopher Street.

26. CHRISTOPHER'S END · 180 Christopher Street
   at Washington Street

After the Stonewall Uprising, one of the most vivid transformations of gay life was the emergence of a visible, public, and aggressive sexuality. (See the Chelsea tour for some of the grittiest of it.) The bar that used to operate here, **Christopher's End,** was merely a coffee shop that summer of '69. But within six months of the protests, Christopher's End was a bar with a dancing area and go-go boys and patrons who might be equally inclined to take it *all* off. It was quickly dubbed "one of the great gay bars in the city," and its pool table, dance floor, and back room (ah yes, an ancient practice) became as busy as bees.

It was also, sweetly, a bit of an old-home-week kind of bar, where everybody knew each other through either happenstance or Linda, the occasional waitress. One regular remembers that Linda thought it "plain foolish for all those nice young guys to stand around staring at each other without *doing* anything about it." She would take it upon herself to arrange introductions. Mostly, though, people remember the go-go boys, who were none too shy in either their own stripping or getting patrons up on the platform with them, equally bare to the world. And, it seems that for a time if you went into the back room, you might find one of the go-go boys sending "the panting audience over the cliff into . . ." well, you can imagine.

Wander up Christopher to Bleecker, then make a right and a short right onto Grove.

27. HART CRANE'S HOME • 45 Grove Street
between Bleecker and Bedford Streets

In many ways our own American Rimbaud, **Hart Crane** was as gifted a poet as he was a troubled soul. Born in Ohio in 1899, he moved to New York during the First World War, and though he lived in various rooms all over the West Village and Brooklyn, he sublet a second-floor room from his friend Gorham Munson in this 150-year-old house in 1919. He liked the room because it had a good writing table and, he wrote, "no inquisitive landlady always looking through the keyhole." It was here that he began to write *The Bridge*, his masterwork about the Brooklyn Bridge, which is considered one of the great twentieth-century American poems. Friends noted that Crane struggled with writing, and a few remembered coming around the corner just in time to see him hurling his typewriter out the window.

But life in New York invigorated the poet, offering the chance to discover his identity in its "sea of humanity." It also offered him the possibility of love, and over the winter of 1919–20 he wrote of his first great affair. "I have never had devotion returned before like this, nor ever found a soul, mind, and body so worthy of devotion. Probably I never shall again." Sadly, love remained unenduring for Crane, a thing he found and lost again with frequency. He eventually became a lover of sailors—lots of sailors—and enjoyed many a drunken night with them. Of those nights he said, "I treasure them against many disillusionments made bitter by the fact that faith was given and expected—whereas, with the sailor no faith or such is properly *expected*, and how jolly and cordial and warm the tousling *is* sometimes, after all."

That treasure was not enough, though. In 1932, returning by ship from Mexico, where he had gone on a Guggenheim Fellowship to write a poem on the Spanish Conquest, Crane threw himself overboard and to his death.

Head west on Grove Street, making a left on Bedford Street and a right on Commerce.

28. THE CHERRY LANE THEATRE and BERENICE ABBOTT'S STUDIO • 38 and 50 Commerce Street
between Bedford and Barrow Streets

The **Cherry Lane** has a rich history dating back to 1924, when **Edna St. Vincent Millay** was involved in its founding. In 1954 **James Dean** appeared in one of his first plays here, and thirty years later **Brad Davis** (*Midnight Express* and *Querelle*) performed in **Joe Orton**'s *Entertaining Mr. Sloane.*

In 1921, according to one biography, Australian **George Orry-Kelly** shared a loft behind the theater with his British boyfriend, **Archie Leach,** and their mutual friend **Charlie Phelps.** All three of them were struggling actors. Phelps, under the name Charlie Spangles, did an act a few streets away called "Josephine and Joseph," in which he appeared half made-up as a woman, half as a man. Orry-Kelly, a handsome, brown-haired, blue-eyed twenty-four-year-old, worked variously as a chorus boy, mural painter, silent-film subtitler, and tailor's assistant. And Leach, who had first found his way to New York at the age of seven as the stilts boy in a traveling burlesque troop from Britain (he sailed on the doomed *Lusitania*), was still walking ten feet up, now as a sandwich-board advertisement in Times Square. They lived and waited for their breaks and had parties here, attended by the likes of George Burns and Gracie Allen, Mary and Jack Benny, and **Moss Hart.** When the big break came, it was Archie Leach who got it. He went from Broadway to Hollywood and from there, with a quick name change, to stardom. The new name: **Cary Grant.**

A couple of loose-cannon Cary tidbits: You may remember the scene in the 1938 film *Bringing Up Baby* where Cary is flouncing about in a woman's nightgown. Asked why, he responds, "I just went gay all of a sudden," and then adds simply to clarify, "I'm just sitting in the middle of 42nd Street [i.e., the center of homo-hustler cruising] waiting for a bus." Oh, a likely story: the line, dear ones, was an ad lib. Anyway, you'll also be happy to know that in 1970, when Cary was sixty-six and retired from the movies, Craig Rodwell's paper *Hymnal* quoted him as saying, "I'm devoting all my remaining energy to the only vice I have left—love-making." To which *Hymnal* replied, "Right on, Cary!"

Around the bend in Commerce, at number 50, **Berenice Abbott** kept her studio, where she worked as both a photographer and a photographic historian. Born in Ohio just before the turn of the century, Abbott left her hometown in 1918, stopping off in New York for a few years and then going on to study sculpture in Berlin and Paris. She ended up becoming the assistant to photographer Man Ray in Paris and then a photographer herself. (The apocryphal story would have us believe that she happily shifted from sculpture to photography when, while switching trains on a trek from Berlin to Paris, she was forced to either catch her train or risk missing it by carting along the sculpture she had just made: she chose the train and a new career.) In Paris, Abbott photographed the likes of **Jean Cocteau, André Gide,** and **Coco Chanel,** as well as most of the members of the Parisian lesbians-abroad set, including **Janet Flanner, Djuna Barnes, Jane Heap, Margaret Anderson,** and **Edna St. Vincent Millay.** (She and Barnes were roommates for a brief time in New York.) In addition, she single-handedly resuscitated the forgotten work of French photographer Eugène Atget, now considered one of the greatest early photographers of any nationality.

When she returned to America in 1929, she devoted herself to documenting a visual history of New York City, of its newly rising skyscrapers and its disappearing marketplaces, peddlers, and tenements. Blue-eyed Abbott was a constant presence in the streets of the city, pursuing what she termed "living photography." It was a spirit of photo taking that she said "acclaims the dignity of man. Living photography does not blink at the fantastic phenomena of real life be it beautiful or disgraceful. . . . It sings a song of life—not death."

When she died in 1991 at the age of 93, Abbott was living in Maine with **Susan Blatchford,** her companion of ten years. My favorite story comes from when she told a Washington, D.C. bureaucrat that she was going down to the Bowery to snap some shots. The bureaucrat said, "Nice girls don't go to the Bowery." Abbott replied, "I'm not a nice girl. I'm a photographer."

Follow Barrow Street west to Hudson; make a left onto Hudson and another onto St. Luke's Place.

29. PAUL CADMUS'S HOME • 5 St. Luke's Place
between Hudson and Seventh Avenue

Before there were **Robert Mapplethorpe** and **Holly Hughes,** before there were **Andres Serrano** and Karen Finley, there was **Paul Cadmus.** Born up on 103rd Street in 1904, Cadmus began his career as a book-review illustrator but quickly left behind commercial illustration for art. In 1937, the first one-man show of his superrealist paintings and illustrations drew record-breaking crowds. Suddenly, his work was everywhere—at the Corcoran in Washington, at the Metropolitan in New York, in magazines and newspapers. His images of men were erotically charged, to say the least: one critic of his first show noted that "around the walls sailors tousled their trollops, perverts beckoned from a cafeteria washroom, sag-bellied Babbitts diddled in the YMCA locker rooms, slatterns rioted on public beaches."

One such painting, *The Fleet's In*, commissioned as part of the WPA's Federal Arts Project, hung briefly at the Corcoran. The press made much of its raciness (the sailors are either passed out or on the verge of debauchery), and so a rear admiral actually sent Henry Roosevelt, FDR's cousin and assistant secretary of the navy at the time, to take it down. Apparently Henry simply walked out with the painting, and it was decades before it was recovered. Cadmus insisted that the painting was relatively tame, stating, "I've seen sailors doing lots of things I couldn't dare paint. On Riverside Drive especially. It's always impressed me as a—well, very sordid place." (You can check out Riverside

Park on the Upper West Side tour.) Interestingly, in both *The Fleet's In* and the similarly themed *Shore Leave* a dapperly dressed man in a red tie is depicted chatting with one of the sailors. In the first, he is extending a cigarette pack and making clear eye contact with the sailor as another sailor lies passed out between them. In the second, he has his hand on the sailor's shoulder. Back then, a red tie meant the same thing a copy of *Giovanni's Room* or a back-pocket bandanna would mean later in the century: this was a man on the prowl.

Cadmus, who lived here for several years with painter **Jared French,** a bisexual man who later married, told me recently that in those days "it was quite easy to be [gay] in the Village. It wasn't much of a problem, but one was secretive: you could get in trouble." He added that while he "approves" of the transformation achieved by gay liberation, something has been lost amid the candor: "in a way it's not so interesting to be gay."

One of the many visitors to Cadmus's studio here (along with writers **Tennessee Williams** and **Donald Windham**) bears special mentioning: **E. M. Forster.** In 1947, at age sixty-eight, Forster came to the States from England. He gave a speech at Harvard, rode a mule down the Grand Canyon, and spent a few days in New York. He had long since given up publishing his fiction (his last published novel was *A Passage to India*, in 1924), complaining at the zenith of his career of a "weariness of the only subject that I both can and may treat— the love of men for women and vice versa." Indeed, Forster's own desires were much like those of the novel (and later movie) *Maurice*. As he wrote in 1935, "I want to love a strong young man of the lower classes and be loved by him and even hurt by him." Sadly, though, he also wanted to write "respectable novels," and so wouldn't allow *Maurice*, or any of his gay stories, to be published until after his death. Of these stories, he wrote in his 1922 diary that "they were written not to express myself but to excite myself, and when first—15 years back—I began them, I had a feeling that I was doing something positively dangerous to my career as a novelist." He added, though, "I am not ashamed of them."

George Platt Lynes, Paul Cadmus, *c. 1942, silver print, 8 × 5½ inches.*

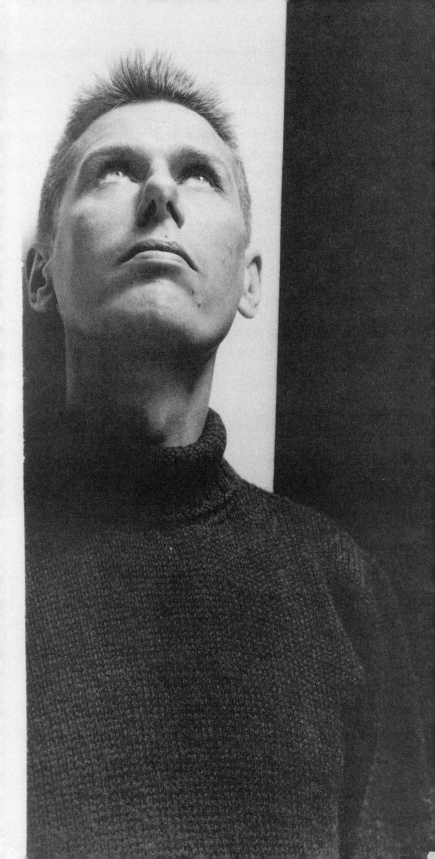

Forster stayed in Cadmus's apartment twice during his visit. Cadmus remembers him as a sharp, if seemingly mild, fellow who was also a bit messy—he left his bed full of chocolate-bar wrappings and torn letters. And he announced at the end of his stay, much to Cadmus's charm, "I have broken nothing. I have impaired everything."

Just to the left, number 3 was the home of Jimmy Walker, the notorious 1920s New York City mayor who, while still in office, loved to get dolled up to go to the drag balls in Harlem—and I do mean *dolled* (check out the Harlem tour). Briefly in 1923 **Sherwood Anderson,** the writer whose *Winesburg, Ohio* collection captured a lost vision of Middle America, made his home farther down the street at number 12. While little is known about Anderson's own attractions, many of the Winesburg stories, and especially the first, "Hands," speak to an impossible and unfathomable homosexual desire.

Turn around.

30. JAMES WALKER PARK
at St. Luke's Place and Hudson Street

All right, sports fans, hold onto your jocks, because this is the one shot you're getting. See the park here? Well, on August 27, 1973, the local Sixth Precinct cops beat the New York Matts 15–0 in a Monday-night softball game. Big deal? You betcha! The New York Matts were the team from the Mattachine Society, and there were some thousand folks gathered to watch. The game had grown out of a weekly rap session that Mattachine was holding with the police force, but was sponsored by a charity for mentally disabled children. One of the cops, Frank Toscano, said that four years earlier, he had been present at the Stonewall raid. Despite the cops' victory, this night's game seemed to be a fair fight: although Matts manager **Jean De Vente** "seared the umps' ears" when the police tried to use a metal bat, she later noted that the police pitcher "has been pitching to the women as if they were men, and that's the way I like it."

That night, with Geraldo Rivera as first-base umpire, a local newscaster calling the shots behind home plate, and tons of press coverage, the police and Mattachine together raised $1,000. As the game ended, one cop said enticingly, "There's going to be a great game in the spring if we can play some touch football."

Follow St. Luke's Place east to Seventh Avenue and turn right. Cross Houston Street, where Seventh turns into Varick; then make a right onto King.

31. PARADISE GARAGE • 84 King Street
between Varick and Hudson Streets

Though it is no longer operating, in the late 1970s an enormous and elaborate members-only disco opened over this taxi garage. Membership was hardly cheap—in 1980, a half-year membership cost $300 just for Friday nights, $400 for both Fridays and Saturdays, and you *still* had to pay a cover at the door—but it made the disco a private club and not subject to the same constraints of the liquor and public events laws. (Lots of discos did this.) And certainly, it was a place of dancing and display. Performers here included Billy Ocean, Chaka Khan, Patti LaBelle, Shannon, Jennifer Holliday, Grace Jones, and **Sylvester.** As far as spectacle: a "jungle" was opened on the rooftop in 1981. Or better yet, one night in 1978 was designated "TUT TUT TUT: An Extravaganza." Gold-leafed invitations with a drawing of King Tut's head were sent out, enticing you to refresh yourself in Cleopatra's Chamber, "relax" in the Rameses' Room, dance the night away in the Pyramid of King Tutankhamen, or pleasure yourself in the Back Tomb. Take your pick, please. Doors, of course, opened at midnight, but you were asked to RSVP, reserving a $20 place for yourself ($30 at the door).

Along with all the show, in the years when activism was on the wane, discos were a place where a surprising sense of community developed. In April of 1982, the Paradise was the site of the first-ever benefit for Gay Men's Health Crisis, raising $30,000 in a single night. And **Keith Haring** once wrote a friend how "important" the Paradise Garage was, "at least for me and the tribe of people who have shared many a collective spiritual experience there." He used to schedule his travel around the Garage, leaving town on a Sunday, returning on or before Saturday. When the club closed, in the fall of 1987, Haring was somewhere between numb and devastated, trying to accept that "there were a whole lot of people I only used to see there, a lot of them I never even spoke to the whole five years I went there, but I feel like I 'know' them 'cause I shared something with them."

Head back to Varick and turn right, then head down to Prince Street, turn left, and walk east to Wooster. Turn right.

32. GAY ACTIVISTS ALLIANCE FIREHOUSE
- **99 Wooster Street**
between Spring and Prince Streets

In the first half of the 1970s, before the disco craze, this old firehouse served as the home of *the* gay political group, and in many ways, of the entire gay community. The GAA, together with the Gay Liberation Front, put gay politics on the map in a way that had never occurred before. Taking the lead from the GLF, the GAA perfected the "zap," the surprising politicized interruption. They used it widely: against City Council members and *The Dick Cavett Show*, interrupting a major mayoral fund-raiser, and holding a kiss-in at a straight bar that had ejected gays. They sat in at George McGovern's state campaign offices and the Republican headquarters. And they interrupted work at *Harper's* magazine in protest of a homophobic article it had run. Weekly general-membership meetings occurred here on Thursday nights, in addition to countless committee meetings. A great deal of effort was spent trying to get "sexual orientation" incorporated into the city's antidiscrimination code. (The founding president of GAA, **Jim Owles,** actually ended up running for City Council in 1973.)

The building itself dates back to the turn of the century, but in the spring of 1971 the GAA transformed it, stripping the floors, cleaning it up. Most dramatically, they painted a mural on the first floor. It portrayed an anguished gay man clutching iron bars; **Walt Whitman** and **Gertrude Stein; Jim Owles** and GAA member **Vito Russo,** and **Allen Ginsberg.** Men were shown embracing, women holding hands, and through it all were woven slogans like "Gay Power," "Gay Pride," and "An Army of Lovers Cannot Lose."

What's more, the GAA set out to make a visible, proud gay social life. They used the ten thousand square feet of the firehouse not only as meeting space but as an essential social space. There were frequent street fairs out front (at one you could kiss Warhol superstar **Holly Woodlawn** for twenty-five cents), and **Jonathan Katz**'s play *Coming Out* debuted here. Every Friday night **Vito Russo** would show old movies, a new development in gay living. One attendee insisted, "Where else but at a Firehouse flick can you hear cries of 'Fuck Streisand!' as **Judy Garland** belts out a heavy number?"

And best of all, every Saturday night there would be dances. At a GAA dance, two dollars got you in the door and all the beer and soda you could drink. There was dancing on the main floor, drinks upstairs, and a dark lounge in the basement. One regular, **Wallace Hamilton,** recalled how on Saturday nights in the summer of 1971, the whole building pulsed with rock music, as the temperature rose—and people stripped down—on the dance floor. But this wasn't the same kind of dancing as was happening at bars on Christopher Street. These dances, Hamilton thought, were "a celebration of post-Stonewall identity. 'We are. We are together. And if you don't like it, *fuck off!*' "

But the GAA emerged, in fact, out of frustration. In part they were impatient with the old homophile spirit of the Mattachine Society and the Daughters of Bilitis and were ready to be reckless and militant and issue "the honest forceful demand for total liberation." They took the lambda symbol as their logo—the first gay organization to do so—because it was the physicists' symbol for change. And GAA exasperation extended also to the GLF, their earlier predecessor: indeed, it was a dozen largely frustrated GLFers who sat down together near the end of 1969, less than six months after the Stonewall Uprising and the founding of the GLF, and determined to try *again* at making a gay liberation organization—one not so chaotic, perhaps, not so interested in nongay issues. Meetings were run by *Robert's Rules of Order*, and you had to attend a certain number in order to become a member.

Nevertheless, by the fall of 1972 the GAA was getting criticized for being its own kind of establishment—too white, too middle-class, too male. Its membership, which stood at 350 in the summer of 1971, dropped to less than half that the following year. By the summer of 1974, groups with names like Faggots' International Revolutionary Movement (of which **Harvey Fierstein** was a member) were criticizing the GAA for having bought in to the big gay sellout and having succeeded only in "creating the same ambiance as the mafia bars." That October, like so many gay homes, bars, and offices around the country, the Firehouse was burned by arsonists, and the GAA, though remaining somewhat active, never fully rose from the ashes; they officially disbanded in 1981.

Indeed, the energy that had motivated gay liberation was redirected during the 1970s, becoming less focused on militancy and increasingly part of a social life and the disco scene. Gay activism lifted its head again when Anita Bryant opened her horrible mouth in 1977 and when *Cruising* was being filmed, but the intensity of gay politics didn't return again until the next decade, when death and disease forced it to do so.

For several years, though, as activist and writer **Arnie Kantrowitz** remembered, "I shared with the members of GAA a single purpose in which I trusted and a single passion to which I surrendered myself. We shared the sacrament of honesty, our coming out. Together we were something significant. We were a part of History, and we knew it. In our minds we were a people struggling valiantly to shed the bonds of oppression, and for every one of us who dared to come out, there were hundreds, no, thousands, awaiting their opportunity to join us."

From Slide to Auction Block:
The Layers of Washington Square

On Sunday, June 29, 1969, the New York Mattachine Society—the local chapter of the nation's principal homophile organization—held a meeting. Mattachine had started in Los Angeles in 1950 and had led the way in the 1950s and '60s across the country in forming what was then known as the homophile movement. As the word "homophile" suggests, their focus was much more the support and acceptance of homosexuals than activism or achieving any civil rights goals; they held lectures and discussion groups and worked to create a sense of a homosexual community, and within that community to develop understanding of a homosexual identity.

But this Sunday, after hundreds of gay men and women had spent the weekend angrily fighting with police in front of the Stonewall Inn, their meeting took on a different tone. A lesbian put forward a proposal: organize a response to the police action, take to the streets in a nonviolent protest, hold a march. And though such an action had never before taken place in New York City, the proposal was unanimously accepted. One month later, after running a small ad in the *Village Voice*, hundreds of protesters, wearing lavender armbands and shouting about "Gay Power," gathered in Washington Square and marched from there back to Sheridan Square and the Stonewall to rally. That was the first official gay gathering in the square, but it was hardly the last. For many years, singers, speakers, and politicians would embrace and exhort the gay community here in the annual Gay Pride rally. (**Bette Midler** joined in one year.)

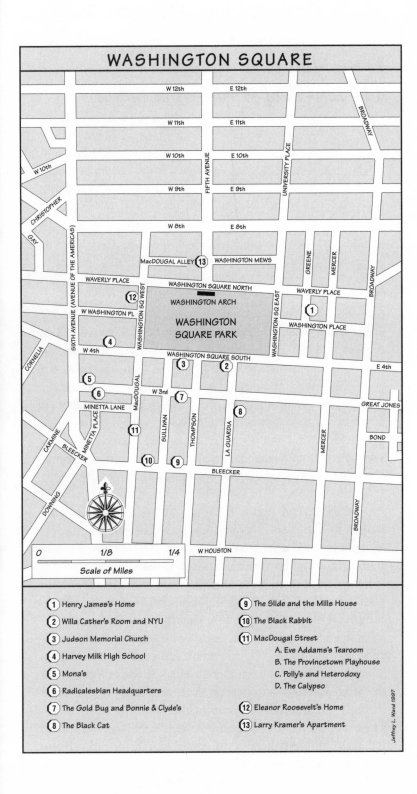

WASHINGTON SQUARE

W 12th   E 12th
W 11th   E 11th
W 10th   E 10th
W 9th   E 9th
W 8th   E 8th

MacDOUGAL ALLEY ⑬ WASHINGTON MEWS
WAVERLY PLACE
WASHINGTON SQUARE NORTH
⑫ WASHINGTON SQ WEST   WAVERLY PLACE
W WASHINGTON PL   WASHINGTON ARCH   ①
④   **WASHINGTON SQUARE PARK**   WASHINGTON PLACE
W 4th   WASHINGTON SQUARE SOUTH
③   ②   E 4th
⑤
⑥   W 3rd   ⑦   GREAT JONES
MINETTA LANE   ⑧   BOND
⑪
⑩   ⑨
BLEECKER

0   1/8   1/4   W HOUSTON
Scale of Miles

CHRISTOPHER · GAY · SIXTH AVENUE (AVENUE OF THE AMERICAS) · CORNELIA · CARMINE · BLEECKER · DOWNING · MINETTA PLACE · MacDOUGAL · SULLIVAN · THOMPSON · LA GUARDIA · MERCER · GREENE · FIFTH AVENUE · UNIVERSITY PLACE · BROADWAY

Jeffrey L. Ward 1997

① Henry James's Home
② Willa Cather's Room and NYU
③ Judson Memorial Church
④ Harvey Milk High School
⑤ Mona's
⑥ Radicalesbian Headquarters
⑦ The Gold Bug and Bonnie & Clyde's
⑧ The Black Cat

⑨ The Slide and the Mills House
⑩ The Black Rabbit
⑪ MacDougal Street
    A. Eve Addams's Tearoom
    B. The Provincetown Playhouse
    C. Polly's and Heterodoxy
    D. The Calypso
⑫ Eleanor Roosevelt's Home
⑬ Larry Kramer's Apartment

Those rallies were hardly the first time there had been a gay *presence* here. In the 1940s and '50s, gay life was centered in the square. The western railing was so cruisy it earned the then new name of "meat rack," and bars could be found on nearby MacDougal and 8th Streets. But even that is just a tiny piece of the square's gay past. No place in Manhattan so clearly epitomizes the wealth of gay history this city holds. And no place better shows how that history is intimately layered with, and actually constitutes an enormous portion of, the larger history of the proud city itself.

The following tour is fairly brief. It begins on the east side of the square, then wanders down beneath the square, exploring Bleecker and MacDougal before circling back around to the arch. But instead of covering vast amounts of physical territory, it moves through huge swathes of gay history, traveling across 150 years of our past. From turn-of-the-century gay men's clubs to 1970s lesbian bars, from **Willa Cather** to **Rita Mae Brown,** from **Eleanor Roosevelt** to **Larry Kramer,** the layering of gay history that it reveals is enormous. And if you're looking for a train ride to get there, you're in luck: almost all the letter trains (A, B, C, D, E, F, and Q) stop at the 4th Street station, just to the west of the square; if you're farther west, the 1/9 train stop in Sheridan Square is just a hop away; and on the East Side, the 6 train stops nearby on Bleecker Street. So don't delay.

1. HENRY JAMES'S HOME • 21 Washington Place
at Greene Street

Though the building is long gone, back in the spring of 1843, the home of our favorite family of geniuses—siblings **Henry, Alice,** and William **James**—stood here. Indeed it was here, that year, that Henry was born. The Jameses were a true Washington Square family, both in style—they had visits from the likes of Emerson and Thackeray, and sent their sons on European tours—and in substance: the family had a home here, and then on Washington Square North (number 1), and the children's grandmother lived on the north side, at number 18, as well. (It's worth peeking over there, for while her house is no longer standing, three of the homes there date back to that time and suggest what the Jameses' domestic life may have been like.)

In his classic novel about a young woman coming of age here, itself entitled *Washington Square*, James presented the square as a place of "established repose" which "has a riper, richer, more honorable look" than could be found on any of the city's avenues. In a charming passage, describing the early years of the plain but good heroine, Catherine Sloper, James equally revealed the details of his own childhood here: the grandmother who "dispensed a hospitality which commended itself alike to the infant imagination and the infant palate"; the first walks in tow with the nanny, "sniffing up the strange odour of the ailanthus-trees which . . . you were not yet critical enough to dislike as it deserved"; and even early schooling under the direction of a "broad-bosomed, broad-based old lady with a ferule, who was always having tea in a blue cup, with a saucer that didn't match."

In addition to *Washington Square* (the play version of which recently starred our own Tony-award-winning **Cherry Jones** on Broadway), James produced volumes and volumes of some of the finest literature in English, from *The Turn of the Screw* to *The Portrait of a Lady*. Despite his literary garrulousness, James was reticent in matters of the heart; one biographer insists he kept himself at a remove from most sexual contact. But it was far from easy being a James: Alice's life is testimony to that. Youngest sibling to four brothers, she was so battered by the large egos in her family that she had a nervous breakdown when she was sixteen. She never fully recovered and remained ill much of the rest of her life. And though she found an intimate companion in **Katherine Loring,** she died at the age of forty-four.

Henry's deepest emotional entanglement, it seems, was with his older brother, William, who became a renowned philosopher and psychologist, but it was hardly a reciprocal or "active" relationship. William aside, James's romantic life never settled into any long-term affairs, but in 1889 he seems to have been rather smitten with a twenty-six-year-old American sculptor named **Hendrik Anderson.** (James was forty-six and living in England when they met.) The few days they first spent together brought an outpouring from James. "I have *missed* you out of all proportion to the three meagre little days," he wrote. And in countless subsequent letters to the "lovable youth," he would repeat, "I feel, my dear boy, my arms around you," or, "I meanwhile pat you affectionately on the back, across the Alps and Apennines, I draw you close, I hold you long." They had only a few more visits over the span of many years, and yet even as James turned seventy, he clung to the hope that they would "meet (and still embracingly) over the abyss of our difference in years and conditions."

Follow the perimeter of the square down to Washington Square South and La Guardia Place.

2. WILLA CATHER'S ROOM and NYU
  * **61 Washington Square South**
  at La Guardia Place

At the turn of the century, where the blue-and-gray-glass New York University Loeb Student Center now stands, Katharine Branchard ran a boardinghouse that came to be known as the House of Genius. (There's a photograph of it on page 63.) Before the building was laid low by NYU in the 1950s, Branchard's roomers had included Stephen Crane, John Dos Passos, Theodore Dreiser, and Frank Norris. And at the outset of the century, two of her boarders were young **Willa Cather** and **Edith Lewis.** Cather, who was born in Virginia in 1873 and grew up in a crowded home in the tiny town of Red Cloud, Nebraska (population 2,500), had always been eager to make a name for herself. (In fact, as a fourteen-year-old, she cut her hair short and started wearing jackets and ties and signing herself "William Cather Jr.") She was wooed to New York in 1906 by S. S. McClure, who had already published her first collection of stories, and now wanted her to join the staff of his eponymously named muckraking magazine. Emotionally, she was hardly unencumbered. By all measures she seems to have still been very much in love with socialite and judge's daughter **Isabelle McClung:** she was living in Pittsburgh with Isabelle and the judge before heading to the city. Meeting Lewis here did not, it seems, immediately shake her of her affection for Isabelle. Though she lived with Lewis for the rest of her life—first in an apartment just to the west of the square, at 82 Washington Place, and then in a famous, though since destroyed, house at 5 Bank Street—she continued to visit Isabelle, go on trips with her, even dedicate a novel to her: she dedicated no books to Lewis.

Nevertheless, once she and Lewis had settled on Bank Street, Cather began to write in earnest (*My Antonia, O Pioneers!, Death Comes for the Archbishop*). And their home, with its constant display of fresh flowers and good French food (they hired a cook), became one of the Village's intellectual and cultural centers. Cather died in 1947, but Lewis kept her flame burning as her literary executor. Though Cather destroyed (and asked her friends to destroy) her correspondence, a few letters from Lewis to a friend remain. In them she describes her abiding affection for Cather and how, for instance, "when we used to go to concerts I was so proud of her. She seemed so fine, so above all that crowd of people."

Interestingly, as the Loeb Center, in 1970, this site was the focus of gay community picketing. NYU's relatively new gay students' organization felt cheated by the administration in their commitment to allow gay dances on campus. Having promised the group five dances, the administration tried to welch after two. A crowd showed up for the third dance, though, so they backed down. In what was one in a series of altercations and confrontations, a number of gay students and supporters occupied the basement of one of the dormitories and demanded a change in the administration's policy, while activists from the larger gay community gathered out here to vent their frustration.

One of the founders, in 1967, of NYU's Student Homophile League was then-student **Rita Mae Brown.** Brown, who'd grown up in Florida, had lost her scholarship at the University of Florida for being too active in civil rights protests and shouting at the head of her sorority. She hitchhiked to New York City and, if her novel *Rubyfruit Jungle* is to be believed, asked to be dropped in Washington Square. Molly, the heroine, says, "I had read somewhere in some trashy book that the square was the hub of the Village, and the Village was the hub of homosexuality." She expects to meet instant friends, but instead meets no one, at least not right away.

Brown got her B.A. at NYU and began to pursue a career in writing (as well as living for a while later on with **Fannie**

The House of Genius at 61 Washington Square South, home to Willa Cather and Edith Lewis.

Flagg, author of *Fried Green Tomatoes at the Whistle Stop Cafe*, and **Martina Navratilova**). In a guide she wrote for aspiring writers, *Starting from Scratch*, she insisted that she didn't know why she was a writer, only that "it never occurred to me to be anything else." Interestingly, *Rubyfruit Jungle*, her best-known work, was turned down by the major publishing houses and finally was published by a small press called Daughters. It then went on to huge success. Rita Mae's response? "Eat your hearts out. You all had your chance."

Head west a block to the church tower.

3. THE JUDSON MEMORIAL CHURCH
- **55 Washington Square South**
between Sullivan and Thompson Streets

The Judson had somehow avoided becoming a denominational church ever since its founding at the turn of the century. In 1961, the senior minister here was looking to hire a junior minister to start a theater group. He found **Al Carmines,** composer, playwright, and freshly ordained minister. Carmines accepted the job with the caveat that none of his scripts could be censored and that none of his shows *had* to be didactic. The productions that the six-foot-two, cigarillo-smoking Carmines put together included *Gorilla Queen,* a story about jungle movies and a dainty ape, and *Joan,* an opera about an East Village girl who bombs a building to protest the Vietnam War. One of Carmines's most famous productions was a staged oratorio called *The Faggot,* whose cast of characters ran from a Fag Hag, Alice B. Toklas, and a Commune Hippie, to The Groped, The Hustled, and The Hustler. In other words, your basic church fare.

Follow Washington Square South two more blocks west, where it turns into West 4th Street.

4. HARVEY MILK HIGH SCHOOL • 135 West 4th Street
between Washington Square West and Sixth Avenue

On April 15, 1985, the Washington Square United Methodist Church assumed yet another identity: home for the first-ever public high school geared for gay and lesbian students. The school took its name from the assassinated San Francisco supervisor, who had grown up on Long Island and discovered his gay identity as a high school student coming in to the city. Initially, the school opened with twenty students, fourteen boys and six girls who, for reason of sexual identity, were having trouble staying in the mainstream schools. For much of that first semester, the school operated (with a single teacher in old schoolhouse style) rather in secret. And then in June, the *New York Times* discovered the story and surprised even the mayor when they broke it. The school was, not surprisingly, both praised and condemned; a group of ministers actually picketed the church for allowing the classes to occur here. But the following fall, classes continued, though at another location. Since 1985, hundreds of students have finished their education thanks to the Harvey Milk.

Make a left on Sixth Avenue and another left onto West 3rd.

5. MONA'S • 135 West 3rd Street
between Sixth Avenue and MacDougal Street

Mona's was one of the oldest known lesbian bars in the city, dating back to around the time of the Second World War. The place was later incarnated as the Purple Onion, and though nothing is running here now, for a long while the neon sign still hung from the wall.

It is hard now to imagine the shock and wonder at the discovery of something so unusual as a lesbian bar in the 1940s or '50s. When novelist **Ann Bannon**'s heroine Beebo Brinker walked into her first women's bar in the 1950s, she was mesmerized, especially by the dancing in the back room—that "mass of couples . . . dancing, arms locked around each other, bodies pressed close and warm." The absence of shame or self-consciousness astounded her. "Beebo watched them for less than a minute, all told; but a minute that was transfixed like a living picture in her mind for the rest of her life. She was startled by it, afraid of it. And yet so passionately moved that she caught her breath and held it till her heart began to pound in protest. Her fists closed hard with the nails biting into her palms and she was obsessed momentarily by the desire to grab the girl nearest her and kiss her."

Walk across the street.

6. RADICALESBIAN HEADQUARTERS • 130 West 3rd Street
between MacDougal Street and Sixth Avenue

On the second floor of this building, for a time, the Gay Liberation Front set up their own community center. Not widely remembered, the center also served as one of the early homes of the **Radicalesbians,** a group that spun out of the male-dominated GLF in 1970 to create an empowered organization for women.

The initial inspiration came from frustration with the GLF dances. According to some women, those dances felt like crowded men's bars where "human contact was limited to groping and dry-fucking," and so the women decided to host their own dance. The event was so successful that they held more, and soon they were meeting and working together regularly. Radicalesbians was born. This combination of rebelling both as gay people and as women would characterize both the Radicalesbians and the Lesbian Feminist Liberation (which emerged out of the Gay Activists Alliance a few years later and is discussed more in the Chelsea tour).

In the spring of 1970, two events brought the Radicalesbians to the public's attention. In May, they issued a declaration entitled "The Woman Identified Woman," which began by asking "What is a lesbian?" They replied that "a lesbian is the rage of all women condensed to the point of explosion" and insisted that lesbians epitomized the woman-centered focus that *all* radical women were then embracing. Additionally, they argued, lesbians needed to stop negotiating compromises with gay men. "Our energies must flow toward our sisters, not backward toward our oppressors."

With that spirit, they launched an attack on the broader women's movement using the code name Lesbian Menace. That same spring, women were gathering in New York for the second annual Congress to Unite Women. Clearly, women's liberation lay at the heart of every lesbian's political concerns, but lesbians had not been made welcome in the early women's movement. In fact, Betty Friedan had made a point of describing lesbians as the albatross hanging around the neck of the movement and had initiated a purge of lesbians from the National Organization for Women. The date of the congress arrived, and suddenly, just before the first planned program got underway, the lights went out. Several seconds later, when they came back on, a group of seventeen Radicalesbians in T-shirts emblazoned with "Lavender Menace" stood before the crowd, while twenty others cheered them on from their seats. They held signs like "Super Dyke Loves You" and "Women's

Liberation Is a Lesbian Plot." First they took over the microphone, and then, by consensus, they took over the meeting. And they successfully brought lesbian issues to bear at the center of the women's rights movement.

Follow 3rd Street east two blocks.

7. THE GOLD BUG and BONNIE & CLYDE'S
- **85 and 82 West 3rd Street**
between Sullivan and Thompson Streets

West 3rd Street seems to have seen a bit of licentious traffic at the turn of the century. Somewhere along this street then stood the Golden Rule Pleasure Club. It was one of many such establishments visited by the reform-minded Reverend Charles Parkhurst, who was seeking out evidence of the kind of muck that Tammany Hall was allowing to stagnate around town. A detective brought him to the Golden Rule, where young men with painted faces and falsetto voices waited in individual cubicles to be hired. Parkhurst lasted a moment before racing out, declaring, "Why, I wouldn't stay in that house for all the money in the world!"

But 3rd Street bubbled most with gay life more recently in this century. Here, in the years surrounding the Stonewall Uprising, the **Gold Bug,** a men's bar at number 85, faced off with **Bonnie & Clyde's,** a women's bar across the street at number 82. The Gold Bug took its name from an Edgar Allan Poe story that the author was said to have written when he lived in the building. It offered up psychedelic lights, plenty of room for dancing, and lots of eager young men. One bar guide from 1971 referred to it as "one of the better known Chicken Coops. . . . A young number picked up here may not be salubrious for your complexion—if you can get past his. These are not sharpies, nor are they out-and-out hustlers, but they are eager."

Meanwhile, Bonnie & Clyde's drew, in the early 1970s, a fairly politicized crowd of women. There was dancing and a minimum charge on weekends. By the end of the decade, the operation had expanded: there were cabaret shows, Sunday brunches, and eventually a full-fledged restaurant upstairs called Bonnie's. Former television producer **Ann Northrop** remembers a clear distinction between the "California wood-and-ferns feel" upstairs and the bar downstairs, which retained a bit of a "raunchy" flavor.

Walk east and turn right onto La Guardia Place.

8. THE BLACK CAT
on the east side of La Guardia Place, just south of West 3rd Street

The **Black Cat** bistro, two doors south of 3rd Street, operated throughout the first half of the century, and its historical record marks the legacy of gay life in the area. It was opened by one Signor Mazzini in 1890 as one of the original bohemian haunts; the decor featured whitewashed brick walls adorned with stenciled black cats, and a pianist who regularly accompanied the drinking and dining. In the 1910s and '20s, it came to be considered the most famous of bohemian restaurants, and even came to feel a bit cliché to some, reeking perhaps of a theatrical Parisian sophistication and an affected air of marginality. Undoubtedly, though, gay life was a part of that atmosphere.

One lesbian remembered that in the late 1940s, the Black Cat still retained its bohemian reputation, but with a much darker allure. It was a place where musicians, artists, communists, and gay people hung out together, all of them, perhaps, feeling equally shunned by society at large. For her, twenty-two years old and hungry for lesbian community, the Black Cat seemed a necessary but "dangerous place." There was the danger of police raids inside, or of being attacked by roving gangs of soldiers outside. And there was the constant presence of drugs, alcohol, and prostitution. "For several years I lived in that dangerous underworld. It seems hard to believe now, but really—what choice did I have?"

Wander down to Bleecker and head right one block.

9. THE SLIDE and THE MILLS HOUSE
- **157 Bleecker Street**

between Thompson and Sullivan Streets

Bleecker Street is a street of transformations. Built up in the nineteenth century with all the trappings and intentions of luxury and respectability, it quickly fell from grace. James D. McCabe, a prolific nineteenth-century writer, offered several moralistic guidebooks to New York. In one, the 1872 *Lights and Shadows of New York Life*, he warned that formerly elegant Bleecker had become "the headquarters of Bohemianism." It wasn't as bad as, say, Houston, Mercer, or Greene Street, he insisted, "but people shake their heads, look mysterious, and sigh ominously when you ask them about it." There is an air of "carelessness" and "independence," a "scorn of conventionality," he warned, and if you dare to walk its length, you must "be prepared for the gossip and surmises of . . . friends."

McCabe never said just what their surmises would be, and he himself demonstrated a rather ready familiarity with "that long-haired, queerly dressed young man" who is "an artist," and that "fresh looking young woman" who, shockingly enough, "meets your glance with composure." Go figure!

Scandal aside, though, what McCabe insisted was that these several blocks, even back in the 1870s, were a place of absolute liberation. "You may dress as you please, live as you please, do as you please in all things, and no comments will be made. There is no 'society' here to worry your life with its claims and laws. You are a law unto yourself." That very freedom meant the possibility for gay life to occur. And it did.

In the very building where Kenny's Castaways now operates, there used to be a place called the **Slide.** Despite its late-seventies-sex-club name, the Slide was popular late in the *previous* century. A slide, in the prostitution jargon of the time, was, simply enough, a place where men dressed as women and solicited other men: a working boy's drag bar. The only surviving descriptions of this place, though exclusively from condemning reports, suggest the name was fairly well earned. It was the "worst dive" and offered "something *outre* in the way of fast life." There were "degenerate" men serving as waiters, and "fairies," though not dressed as women, wore rouge and powder and sang dirty songs in falsetto to entice potential customers.

But behind the horror emerges a description of gay men enjoying themselves. One police account indicated that each night, between one hundred and three hundred men would pour in. There was joking and singing among old friends and future lovers, and "vices which are inhuman and unnatural." What's more, the bar was not only very popular among gay men, it became a necessary stop on any good straight host's tour of just how low New York life could be.

Before leaving this corner, look across Bleecker at the massive "Atrium" building. At the end of the nineteenth century, the good-deed forces were at work throughout the city to rescue the moral lives of the single workingmen who made up the new work force of urban industry. By some strange irony (and a healthy dose of poor planning), philanthropist Darius Mills decided to build the first of his YMCA-like housing structures on this very stretch of notorious Bleecker Street, directly across the street from where the Slide had operated. (The Slide was shut down by the police in 1892.) The Mills House was meant to be a home of quality for young men on their own, but the neighborhood caught up with it: according to historian George Chauncey, the building became an attractive home for working-class gay men.

Stroll west on Bleecker.

10. THE BLACK RABBIT • 183 Bleecker Street
between Sullivan and MacDougal Streets

Up the street from the Slide, the **Black Rabbit** operated here, where the clothing store is, at about the same time and had a similar feel to it, although it seems to have been more explicitly a sex club. Its high-draw entertainment included the French floorman known as the Jarbean Fairy; a twenty-year-old woman who performed sodomy with two men as part of the floor show (and was eventually arrested as a result); and a "hermaphrodite" who displayed his/her genitals to round out the night. Talk about fin-de-siècle, huh? The club was raided in 1900 as part of an effort by Anthony Comstock and his Society for the Suppression of Vice to clean up the city.

Turn right at MacDougal.

11. MACDOUGAL STREET
at Bleecker Street

Like Bleecker, MacDougal is a street with a reputation. The stretch from where you are now up to the square was a center for gay and lesbian life dating back at least to the 1910s, when the Provincetown Players set up their shop here. From then on, this street seemed to draw the gay and bohemian worlds for drinking, dining, arguing, philosophizing. Much that once stood here is now gone, and NYU casts a large shadow, but even the coffeehouses that now dominate the intersection with Bleecker Street suggest our own modern version of the aesthete living that long reigned here.

Pick a decade and there's some reference. Author **Charles Henri Ford** lived on MacDougal (number 144) in the 1930s, when he first moved to New York and the block was speckled with his favorite speakeasies. When writer **May Sarton** first moved here, she also lived in a boardinghouse along here while she tried to succeed as an actress in **Eva Le Gallienne**'s Civic Repertory Theater. In the 1940s and '50s, writers **Allen Ginsberg, James Baldwin,** and Jack Kerouac, choreographer **Merce Cunningham,** and composer **John Cage,** among others, hung out at the San Remo bar on the corner here. **Ann Bannon** placed the beautiful redhead Paula Ash in an apartment along here in her 1950 Beebo Brinker novels. A lesbian bar called El Cafe operated at number 116 in the 1970s, in exactly the spot where in the 1930s Louis' Luncheon had become a regular hangout for gay men and women; in the late 1940s, the Swing Rendezvous opened as a lesbian bar at number 117, just across the street.

The density of gay life in these few blocks has been incredible; this was gay territory that was earned, held on to, and invested in. According to historian **Lillian Faderman,** the one block between Bleecker and 3rd was so cruisy with gay men that for a time it was known as the Auction Block. The nickname suggests not just the lustiness of gay men, but the avidity with which this area was attended.

Here are a handful of my favorite MacDougal memories:

Old MacDougal Street, around 1940, before the NYU construction.

11A. EVE ADDAMS'S TEAROOM • 129 MacDougal Street

Many of the little hole-in-the-wall places along and off this street catered primarily to gay men and women. Around 1925, a Polish-born Jewish émigrée named **Eva Kotchever** set up a tearoom and speakeasy in this building. Inside, she offered poetry readings, discussions and musical shows. And she hung a sign on the door that stated in no uncertain terms, "Men are admitted but not welcome." In the summer of 1926, the place was raided and closed, and Kotchever was sentenced to a year in a workhouse for disorderly conduct and allegedly writing an "obscene" collection of stories called *Lesbian Love*. She was deported the next year, but interestingly, it seems that a few years later a group of actors performed a play based on her stories in a local basement theater. She was gone but much remembered.

11B. THE PROVINCETOWN PLAYHOUSE
 • 133 MacDougal Street

Formed in 1915, the Provincetown Players brought together the minds and work of **Djuna Barnes,** Eugene O'Neill, John Reed, and **Edna St. Vincent Millay. Bette Davis** joined their ranks briefly at one point, and, I'm happy to report, the photographer **Berenice Abbott** even did a little acting here. This building, to which the Players moved in 1918, had been a storehouse, a stable, and even a bottling works (making sparkling water called "Champinette") before the theater crowd showed up. Initially, there were twenty-five members in the company (they all did everything), and the theater could seat 182 people.

You can read about Barnes and Abbott in the West Village tour. Millay, well known for her poetry, also had a rich reputation among her peers. Born in 1892 in Rockland, Maine, she was a great admirer of the ancient poet **Sappho** and kept a bust of her on a marble pedestal. Back when she was a student at Vassar College, all of Millay's sweethearts were women. When one of them planned to marry, the young writer penned her a note which read in part, "I love you very dearly. Don't forget me entirely, just on account of that Mac Sills." According to historians, around the turn of the century such affections among women, especially younger women, were not unusual. As men became increasingly focused on work and the male work world, women turned to each other, often developing extremely deep, even romantic friendships. An 1873 Yale newspaper described what happens when one "Vassar girl takes a shine to another": a steady stream of candies, notes, bouquets, even locks of hair, "until at last the object of her attentions is captured, the two women become inseparable, and the aggressor is considered by her circle of acquaintances as—*smashed.*"

By the time Millay moved to the city, she seemed to save her smashes for men. Nevertheless, she remained one of the earliest mouthpieces of sexual liberation. At one Village party, it's said, a psychoanalyst attempted to determine the cause of her headache. "I wonder if it has ever occurred to you," he asked, "that you might perhaps, although you are hardly conscious of it, have an occasional impulse toward a person of your own sex?" To which Millay replied, characteristically nonchalantly, "Oh, you mean I'm homosexual! Of course I am, and heterosexual too, but what's that got to do with my headache?" (Perhaps this was the hidden message in her famous poem about how her "candle burns at both ends"!) Some of the clearest thinking on Millay came from a friend who wrote a series of limericks about her. One simply began:

> *There was a young woman named Saint,*
> *Who was named for something she ain't. . . .*

11c. Polly's and Heterodoxy • 137 MacDougal Street

Next door to the Playhouse in the 1910s stood **Polly's Restaurant** in a corner building long gone. It was part tavern, part cafe, part intellectuals' inspiration—an institution of early bohemian life. The owner, Paula Holladay, was an anarchist from Evanston, Illinois, who served good cheap food downstairs, and upstairs hosted the Liberal Club, which held poetry readings, exhibitions, speeches from **Emma Goldman** and Margaret Sanger, arguments, debates, what have you. Polly and the Liberal Club are inscribed in every good account of New York bohemia.

Less discussed, though, is another intellectual club, Heterodoxy, which also gathered first at Polly's and had as a charter member the same Henrietta Rodman who founded the Liberal Club. Heterodoxy, however, was exclusively a women's club. Formed in 1912, the organization brought together a wide array of professional women—authors, lawyers, actresses, educators—for regular luncheon meetings where they could drop the social constraints of "feminine" politeness and have honest arguments and debates.

The salon diva **Mabel Dodge Luhan** wrote that Heterodoxy was for "unorthodox women, women who did things and did them openly." At least a quarter of Heterodoxy's members were lesbians, and their relationships were welcomed into the club and celebrated there. And these were women who led important lives.

Take, for instance, **Elisabeth Irwin** and **Katharine Anthony:** Irwin was an innovative progressive educator who ran

Sara Josephine Baker.

Ida A. R. Wylie.

the experimental (and still prestigious) Little Red School-house. Anthony was both a social researcher, who did early studies of poor working mothers, and a feminist biographer, writing about **Margaret Fuller, Susan B. Anthony,** Catherine the Great, Dolley Madison, and Louisa May Alcott. One club member described Anthony as "a wise woman with a philosophic outlook and a delicious sense of humor." Irwin, by contrast, was more of a "warm, earthy type," but an "iconoclast" all the same. They lived together in the Village for thirty years and raised several children whom Irwin adopted.

Or **Sara Josephine Baker** and **Ida A. R. Wylie:** Baker was a physician who ran a large part of the New York Public Health Department. Initially to supplement her private-practice income—which in her first year came almost entirely from poor obstetrics cases and amounted to only $185—Baker signed up to do medical exams for an insurance company and then the city's health department. In 1908 she began developing a plan to reduce infant mortality on the Lower East Side by teaching immigrant mothers how to care for their newborns. Her success led the city to establish a Division (and then a Bureau) of Child Hygiene, the first such in the world, and by 1918 infant deaths in the city had been cut in half and were continuing to decline. Wylie was an Australian-born novelist and screenwriter, whose works included *Keeper of the Flame.*

Despite her successes, Baker used the professional name of S. J. Baker and attired herself as much like a man as possible. "The last thing I wanted," she later wrote, "was to be conspicuously feminine when working with men." At home, though, it was a different matter. Indeed, in their relationship, Wylie described herself as "faintly masculine . . . I like to be taken care of, to have my clothes mended . . . my hand held when my head aches . . . in the grand manner I want to be It." It seems she was: their relationship lasted some twenty-five years.

As historian **Judith Schwarz** has pointed out, these women were accepted into the Heterodoxy community, and their concerns meshed with the other women's concerns. They weren't there to fight for lesbian political activism: they were there as women concerned with feminist issues. That they were lesbians was beside the point.

Cross the street.

11D. THE CALYPSO • 146 MacDougal Street

The building itself was lost to NYU's expansion, but you can imagine it from the photograph of old MacDougal. Connie Williams, a Trinidadian woman, ran a Caribbean restaurant here around the time of the Second World War called the Calypso. She served West Indian curry, considered the best in New York City, had calypso singing and Trinidadian dancing, and she hired as a waiter young **James Baldwin,** who had just left his church and family in Harlem and moved to the Village. At the time, Baldwin was struggling with his life—his finances, his writing, his sexuality. He lived all over the Village in various rooms and apartments, and for a year he kept house with a woman he nearly asked to marry him. Ultimately, though, he decided she was "many light-years too late." His best friend, **Eugene Worth,** was apparently smitten with him, but Baldwin was blind to Worth's emotions, "unable to imagine that anyone could possibly be in love with an ugly boy like me." Tragically, Worth committed suicide.

Amidst all this turmoil, Baldwin developed a group of friends—seamen and would-be artists and intellectuals—with whom he'd hang out at the Minetta Tavern down the block or at the White Horse Tavern over on Hudson. And when he began working here, at the Calypso, they came to see him, even called ahead to see if it was his shift: Henry Miller, **Alain Locke,** and Paul Robeson, Baldwin's mentor **Beauford Delaney, Marlon Brando** (his friend from theater classes at the New School), and Eartha Kitt. Here young Jimmy held court.

Continue heading north on MacDougal as it turns into Washington Square West.

12. ELEANOR ROOSEVELT'S HOME
- **29 Washington Square West**
  at Washington Square North

Though remembered by many as First Lady to FDR, **Eleanor Roosevelt** was her own woman long before, and after, meeting her husband. Indeed, many historians view their marriage as more of a powerful political partnership than an affair of the heart. Born in New York City in 1884, Roosevelt has come to be seen as one of the most powerful and successful politicians of the century, taking her role as wife and transforming it into a platform from which to advocate the causes and changes she believed in: civil rights for black Americans, an expansive liberal government, labor reform. After FDR died in 1945, she returned to New York, living in this building for several years before moving uptown.

Roosevelt also came of age with a close group of lesbian friends, and during much of her adult life she was sustained by a long-standing relationship with **Lorena Alice Hickok,** an Associated Press reporter. Hickok, an ambitious, hard-drinking, chain-smoking journalist—apparently the first woman whose byline ran above a page-one story in the *New York Times*—gave up her career so that she wouldn't have to write about Roosevelt; instead she wrote for various public and private organizations.

The women met in 1928 and exchanged passionate correspondence whenever they weren't together. At FDR's 1933
inauguration, Roosevelt wore a sapphire ring Hickok had
given her. In a letter that evening, Roosevelt wrote, "All day
I've thought of you. . . . Oh! I want to put my arm around you.
I ache to hold you close. Your ring is a great comfort. I look at
it & think she does love me or I wouldn't be wearing it!" The
rest of Roosevelt's correspondence was littered with endear-
ments and entreaties like "I want to put my arms around you
& kiss you at the corner of your mouth" and "Oh! dear one, it
is all the little things, tones in your voice, the feel of your hair,
gestures, these are the things I think about & long for."

In 1954, the two women collaborated on a book called
Ladies of Courage, largely devoted to the struggle for women's
suffrage, as well as the contributions of various women to party
politics. Intriguingly, there is a chapter about Roosevelt, which
Hickok alone wrote. Of the many anecdotes related, one of the
most striking describes Roosevelt's friendship with **Elizabeth
Read** and her live-in companion, **Esther Lape.** Early in Roosevelt's political career, Read served as her legislative tutor. But
Hickok also noted that together Read and Lape were the first
"independent, professional women" (i.e., lesbians) Roosevelt
had ever known. "And she was as awed as she was fascinated by
them. Her diffidence soon melted under the warmth of their
friendship, and dining with them in their apartment evenings
when her husband was out became a treat to which she would
look forward for days." There, just beneath the surface, lay all
the truth about the nation's adored First Lady.

Roosevelt died in 1962; Hickok died six years later. Before
her own death, Hickok deposited their letters in the FDR
archives in Hyde Park, New York—both inviting and post-
poning their discovery.

Walk east on Washington Square North to Fifth Avenue.

13. LARRY KRAMER'S APARTMENT • 2 Fifth Avenue
   at Washington Square North

Writer and activist **Larry Kramer** made his early career in the
1950s and '60s in the film industry, including writing and

producing the Oscar-winning adaptation of D. H. Lawrence's *Women in Love*. At the end of the 1970s, during the heyday of disco, Kramer wrote a novel called *Faggots*, which was extremely critical about New York's gay life becoming ghettoized and sex-obsessed. The book won him few admirers in the community (**Martin Duberman** blasted it in *The New Republic*), but as he explained in an interview at the time, "I have seen very few couples who have what I think I want, who are *lovers*, who have a settled relationship where they love each other and care. I'm sure they're there, but I haven't seen them! And it's their responsibility to come out so that people who are fucking in the Mineshaft can see them and know that that sort of thing exists!" (You can find the Mineshaft in the Chelsea tour.)

But as the 1980s unfolded, Kramer's outrage shifted from the absence of role models to the horror of AIDS, and it is as an activist and playwright daily fighting with AIDS that, over the last fifteen years, he has truly come into his own. In 1981, when the *New York Times* ran an article on a "rare cancer" found in forty-one gay men, Kramer's home served as a gathering point for a meeting between gay men and scientists; out of that meeting came the Gay Men's Health Crisis. Kramer wrote angry essays for publications like the *New York Native*, including one called "1,112 and Counting," which insisted, "If this article doesn't scare the shit out of you, we're in real trouble. If this article doesn't rouse you to anger, fury, rage and action, gay men may have no future on this earth. Our continued existence depends on just how angry you can get."

Out of his frustrations with GMHC, which he eventually left, and his ongoing exasperation as AIDS became pandemic, Kramer helped form ACT UP, issuing the rallying cry that caused the first meeting. (See the West Village tour.) And he has continued to write—plays primarily, including *The Normal Heart* and *The Destiny of Me*, both of which confront his personal struggle with AIDS.

For years, Kramer boasted that he and the city's iconoclastic former mayor Ed Koch were neighbors. Koch, consistently rumored to be gay, just as consistently has denied those rumors—and as mayor, he was hardly everything the gay community had hoped for. But before that, when he was a mere junior congressman in 1975, he, together with Bella Abzug, introduced a gay rights bill into Congress.

In recent years, Fifth Avenue has been the route of the Gay Pride Parade, and in 1990, Kramer and film historian **Vito Russo** stood together on one of the tower terraces of this building and watched the parade. Russo was already quite sick from AIDS-related diseases, but the marchers stopped to applaud him as they walked by. He was their gay past; they, his future.

This, then, brings you to the top of Washington Square, with the familiar icon of the arch in back of you. From Henry James's novel to the opening sequences of *When Harry Met Sally*, it is a location that has been fixed in the American imagination. But it is appropriate that you leave the arch behind you. For well beyond that Washington Square image lie years and years of rich, fascinating, insufficiently explored gay and lesbian living. You have begun to see that past.

Love American Style: The Wilde Past of the East Village

Ah, the East Village . . .

Mood setters: Think black—turtleneck, jeans, boots (the last are crucial: big, heavy, high-lacing or huge-buckling, shit-kicking boots). Think cigarettes. Think punctuation-free (let alone rhyme-free) poetry. Think coffee-shop tables with stacks of Sartre and Habermas. And think pierced—ears, noses, navels, tongues, nipples, you name it—flashing startling moments of metallic glory.

Truth be told, that lets you in on only a tiny window of life in the East Village. You might get a better sense of the variety from sweet Newbie and his neighbors in **Andrew Holleran's** novel *Nights in Aruba,* who all lived down on St. Marks Place for a time (we'll get there). They occupied an old German high-school building that had transformed itself first into a home for Ukrainian immigrants and then again into cheap apartments for seekers of bohemia. It oozed living. Across the hall from Newbie, there was a lesbian who "every year acquired a thin lover whom she took in and fed foods she would not allow herself to eat—cakes, pies, cookies, pasta, homemade bread, ice cream, rice pudding—until the woman became obese, and then she kicked her out." Farther down the corridor a male hustler raised all sorts of flowers but never went into the sun, guarding his skin "for the same reason my mother covered the sofa on her porch in Jasper with a sheet: so it would last forever." Downstairs lived the drag queens, the drug dealer, and the screaming straight couple.

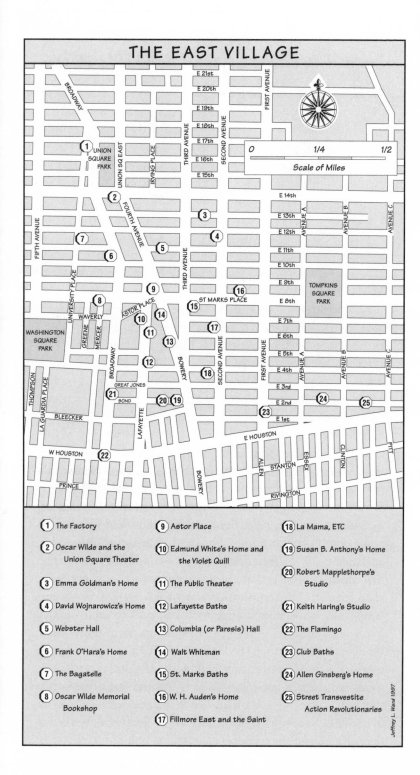

THE EAST VILLAGE

0   1/4   1/2

Scale of Miles

Jeffrey L. Ward 1997

① The Factory

② Oscar Wilde and the Union Square Theater

③ Emma Goldman's Home

④ David Wojnarowicz's Home

⑤ Webster Hall

⑥ Frank O'Hara's Home

⑦ The Bagatelle

⑧ Oscar Wilde Memorial Bookshop

⑨ Astor Place

⑩ Edmund White's Home and the Violet Quill

⑪ The Public Theater

⑫ Lafayette Baths

⑬ Columbia (or Paresis) Hall

⑭ Walt Whitman

⑮ St. Marks Baths

⑯ W. H. Auden's Home

⑰ Fillmore East and the Saint

⑱ La Mama, ETC

⑲ Susan B. Anthony's Home

⑳ Robert Mapplethorpe's Studio

㉑ Keith Haring's Studio

㉒ The Flamingo

㉓ Club Baths

㉔ Allen Ginsberg's Home

㉕ Street Transvestite Action Revolutionaries

According to Newbie, the neighborhood police referred to his building as "Love American Style." But that name—suggesting some topsy-turvy mix of cultures, styles, attachments, and liaisons (as well as that wacky TV show)—is just as accurate for the East Village as a whole. The tour that follows takes you through some of the high points of this bohemia: from **Andy Warhol**'s Factory to **Keith Haring**'s headquarters, from **Walt Whitman**'s cruising ground to **Susan B. Anthony**'s home, and from a turn-of-the-century drag club to one of the most popular (and somewhat visitable) 1970s bathhouses.

To start, we'll meet on the northwest corner of Union Square. The 4/5/6 trains will drop you off there directly, as will the N-and-R line, or even the L. If you're over on the west side of town, you can take either the A/C/E line, the 1/2/3/9 line, or the F line to their 14th Street stations and walk east a few blocks; it's not far.

1. THE FACTORY • 33 Union Square West
in the Union Building between 16th and 17th Streets

Andy. How can we ever be grateful enough? *Interview* magazine. Fifteen minutes of fame. Enormous Campbell's soup cans. Multicolored Marilyns. The diaries. The list is so long.

Born Andrew Warhola in Pennsylvania, **Andy Warhol** was an unlikely candidate to lead the charge of the Pop Art movement. He was the son of Czechoslovakian immigrants, and his father was a coal miner. But in 1949 he moved to New York and started working as a fashion illustrator at places like Tiffany's, Bonwit Teller, *Vogue*, and *Glamour*. He was successful enough to buy a townhouse, but he wanted more. In a 1962 Los Angeles art show, his soup cans got noticed, and Warhol had his ticket. The following year he began silk-screening the soup cans and mass-producing them—hence the name of his studio, the Factory. He also branched out and started filming.

The Factory had various homes in the city: its first up in Midtown; later, down on Broadway. But from 1968 to 1973, in the years bracketing Stonewall, the Factory was here on the sixth floor in an enormous white-walled loft. Warhol and the Factory were magnets for the poet-waifs and transvestite wannabes of the city. **Truman Capote** described them as "desperate, lost people [who] find their way to him, looking for some sort of salvation, and Andy sort of sits back like a deaf mute with very little to offer." Their names are familiar enough: Edie Sedgwick, **Holly Woodlawn**, Viva, **Candy Darling.**

On June 5, 1968, the day before Bobby Kennedy was killed, Valerie Solanis, the founder and sole member of SCUM (the Society to Cut Up Men), walked in. Angry because Warhol had rejected a screenplay of hers, she shot him. He survived (with a bevy of beautiful scars), but began to change the company he kept, leaving the poets behind and linking up with the Beautiful People (you *have* seen *Interview*, haven't you?) During his recuperation, he also left young **Paul Morrissey** to direct **Joe Dallesandro,** first in *Flesh* and then in *Trash* and *Heat.* Tasty, tasty, tasty. (To see how well Morrissey took his training in the treatment of lovely human forms, rent *Spike of Bensonhurst.*)

Oh, and about being gay, Andy wrote in his book *Popism*, "I liked the swish. I liked the way people react." He died in 1987.

Head southeast across the grassy plaza. As you walk, you should know that for a number of years Union Square has been the site of New York's annual rhetoric- and cruise-filled Gay Pride Rally. In this square, writer and activist **Larry Kramer** has spoken, comediennes **Lea DeLaria** and **Kate Clinton** have squawked and charmed, respectively, and AIDS activist and musician **Michael Callen** sang shortly before his death. As for the other weekends in the year, it's a farmers' market, and there's more fresh fruit(s) here than you could ever take home.

2. THE UNION SQUARE THEATER
- **formerly 56 East 14th Street**
  between Broadway and Fourth Avenue

Before diving fully into American bohemia, let's take a moment to step into the pantheon of gay patron saints and visit with a legend: **Oscar Wilde.** Born in Dublin in 1854, he was blessed with a hearty name—Oscar Fingal O'Flahertie Wills Wilde—and a sharp wit. You no doubt know something of his plays, most especially *The Importance of Being Earnest* or *An Ideal Husband*, as well as his novel *The Picture of Dorian*

Oscar Wilde shortly after his arrival in New York, 1882.

Gray. One of his plays, *Vera*, was given a production where this new development is, at what was then the Union Square Theater in 1883; it was the only American production that he oversaw, and it was a miserable flop, closing in a week's time.

More, though, I want to tell you about Wilde the tourist. Because prior to *Vera*'s production, Wilde spent all of 1882 traveling the United States on a lecture tour. He arrived in New York on January 2, and famously told the customs officer, "I have nothing to declare except my genius." Officially, his lecture topic was the English Renaissance, but he was an object of interest even separate from his commentary. His lecture in New York, delivered at the old Chickering Hall (on the northwest corner of Fifth Avenue and 13th Street), received one write-up that deemed him "well worth seeing, his short breeches and silk stockings showing to even better advantage upon the stage than in the gilded drawing room."

Brilliantly, Wilde declaimed not only in East Coast culture capitals like New York and Boston, where the leading figures (Oliver Wendell Holmes, General Ulysses S. Grant, Louisa May Alcott, Henry Wadsworth Longfellow) all came to hear him—he also went out west to Salt Lake City; Topeka, Kansas; Sioux City, Iowa; and San Francisco. My favorite excursion is the one he described when, after lecturing in Denver, he was lured down to the tiny—if famously dangerous—mining town of Leadville and called upon to lecture. The miners, he wrote, "sat there, rows and rows of them, enormous, powerfully built men, silent as the grave, their eyes watchful, their brawny arms folded over their muscular chests, a loaded gun on each thigh . . . I spoke to these delightful fellows of the early Florentine Schools, and they slept as peacefully as though no crime had ever stained the ravines of their wild mountain home."

Wilde left the States at the end of 1882, returned briefly for the *Vera* production, and did not return again. In 1895, he was accused by Lord Alfred Douglas's father, the Marquis of Queensberry, of having had sex with his son. Though indeed he had been Douglas's lover, Wilde sued for libel, and the matter ended up before the courts. In the twisted outcome, Wilde was found guilty of sodomy and sentenced to two years' hard labor. He died in 1900, three years after his release.

Follow 14th Street east to Third Avenue, then drop down to 13th Street and turn left.

3. EMMA GOLDMAN'S HOME • 208 or 212 East 13th Street
between Second and Third Avenues

Some debate remains about precisely where **Emma Goldman** lived, but then Goldman defies simple characterization. An essayist, lecturer, and anarchist, Goldman, though not decidedly homosexual, gave voice and place to much that early-twentieth-century American society excluded. Born in Lithuania in 1869, she came to the United States at the age of sixteen and quickly became a critic of the American way. She lived on the sixth floor of a building here from 1903 to 1913. In 1906 she started publishing her own journal, *Mother Earth;* that was also the year her well-known lover Alexander Berkman was released from prison after having served fourteen years for attempting to assassinate industrialist Henry Clay Frick. (Goldman herself was implicated in the assassination of President William McKinley.) The apartment here became a haven for radicals and intellectuals, and, as she said, "a home for lost dogs."

Goldman, who was one of Oscar Wilde's loudest defenders, frequently traveled the country lecturing about birth control, "free love," and homosexuality. After her homosexuality lectures, she later wrote, she was approached by men and women who "confided to me their anguish and their isolation" and who "were often of finer grain than those who had cast them out." One woman struck her particularly. "She had never met anyone, she told me, who suffered from a similar affliction, nor had she ever read books dealing with the subject. My lecture had set her free, I had given her back her self-respect."

Another woman, **Amelda Sperry,** a former prostitute, was so moved by Goldman's words that she fell in love with her and became an anarchist herself. She wrote passionate letters to Goldman (which Goldman saved), and they went on vacation together. Before the trip Amelda wrote how as she drifted off to sleep, she imagined that "I kiss your body with biting kisses—I inhale the sweet pungent odor of you and you plead with me for relief." Afterward, Amelda no longer needed to imagine. She vividly recalled being in Goldman's arms, "your beautiful throat that I kissed with reverent tenderness . . . And your bosom—ah, your sweet bosom, unconfined."

Goldman, who lived until 1940, would no doubt have remained a powerful force in American cultural and political life. During the First World War, however, she was arrested for having coordinated an antidraft campaign. After the war, she and other anarchists were deported to Russia.

Head to Second Avenue and hang a right.

4. DAVID WOJNAROWICZ'S HOME
- **189 Second Avenue, Apt. 3**

at 12th Street

David Wojnarowicz was a photographer, painter, activist, polemicist, and performance artist who, like Goldman, practiced his life and his craft fearlessly. His visual work had searing images of animals, erotica, industrial wastelands, and skeletons; and his writing was as honest and demanding as it was troubling. Having grown up in New York, Wojnarowicz lived always on the edge; he placed himself there. In one reminiscence of childhood he described crawling onto the ledge of his family's seventh-floor apartment and then, holding on just with his fingers, suspending himself over Eighth Avenue. Over and over again, he would do it: "testing testing testing how do I control this how much control do I have how much strength do I have."

In *Close to the Knives*, essays he wrote while contemplating AIDS and his own mortality, he described his life and his world: grim and garish, full of transvestites and drugs and waterfront pickups. Out of it emerged extraordinary brilliant visions, as when walking through a sexually busy warehouse along the river, Wojnarowicz spied men who became "glimpses of frescoes, vagrant frescoes painted with rough hands on the peeling walls."

And there was uncomprehending sickness and rage, fueled by the memory of losses to AIDS, of "faces and bodies of people I loved struggling for life." At one point he wrote, "I've been trying to fight the urge to throw up for the last two weeks. At first I thought it was food poisoning but slowly realized it was civilization. Everything is stirring this feeling inside me, signs of physical distress, the evening news, all the flags in the streets and the zombie population going about its daily routine. I just want to puke it all out like an intense projectile."

Wojnarowicz died of AIDS-related illnesses in July 1992.

Walk down to 11th Street and turn right.

5. WEBSTER HALL • 125 East 11th Street
between Third and Fourth Avenues

The history of this hall, from dance hall to concert hall to disco (even church thrown in there somewhere) is fascinating in itself. Back in the 1970s and '80s it was called the Ritz, and hosted performers ranging from Jefferson Starship and Jerry Lee Lewis to Prince and the Rolling Stones. But well before that, back in the 1920s, **Webster Hall** was the site each year of an enormous gay and lesbian drag ball. The tradition actually began in the 1910s, when masquerades and drag balls for the world at large (i.e., straight) started taking place here, and were found to be both successful and quite lucrative. The fêtes also began to attract gay men and women, who were frequently included in the ball pageants. And by the next decade, the gay men and lesbians were organizing their own parties here.

Although it's a couple of decades too early, and he's merely describing balls in general, listen to James D. McCabe as he describes the city's great balls in *New York by Sunlight and Gaslight:* "Upon the night of the entertainment a carpet is spread from the doorway to the edge of the sidewalk, and a temporary awning is erected over this. A policeman is provided to keep off the crowd of lookers-on which such an occasion invariably draws, and the sexton in charge takes his place at the door to receive the cards of invitation as the guests arrive. Between nine and ten, handsome carriages, with servants in livery, drive up and deposit their inmates at the awning." So romantic a setting! Now a close-up on the guests: beautiful boys in gowns and flapper dresses, stunning girls in top hats and tails, stepping from their coaches, filling the street, overwhelming in their elegance, style and savoir-faire. Kind of swell, no?

Okay, wipe your mouth and keep moving. Head down Fourth Avenue, around Grace Church on 10th Street, then on to Broadway on the other side.

6. FRANK O'HARA'S HOME • 791 Broadway
between 10th and 11th Streets

Frank O'Hara was born in March 1926, six months after his parents got married. His youth was hardly easy (although there was a stimulating encounter with a stable boy when he was sixteen): his mother was a bitter alcoholic and his father died while he was in college. He fled from his family as soon as he was able, and established himself in New York. Initially, he made a name for himself as a poet, founding the New York School of poets with John Ashbery and Kenneth Koch (who was a close friend). Their poetry and the poetry they encouraged, especially that of the younger beat poets like **Allen Ginsberg,** gave the East Village its bohemian flavor. O'Hara, along with Ginsberg and others, was a regular at the Cedar Tavern over on University Place, and he organized weekly poetry readings at St. Mark's Church in the Bowery (where **W. H. Auden** was also an habitué). And he lived all over the East Village in the 1950s and '60s, ending up here, in an all-white loft.

In addition to his poetry, O'Hara became an art curator. According to painter **Larry Rivers,** his career was an easy ascension. Apparently, Rivers and O'Hara started reading a lot of art criticism together, and then O'Hara got a job at the Museum of Modern Art. "He started out there selling postcards for Christmas," Rivers said. "He got to know so many artists and so much about art and what was going on in the art world that he became completely invaluable to the Museum and finally he was given the job of curator—my version of Horatio O'Hara."

O'Hara's career, sadly, was cut short. In July 1966, he was out alone at night on the beach at Fire Island and was run down by a beach buggy; he was just forty. In a eulogy for O'Hara, Rivers described O'Hara as his best friend and then added, "There are at least sixty people in New York who thought Frank O'Hara was their best friend. Without a doubt he was the most impossible man I knew. He never let me off the hook. He never allowed me to be lazy. His talk, his interest, his poetry, his life was a theater in which I saw what human beings are *really* like. . . . It is easy to deify in the presence of death, but Frank *was* an extraordinary man—and everyone here knows it."

Walk west on 11th Street one block to University Place.

7. THE BAGATELLE • 86 University Place
between 11th and 12th Streets

Audre Lorde was a poet and essayist who candidly portrayed
the rich diversity of her life experiences as a woman, a mother,
a lesbian, an African-American, and a cancer patient. She
wrote with a powerful clarity, simplicity, and honesty. (If you
haven't done so, take a look at *Sister Outsider,* or *The Cancer
Diaries,* about her experiences with the disease.) Born in 1934,
Lorde grew up in Harlem. She left New York as a young
woman, living for a time in Mexico, but she returned to the
Village in the 1950s and struggled to find a place for herself in
its lesbian community.

One of the places she went to was a lesbian club called
the Bagatelle, which operated in this building. She didn't go
often: she didn't like beer, and the bouncer always carded her.
But as she wrote in *Zami,* her autobiographical work about
that time, she did go. She described "the Bag" as "fast and
crowded . . . a good place for cruising." While there were
other lesbian bars in 1954, "the Bag was always The Club."
It was divided into two rooms by an archway. The first was
smoky and "smelled like plastic and blue glass and beer and
lots of good-looking young women." The second held a tiny
dance floor in the back. Elsewhere Lorde described how
she and friends would stand around deliberating "whether to
inch onto the postage-stamp dance floor for a slow intimate
fish, garrison belt to pubis and rump to rump, and did we
really want to get that excited after a long weekend with
work tomorrow." Inevitably Lorde decided not to: she never
danced, she was too scared. "Every other woman in the Bag,
it seemed, had a right to be there except us; we were pre-
tenders, only appearing to be cool and hip and tough like all
gay-girls were supposed to be."

Among the handful of "out" black lesbians at the time,
Lorde said, there was neither solidarity nor community. "We
acknowledged each other's presence by avoiding each other's
eyes, and since all too often we found ourselves sleeping with
the same white women, we recognized ourselves as exotic sister
outsiders who might gain little from banding together. It was as
if we thought our strength might lie in our fewness, our rarity."

It was against such isolation that Lorde fought constantly in her later years. Over the course of her full life—training as a librarian, having lovers, a husband, and two children—she continually inspired others by her example. And as a college instructor and a publisher, she demonstrated how people could support each other. At a lecture before a gathering of black women, she declared, "I do not want to be tolerated, nor misnamed. I want to be recognized. I am a Black Lesbian, and I *am* your sister." As she argued in a poem, all our battles are shared; if we lose those fights, she wrote, "someday women's blood will congeal / upon a dead planet / if we win / there is no telling."

Late in her life Lorde lived with **Dr. Glira I. Joseph** in St. Croix, where she was embraced by parts of the community, doing readings and joining the beekeepers' collective. When Lorde was dying with liver cancer, the fruit seller would ask Joseph where her friend was. "How she be? Here, take this papaya to her. It good for her." Lorde lived to be fifty-eight.

Follow University Place down to 8th Street and then walk east two blocks to Mercer Street.

8. Oscar Wilde Memorial Bookshop
• **291 Mercer Street (now at 15 Christopher Street)**
between 8th Street and Waverly Place

Though the shop has since moved, twenty-seven-year-old **Craig Rodwell** opened the Oscar Wilde here in 1967. It was the first gay bookstore anywhere in the United States and it was initially subjected to bomb threats and phone harassment; once its windows were smashed, and swastikas and "Kill Fags" were occasionally scrawled on the wall. But Rodwell was a committed gay activist: he had moved to New York when he was eighteen and quickly became active in the Mattachine Society. In 1966 he was one of three gay men to drink and identify themselves as gay at Julius' bar (in the West Village) in order to challenge the state's liquor authorities. And in 1969 and 1970 he became an active participant in both the Stonewall Uprising and the first Gay Pride Parade. He was not a man to be easily deterred. (Just for the gossipy set: One of Rodwell's early squeezes was **Harvey Milk,** the martyred San Francisco supervisor. He and Rodwell had picked each other up on Central Park West and quickly become lovers— small, if sad, world.)

Both before and after the Stonewall riots, the bookstore Rodwell ran was as much a community center as anything else. He served coffee on the weekends and gave discounts to gay activists. He organized a gay youth group out of it, and the first Gay Pride Parade was planned here. Early in 1968, well before Stonewall, he began publishing a newsletter that was both informative (with reviews and news and bar details) and motivational (trying to get "our people to join and support the work of the movement"). In that spirit, he gave it the name *Hymnal.* "We will make no pretense of speaking to the heterosexual," he wrote, "in trying to persuade him to 'accept' homosexuals. HYMNAL is solely concerned with what the gay person thinks of himself. The community has the economic, political, and social potential to shape its own future. This potential only needs to be encouraged and channeled."

In May 1973, Rodwell moved his shop to Christopher Street. For a while both stores stayed open, and there was talk of opening a shop in California as well. It was a dream that remained unfulfilled. Rodwell passed away in June 1993, but the Oscar Wilde remains a powerful presence in the community to this day.

Heading east on Waverly Place, cross Broadway and saunter up the angled Astor Street.

9. ASTOR PLACE • Astor and Lafayette Streets

As you approach this funky intersection, recognize that there's a real butchness opportunity here: the cube turns. Go ahead. Impress your date. Impress your friends. Or, better still, impress passersby. Why else do you waste all that time at the gym?

Stroll down Lafayette for just an instant.

10. EDMUND WHITE'S HOME and the VIOLET QUILL
- **434 Lafayette Street**

between Astor and 4th Street

Author **Edmund White,** whose range extends from *A Boy's Own Story* and *The Beautiful Room Is Empty* to *States of Desire* and *The Joy of Gay Sex*, long kept an apartment here, in the back, on the second floor. And it was here in 1980 and '81 that White gathered with his friends and colleagues who made up the Violet Quill writing group: **Andrew Holleran, Christopher Coe, Robert Ferro, Michael Grumley, George Whitmore,** and **Felice Picano.** They met fewer than a dozen times, taking turns in each other's apartments to read aloud, over dessert, their new short stories and novel chapters. But their coming together marked a new moment in gay literature. With White's novels, Holleran's *Dancer from the Dance*, Whitmore's *Confessions of Danny Slocum*, Ferro's *The Family of Max Desir*, and Picano's collection *Slashed to Ribbons, in Defense of Love*, gay writing ceased to be closeted, ceased to be simply self-hating, and truly began to emerge as a significant, self-respecting cultural presence.

Turn around.

11. THE PUBLIC THEATER • 425 Lafayette Street

A brief theatrical note: Joseph Papp's New York Shakespeare Festival empire was based just across the street here. Papp's productions went well beyond Shakespeare, ranging from *Hair* to **Larry Kramer**'s *The Normal Heart* to **Michael Bennett**'s *A Chorus Line*. In fact, for years *Chorus Line* was the breadwinner that allowed the company to front many other shows, including putting **Tony Kushner**'s *Angels in America* on Broadway. **George C. Wolfe,** who directed that production of *Angels*, is the second person to run the company since Papp's death in 1991. The theater has also, for several years, been home to New York's Lesbian and Gay Film Festival.

Wander down Lafayette a few steps.

12. LAFAYETTE BATHS • 403–405 Lafayette Street
between 4th and 5th Streets

We've been taught so well that no gay community existed before the Stonewall riots that it's hard to believe otherwise. But back in the 1910s, '20s, and '30s, before it closed, the **Lafayette,** one of the city's many bathhouses, was a central institution in just such a gay world. Importantly, while there is much to be said about the liberating vision of sexuality that the baths offered, they were not simply or exclusively places for anonymous sexual encounters. According to historian George Chauncey, especially in the early part of the century, the baths provided a social center, serving at least as much as a place for making friends, networking, and creating and discovering social circles. (If you were a regular in those early decades, your friends might refer to you as "Bathsheba" or "Our Lady of the Vapors.")

Operating where the parking structure now is, the management here catered to their clients and made certain that the baths were a safe, comfortable environment for them: this alone made the Lafayette a unique place for gay men to be, let alone to be gay. It also attracted a wide variety of clients, from an array of ethnic and economic backgrounds. These were men, in other words, who would not have considered each other part of the same community *outside* of the bathhouse. Inside, though, some of their differences disappeared and they became equals in a new community. Chauncey describes how the young composer **Charles Tomlinson Griffes** "was drawn into the gay world by the baths not just because he had sex there, but because he met men there who helped him find apartments and otherwise make his way through the city, who appreciated his music, who gave him new insights into his character, and who became his good friends." Griffes found a community here that sustained him well beyond the walls of the Lafayette.

And get this: back around the First World War, for a while the place was run by the Gershwin family, who lived not far from here. This was before George and Ira had made it big in the music world, and Ira, the lyricist brother, was manager. Far from wasting his time, the job, no doubt, gave young Ira the chance to peruse romance and seduction up close. Certainly in the song "The Man I Love," when that loving man finally does come along, he wins his paramour in a manner all too familiar: without speaking, with just a knowing look and an enticing smile. Hmm, wonder what could've inspired Ira for that. . . .

Make a left at 4th Street and then another quick left on the other side of the block.

13. COLUMBIA (OR PARESIS) HALL
  • **32 Cooper Square (formerly 392 Bowery)**
  near 6th Street

> *The Bow'ry, the Bow'ry! They say such things, and they do strange things on*
> *The Bow'ry! The Bow'ry! I'll never go there any more!*

How it is that it took me so long to figure out that the places I was warned away from were *exactly* the best places to go to, I'll never know. Nevertheless, around the turn of the century—that is, in the late 1800s—the Bowery, and on down into the Lower East Side, was precisely such a place. With the elevated train on Third Avenue running overhead, the Bowery was notoriously full of workingmen's pleasures: theaters, dime museums, saloons, dance halls, prostitutes and quickie hotels. This was the part of the city that made out-of-towners think of New York as a "wide open town." It was the kind of place that could inspire some people to call the Bowery "the flashiest of all flash streets in the metropolis," and other folks, like moralist James D. McCabe, to announce that "respectable people avoid the Bowery as far as possible at night. Every species of crime and vice is abroad at this time watching for its victims. Those who do not wish to fall into trouble should keep out of the way."

If trouble and vice hold even a little interest for you, though, then step up to this building—the home of **Columbia Hall**, a gay bar and club owned by one **Biff Ellison**. If you've read Caleb Carr's *The Alienist*, you've encountered Mr. Ellison and his club already; if you haven't, pick up a copy: it's an invitation into a world you're only beginning to discover. The

Hall, as the regulars called it, was the constant recipient of pulpit condemnations. Its nickname, **Paresis Hall,** was taken from the stage of syphilis that causes insanity, only the implication was that *homosexuality* was caused by insanity. Police reports described it as a place for "male degenerates," where they used names like "Princess this and Lady So and So and the Duchess of Marlboro," and where they "get up and sing as women, and dance; ape the female character; call each other sisters and take people out for immoral purposes."

Downstairs, there was a barroom and a beer garden. According to the police (a not altogether unimpeachable source), men "worked" the tables as prostitutes, earning drinks at the very least. Upstairs, though, there were small rooms for rent, including one room permanently rented by the Cercle Hermaphroditos. According to one regular, the Cercle was a small group of self-identified "extreme types—such as like to doll themselves up in feminine finery" and had formed their klatch "to unite for defense against the world's bitter persecution of bisexuals." The men had lockers there to store their feminine wardrobe and padding, and in their group, they found support, chatter, banter, and community. Across the street was another gay bar, called Little Bucks. This neck of the woods, then, in the 1880s and '90s was a bit of a night-out, a little gay bar strip.

Follow Cooper Square up toward Astor Place.

14. WALT WHITMAN • roughly 82 Cooper Square
just south of Astor Place

I don't know what your feelings are about poetry. Maybe you're still scarred from all that grade-school memorization. Maybe you find poetry too small, too precious: your tastes run more toward bravura and adventure. Well, before you go off to the new Jean-Claude Van Damme flick, you have to try some **Walt Whitman,** the great Gay Bard. This man lived and wrote fully, richly. Born in 1819, he spent much of his life in New York—primarily in Brooklyn, though also in Manhattan—writing and editing for magazines. He lived through the great changes of the nineteenth century—industrialization,

the Jacksonian era, the Civil War—but he wrote with a kind of populist spirituality, envisioning people as deeply natural and sexual beings. During the Civil War, Whitman went down to Washington, D.C., and, serving as nurse, healer, counselor, and shrink, cared for the wounded in the camps and hospitals—kissing, holding, listening, and orating. One eighteen-year-old Confederate soldier eventually moved to New York just to be near him. (You can find out about Whitman's relationship with some of the soldiers in the Midtown tour.)

Few writers before or after Whitman have so passionately, so unabashedly, so fearlessly told the gay romance of New York City, from the cruising ("as I pass, O Manhattan, your frequent / and swift flash of eyes offering me love") to the abiding love ("But more of two simple men I saw today on the pier / in the midst of the crowd, parting the parting of dear friends, / The one to remain hung on the other's neck and / passionately kissed him, / While the one to depart tightly pressed the one / to remain in his arms").

Roughly in the middle of this parking lot on Cooper Square, there once stood a house where Whitman stayed. He was not alone. According to historian **Jonathan Katz,** Whitman mentioned in his journals a few of the men he spent the night with; in one entry, he noted sleeping with **Horace Ostrander,** whom he met on October 22, 1862, and slept with, here, on December 4th. With that in mind, try this:

> *And when I thought how my friend, my lover, was*
>   *coming, then O I was happy . . .*
>   *and with the next, at evening, came my friend.*
> *And that night, while all was still, I heard the waters*
>   *roll slowly continually up the shores,*
> *I heard the hissing rustle of the liquid and sands,*
>   *as directed to me, whispering, to congratulate me,*
>   *—For the friend I love lay sleeping by my side,*
> *In the stillness his face was inclined towards me,*
>   *while the moon's clear beams shone,*
> *And his arm lay lightly over my breast. And*
>   *that night I was happy.*

Walt Whitman, the Great Gay Bard.

Late in his life, Whitman moved to Camden, New Jersey, where he lived out his days until 1892. **Oscar Wilde** twice made the pilgrimage to Camden to see Whitman on his great American tour, and later wrote him, "My Dear, Dear Walt. There is no one in this great wide world of America whom I love and honor so much." He also boasted afterward that "the kiss of Walt Whitman is still on my lips." At Whitman's funeral, three tents were set up: one for his body, one for food (including barbecued ox and ram), and one for drinks (barrels of whiskey, beer, lemonade). According to one attendant, "Homosexuals came in crowds and the most courted among them was Peter Cornelly, a young Irishman famed for his beauty, once a horsecar driver in Washington, whom Whitman had dearly loved. Everyone remembered having seen Whitman and Cornelly together often, sitting on the curbstone eating watermelon. Hence, at this funeral festival, great heaps of watermelon were available to one and all."

A quick historical note: **Abraham Lincoln** (as well as **Susan B. Anthony, Emma Goldman,** and many others) spoke at Cooper Union, the big brick building across the street, and won the Republican Party's presidential nomination because of it. (Come on, you do so care: as if he isn't your favorite presidential fantasy. You know what they say: Big hat, big . . .) Whitman said of Lincoln: "He has a face like a Hoosier Michelangelo, so awful ugly that it becomes beautiful." But Lincoln himself kept a well-thumbed copy of *Leaves of Grass* at the White House and had an aide alert him whenever Whitman would walk by the window on his way back from caring for the Civil War soldiers. Still uninterested? Try this: For three years, as a young attorney in Springfield, Illinois, Lincoln was not only housemates with shopkeeper Joshua Speed, he was bedmates. That was the practice in those days. What happened in that bed? Who knows? They both eventually married, but you know how young men can be, especially on those cold Illinois nights. And when Speed did go off and get married, Lincoln said he was more depressed than he had ever been before or ever would be again. Breaking up, it's hard to do.

Head back across this crazy intersection, crossing Third Avenue to go east on St. Marks Place (actually 8th Street).

15. ST. MARKS BATHS • 6 St. Marks Place
between Second and Third Avenues

Like most of the bathhouses in the city, the St. Marks has long since closed. Having been boarded up for quite some time, it recently re-emerged as a video and music store and cafe. But in 1915, a Jewish bathhouse opened up here and continued to operate in that capacity well into the 1970s—at least, that is, during the daytime. By the Second World War, though, its evenings were peopled by gay men, whom the management catered to and cared for well. And when the very gay Everard Bathhouse in Chelsea burned in the mid-1970s, much of its clientele began coming here.

There was no disco music or TV here, although there was food to be had. Instead, on the top three floors, as **Edmund White** has written, there was "sound like the galleys of a slave ship"—obscenities, slaps, belts, heavy breathing, moans, and cries. In the 1980s, patrons began receiving condoms and safe-sex pamphlets and were required to sign contracts agreeing to practice safe sex. Nevertheless, early in December 1985, the city shut the place down, and quickly graffiti went up, shouting "Finally!" and "Fuck Fags!" You might wander inside, though, and try to imagine the old atmosphere.

Follow St. Marks Place across Second Avenue (and remember, this is the block Newbie and his friends lived on).

16. W. H. AUDEN'S HOME • 77 St. Marks Place
between First and Second Avenues

One of the century's great English-language poets lived here from 1953 until 1972. Born in Britain, **W. H. Auden** traveled the world with fellow writer and close friend **Christopher Isherwood** before settling in New York at the outset of the Second World War and eventually taking American citizenship. He lived in a variety of places in the city and finally moved into the second-floor apartment here. (One of those was a communal house in Brooklyn, discussed a bit in the Battery tour, that he shared with **Carson McCullers, Jane** and **Paul Bowles,** and **Thomas Mann**'s son **Golo.** Auden was

From left to right: *Christopher Isherwood, W. H. Auden, and Chester Kallman out on Fire Island, 1940.*

close with the Manns and married Golo's sister **Erika,** a lesbian, to secure a British passport for her.)

But it was primarily with **Chester Kallman,** for better or worse, that Auden shared much of his life. They met in 1939, a few months after the poet's arrival in New York. By then, Auden already had quite a reputation, and one night he and Isherwood were invited, with others, to speak to the League of American Writers. Isherwood talked about their recent trip to China, and Auden read a poem about Yeats. In the audience was eighteen-year-old Kallman, then the managing editor of Brooklyn College's literary magazine, the *Observer.* Kallman arranged for himself and a friend to interview the poet two days later, but on the day of the interview, the blond, five-foot-eleven college junior arrived alone. And although at first the interview barely puttered along, eventually, it seems, things picked up.

The next month, Auden wrote a poem about his romantic fantasies called "The Prophets." He wrote that previously his dreams had all been exclusively inspired by books and had remained unfulfilled. But then Kallman arrived, and all his fantasies seemed "true," he wrote.

> *For now I have the answer from the face*
> *That never will go back into a book*
> *But asks for all my life, and is the Place*
> *Where all I touch is moved to an embrace,*
> *And there is no such thing as a vain look.*

Not to give too serious an impression of dear Auden, you should know that for most of the time he lived here, he was accessible to the world, even listed in the New York phone book. You might also be amused to know that in 1948 he composed a poem called "The Platonic Blow" that for years circulated only among his friends. It began: "*It was a spring day, a day for a lay, when the air / Smelled like a locker-room, a day to blow or get blown.*"

Poets, I hope you're finding, do have their pleasures.

Head back to Second Avenue and then down.

17. FILLMORE EAST and THE SAINT • 105 Second Avenue
between 6th and 7th Streets

In the early 1970s, most of this block was filled by a huge theater known as the **Fillmore East,** San Francisco music impresario Bob Graham's New York digs, where the showcased talent ranged from **Janis Joplin** to **Elton John.** The interior has recently been renovated, but the entrance here next to the bank remains the same.

Elton actually made his New York debut here, in the fall of 1970, at the tail end of his first major American tour, the one that catapulted him into stardom with a hit tune called "Your Song." Born Reginald Dwight in postwar England, Elton suffered through an unhappy childhood (overweight with a nasty father). At the age of twenty, though, he and soon-to-be lifetime writing partner Bernie Taupin answered the same record company ad for songwriters. Bernie was seventeen, but they were a match for success. Bernie moved into Elton's room in his mother's flat; two years later Elton had his debut album, and the following summer began his outrageous performing career. Shortly before the debut show here, Elton and Bernie were walking along St. Marks Place on their way to a rehearsal. With an eye to the future, Elton told his friend, "I think you'd better savor your anonymity now. It'll be gone soon enough."

Janis, whose career shot like a three-year meteor across the musical scene, was born in 1943 in a Texas oil town. She ran away when she was seventeen, explaining, "I read, I painted, I thought, I didn't hate niggers. There was nobody like me in Port Arthur. It was lonely, those feelings welling up and nobody to talk to, I was just 'silly crazy Janis.' " Though she wandered around, even going back to Port Arthur sometimes, by 1966 she was up on stage in San Francisco's Haight-Ashbury. "I couldn't believe it, all that rhythm and power. I got stoned just feeling it, like it was the best dope in the world. It was so sensual, so vibrant, loud, *crazy!* I couldn't stay still; I had never danced when I sang . . . but there I was moving and jumping. I couldn't hear myself, so I sang louder and louder, by the end I was wild."

That year she also met **Peggy Caserta** (who eventually wrote a memoir about her on-and-off four-year relationship with Janis). For neither woman was the relationship monogamous, nor were their attractions exclusive to women. And, wrote Caserta, "I had not been the first woman to slip down between her legs and send her with tongue flicks and finger insertions to some place in the sky where even the moon is warm." But for a while, it seems, she was the best. Two years later, Janis debuted in New York, at a club just up the street. And, in 1969, she played here. The year after that, sadly, she was dead from too many drugs.

For much of the 1980s, the Fillmore East was the **Saint,** a members-only men's disco. There were two thousand revolving lights, a 76-foot-high dance-floor dome—it was, after all, still a theater building—and a centerpiece planetarium projector. (If you walk around the back, you can still see how enormous the club was.) When the doors opened the first night at midnight, three thousand men were ready to pay $250 to join. It then cost them only $10 to get in (their guests—one each—cost $20), and the waiting list remained long.

Essayist and novelist **Ethan Mordden** once wrote, "There are three memories that every gay lives on—the first Gay Pride Parade, the first sight of the Saint, and the first trip to the Pines." Saint members could rent lockers, get free beer, sign up for computer dating. They were mailed DJ schedules and membership cards and even a newsletter that encouraged them to compete in cartoon and short-story contests that featured the club. Special occasions here were elaborately planned, including sending out ornate invitations: the invite for the first Halloween party (graced by Nona Hendryx) included a narrow leather face mask; New Year's Eve was gold leaf and black enamel; and the 1987 Black Party invite came with a Trojan. Performers here included **Sylvester,** Thelma Houston, even Tina Turner. One infamous Black Party went for two nights, and according to the invitation, featured **Robert Mapplethorpe** on hand to photograph "selected guests."

Walk down to 4th Street and turn right.

18. La Mama ETC • 74A East 4th Street
between Second and Third Avenues

Just a quick stop. The "ETC" here is as in "Experimental Theatre Company." Two experiments worth noting: May 9, 1971, the opening of *Pork*, a show by **Andy Warhol** that featured a sixteen-year-old **Harvey Fierstein,** even then a drag queen (although perhaps at that age "drag princess"?). Before the decade's end, Fierstein would return here as a playwright and more consummate performer. He presented, as individual shows, each of the three parts that later came to constitute his *Torch Song Trilogy.* As a whole, they traced the struggles of a drag performer to find love and craft a family, even as he struggled with loss and making peace with his own family. (When it was made into a movie in the 1980s, Fierstein starred in it opposite Matthew Broderick and Anne Bancroft.)

Once asked how a nice boy from Brooklyn becomes a drag queen, Fierstein deftly replied, "You get a nice dress, shoes to match, and a purse. If you pick the right gloves, you're a drag queen."

Walk west to the end of the block and hang a left down Bowery to Bond on the right.

19. SUSAN B. ANTHONY'S HOME • 44 Bond Street
  between Bowery and Lafayette

Although there's no building here now, the woman who lived here in the previous century was more than just another pretty silver-dollar face. **Susan B. Anthony** was a powerful figure who fought tirelessly for women's rights, working on the first laws giving women legal control over children and property in New York State as well as organizing the National Woman Suffrage Association.

Born in 1820, Anthony's earliest political activity involved working for the abolition of slavery—including assisting with the underground railroad—and fighting for temperance. For her, as well as for the many other women involved in those causes, these experiences made the possibility of women fighting together for their own liberation seem reasonable. And by her early thirties, Anthony had embarked on just that effort, taking up the causes that were to remain fundamental issues for modern women: domestic violence, sexual harassment, the victimization of prostitutes, equal pay—and suffrage. Anthony was arrested in 1872 for daring to vote, although she refused to pay the fine she was levied.

Anthony's marital status—unmarried till the end—was apparently a subject of unending interest to the press. Asked about it yet again in an interview in her seventies, Anthony replied, "I'll say that a good many men have done me the honor to ask me to marry them. Why did I refuse them all? Why, child, it was simply that I never met a man whom I thought I loved well enough to live with all my life, and for that matter, I never met one whom I thought loved me well enough to live with me all his life. That marriage proposition has two sides."

Instead her life was filled with the love of women. Her letters to abolitionist **Anna Dickinson** were loaded with protes-
tations of love and often began, "My Dear Chicky Dicky
Darling." One went on, "I have *plain quarters*—at 44 Bond
Street—*double bed*—and big enough & good enough to take
you *in*—So come & see me." After a thirty-year hiatus
between them, Anthony still maintained her affections. "My
Darling Anna," she wrote, "I'm awfully glad to know you still
live—and that I have chance to tell you that my *motherly love*—
my elderly sister's love—has never abated for my *first Anna*. I
had had several lovely *Anna* girls—'nieces,' they call themselves now-a-day—since my *first Anna*—but none of them—
ever has or ever can fill the niche in my heart that you
did—my dear."

Anthony died in 1906, fourteen years before the Nineteenth Amendment guaranteed women's right to vote.

Keep walking west on Bond Street.

20. ROBERT MAPPLETHORPE'S STUDIO • 24 Bond Street
between Bowery and Lafayette

Born in Queens (just across the East River) in 1946, by the
early 1970s photographer **Robert Mapplethorpe** had set up
shop here, no doubt inspired by ghostly neighbor Anthony's
push-the-envelope spirit; it remained his studio space until the
end of his life in 1989. Mapplethorpe turned to photography
in the early 1970s, having studied painting and sculpture at the
Pratt Institute and grown tired of them. (It was also at Pratt
that he met poet and musician Patti Smith, who became his
closest friend and housemate.) And when his photographs first
received solo public viewings in 1976 and 1977, they turned
the photo world on its ear—particularly his classically stylized
images of the gay S&M world, which he said stood for "sex &
magic." He later told **Ingrid Sischy** of *Interview* that in his
photography he was trying to recapture the experience he had
as a kid looking at porn magazines in Times Square. "A kid
gets a certain kind of reaction, which of course once you've
been exposed to everything you don't get. I got that feeling in
my stomach; it's not a directly sexual one, it's something more

potent than that. I thought if I could somehow bring that element into art, if I could somehow retain that feeling, I would be doing something that was uniquely my own." The Mapplethorpe vision became a union of cool formality and extreme sexuality, visible in his nudes, his portraits, and his flower studies.

Mapplethorpe died of AIDS-related illnesses in the spring of 1989, but the rest of that year and well into the next, his name and work were continually in the press. A Philadelphia museum organized a retrospective show of his work, with funding by the National Endowment for the Arts. Though that show went forward, a flood of angry criticism about NEA funding for Mapplethorpe and **Andres Serrano**—pouring most loudly from Senator Jesse Helms—prompted the Washington, D.C. Corcoran Gallery, which had been scheduled to pick up the show that summer, to back out. In the ensuing furor, the Corcoran director was forced to resign. The next spring, however, Cincinnati's Contemporary Art Center decided to put up their own Mapplethorpe exhibit of 175 photographs. When that show opened, the museum and its director, Dennis Barrie, were indicted on obscenity charges (prosecutors alleged that seven of the photos were obscene—two showed naked kids, five depicted homosexual acts). Although they were eventually acquitted, these controversies added extra sparkle to Mapplethorpe's notorious star and marked the beginning of the all-too-rapid decimation of the NEA.

Follow Bond out to Broadway and turn right.

21. KEITH HARING'S STUDIO • 676 Broadway
between Bond and Great Jones Streets

Keith Haring lived nearly half his short life in New York, and much of that in and around the East Village. He moved here from Pittsburgh in 1978, eager to jump into life. Growing up watching TV and reading magazines, he eagerly observed the upheaval of the 1960s and '70s. "I couldn't be a part of it," he once said, "but I was watching, and so I had some sort of consciousness. The older I got, the more I wanted to participate."

Once here, he dove in. Starting with a weekend stay at the

Chelsea Y, Haring was a busboy at Danceteria, did perfor-mances at Club 57 (57 St. Marks), and worked at the Mudd Club. He also became a regular at the Paradise Garage dance club on the edge of the West Village. By 1981, he was an habitué in the city's underground channels and passageways, spraying his artwork on the walls of subway cars. Five years later, when that work appeared aboveground, it was selling for, at the least, $60,000 a pop, and Haring was friends with the likes of **Madonna** and **Andy Warhol.** He went on to paint **Grace Jones**'s body, a blimp, a church, even the Berlin Wall. (You can see some of his work in the men's room at the Lesbian and Gay Community Services Center in the West Village.)

Haring's steadiest love affair was with **Juan Rivera,** in the mid-1980s—a man he described in his journal as "forever handsome with a chameleon face that adapts to every place we go, making him look Brazilian, Moroccan, or in this case part Japanese." But Haring was also a fan of anonymous encoun-ters and rich mental fantasies. "I can have these boys," he wrote once, "any of them, all of them, tonight alone in my lit-tle room in the dark."

Although he died of AIDS-related complications in 1990, at the age of thirty-one, his artwork continues to support a foundation funding children's and AIDS organizations in his name. The foundation runs out of his old studio up on the fifth floor. (Check out his Pop Shop over at 292 Lafayette, below Houston.)

Head down Broadway and cross Houston.

22. FLAMINGO • 599 Broadway
at Houston Street

On the two floors above the bank here, the **Flamingo** ruled in the late 1970s as *the* most celebrated men's disco in the city. It was restricted to members, like the Saint and the Paradise Garage, and its waiting list was always long. The club was reg-ularly packed with dancing, shirtless men pressed against each other by the sheer enormity of the crowd, fogging the mir-rored panels and staining the air. It was frequented by folks like novelist **Felice Picano** and editor **George Stambolian.**

To succeed at the Flamingo, **Edmund White** wrote, "one must have the drive of a tycoon, the allure of a kept boy, the stamina of an athlete, the bonhomie of a man of the world." (Is that all? No problem.)

According to writer **George Whitmore,** the inside was relatively uninteresting, your basic warehouse turned disco: industrial carpeting, an enormous polished dance floor, a few raised platforms, and lots and lots of lights. As for the people, they began arriving at one A.M., although the best music didn't play until six. Some came in limos. On special occasions, the staff stood outside in tuxedos to greet them. There were hanky models, writers, clerks, you name it. But what made the Flamingo unique is that they were all there to dance, truly. Wrote Whitmore: "That dance floor, that pedestrian square of parquet, is situated directly between the *Inferno* of 'real life' and the *Paradiso* we've all come here to achieve. On the right night, with the right drugs and the right music, a membership card to Flamingo can be a visa to a disembodied and transcendent state, beyond the Iron Curtain of individual identity, through a looking glass of ego, into the Land of Nod."

Remember, this was truly the dawning of the age of disco. When gay guides recommended the Flamingo, they warned their readers to go only to dance, not to cruise. One 1975 rag, *Man Alive!*, breathlessly insisted that a night at the Flamingo could be wild, but that it was all driven by "disco-energy, a phenomenal human force that, if harnessed, could alleviate any crisis real or imagined." Between the music and the drugs, they insisted, you could "generate enough energy to get everyone airborne. $E = MC^2$." Oh, that disco fever!

Walk east on Houston a few long blocks to First Avenue and turn left.

23. CLUB BATHS • 24 First Avenue
between 1st and 2nd Streets

Okay, just one more bathhouse on this round, I swear. Although now disguised as the fabulous, drag-staffed restaurant Lucky Cheng's, there was a bathhouse in this very building from the turn of the century until the closing of the baths in 1985. At the end of World War II, it was remodeled and called Gordon's, but in the 1970s and 1980s, it was renamed the **Club Baths.** There were four floors of activity: 50 private rooms, 50 walk-in lockers, 50 gym lockers, a maze, and a capacity of 250.

More than just a bathhouse, the Club Baths strove for respectability. The outside of the building was green with black shutters, with the name in stained wood letters on the brass-studded front door. The lobby had brick walls, plush carpeting, brass antique chandeliers, tropical plants, and male statues. Visitors were given towels and sarongs—stain-resistant, lined with terry cloth, and emblazoned with the club signet of an orgy scene. The private rooms had marble-top tables, walnut headboards, foam-rubber mattresses, and goose-down pillows. And in the basement, there was an octagonal shower, two chambered steam rooms, a whirlpool bath, and a swimming pool fed by natural springs and good enough for a dive.

As for hard statistics: In 1976, the baths hosted 5,000 customers each week. The typical client was a white male in his early thirties who earned about $12,000 a year, stayed five hours, and had three climaxes. One atypical visitor in 1975, though, was the young writer **Rita Mae Brown,** done up in mustache, codpiece, and robe. She wrote about her surreptitious (though undiscovered) visit: "Inching around the bed, I felt like I was sliding by a picket fence—all the erect penises behind me were hitting me in the small of my back. People reach for your genitals as you pass. My first response was to turn around and smash the offender's face in. I had to keep reminding myself, like a mantra chant, that these men thought I was a man and being a man is much safer than being a woman."

The Club's success meant that the owners, lovers **Bill McNeeley** and **Bob Moberg,** had half a million dollars to reinvest in new decorations in 1976. One addition: a room with a glass roof and a waterfall at one end. Go in, have a drink, flirt with the waitresses, and wander around, especially into the basement: you'll see that there are enough remnants of its previous life to give you a hint of the show. One oldtime regular: a young **Keith Haring.** After the Club Baths closed, a restaurant/bar called Cave Canem was set up here where, at least on lesbian nights, the downstairs facilities were kept in good use.

Follow 2nd Street east.

24. ALLEN GINSBERG'S HOME
- **170 East 2nd Street, Apartment 16, "The Croton"**
between Avenues A and B

The father of the beat generation, **Allen Ginsberg** was born in Newark, New Jersey, in 1926, the son of a poet and a Russian émigrée. He attended Columbia University for a while in the 1940s, but he was kicked out for writing graffiti and making inappropriate remarks about the university president. But while he was up there, through his friend Edie Parker, he got to know Jack Kerouac and **William Burroughs,** and the three of them became the great icons of a new literary avant-garde.

It was also at Columbia, when he was twenty, that Ginsberg came out. The first person he told was Kerouac; he had known him then for about a year. Why Kerouac? "Cause I was in love with him. He was staying in my room up on the bed, and I was sleeping on a pallet on the floor. I said, 'Jack, you know, I love you, and I want to sleep with you, and I really like men.' And he said, 'Oooooh, no . . .' " Eventually, though, Kerouac's initial dismay gave way, and he and Ginsberg spent many a night together.

When Ginsberg moved into the East Village (first at 206 East 7th Street) in the 1950s, he brought Kerouac, Burroughs, and the beat scene with him. He went off to San Francisco for a few years and, most famously, wrote *Howl*, the epic poem, introduced by William Carlos Williams with the line "Hold back the edges of your gowns, Ladies, we are going through hell," and whose publication radicalized young writers and ultimately resulted in an obscenity trial. (The homoerotics of Ginsberg's poetry are hardly subtle.) In 1959, Ginsberg and his long-term lover, **Peter Orlovsky,** moved in here and remained for quite some time. One poem he wrote described sitting in his window, high, at three o'clock in the morning, "gazing at Blue incandescent torches / bright-lit street below."

A cat crosses the street, "I meow / and she looks up, and passes a / pile of rubble on the way / to a golden shining garbage pail." (Interestingly, it was the view from Ginsberg's 7th Street apartment that inspired Burroughs's *Naked Lunch* vision of a city of catwalks and boardwalks.)

Ginsberg performed as a vital bridge between homosexuality, the literary avant-garde, and, in the 1960s, the antiwar movement. His work redefined poetry and at the same time made a place for homosexuality within the new definition. A few months after the Stonewall Uprising, Ginsberg gave a reading at New York University. He read a six-minute poem which the never unopinionated *New York Post* said "could easily pass for a homosexual's handbook on lovemaking." But the *Post* also noted that "if there's one thing the beat generation taught these kids, it's not to discriminate against homosexuals." That lesson is Ginsberg's doing.

Head east one more block.

25. STREET TRANSVESTITE ACTION REVOLUTIONARIES
- **213 East 2nd Street**
  between Avenues B and C

The gay liberation movement of 1969 and 1970 made few political entrees into the East Village, but one of the exceptions was STAR. Set up in 1971 by nineteen-year-old **Ray "Sylvia Lee" Rivera,** STAR focused on empowering and uniting drag queens, especially those who lived and worked on the streets. Rivera was a dynamic, if contentious, presence in the early liberation activities. Historian **Martin Duberman** has written much about Rivera, especially as a participant in the Stonewall riots. Of himself, Rivera once said, "I started wearing makeup to school in the fourth grade. I had no hassle until some kid on the playground called me a faggot and I had to beat him up. I stood there in full face makeup and the tightest pants I could squeeze into and said: nobody calls me a faggot."

Rivera was committed to making a safe space for young drag queens, a place to escape the streets and the life, and initially operated a refuge out of an abandoned trailer truck in the West Village. One morning, though, while twenty kids were asleep

Members of the Street Transvestite Action Revolutionaries, 1970. Sylvia Rivera, organizer and Stonewall rioter, is sitting in the middle.

inside, the truck was unabandoned and the operation moved here. Although the structure is now long gone, even then the building was barely a shell—no plumbing, electricity, or working boiler. But STAR cleaned it up, and though they were eventually evicted for failing to pay rent, for a time this served as a community center for young drag queens.

The following decade, drag queens again became a dynamic presence in the East Village, starting up Wigstock, the annual drag festival, a few blocks north of here in Tompkins Square Park. Wander around: there are bits of bohemia everywhere.

The Frontier Old and New: Chelsea

Since early in the 1990s, a gay explosion has been happening in Chelsea. If you've been around at all the past few years, you've seen it happen, especially in the commercial rebirth of Eighth Avenue. It's safe to say that while the West Village and Christopher Street have remained the center of the gay city—and especially so for the early generation of gay liberationists—Chelsea has risen to the status of Second City. Somewhat more affordable, it has attracted a new, younger, professional gay community.

I once told a friend how dramatic and exciting I found the transformation of Chelsea. He reminded me, though, that Chelsea's gay gentrification wasn't occurring in a vacuum: each gay boy or girl who moved in, each swanky new boîte that opened, each rent hike that occurred meant that someone else moved out, perhaps was forced out. In truth, he reminded me that Chelsea is a neighborhood with a past and that in that past being gay was not Chelsea's central identity. But the identity that Chelsea did form for the early gay community was important exactly because it was *not* central. Chelsea was off the beaten residential path. It was active in the day with commerce and industry, but quieter at night, removed from the action.

And because of that removal, it became a frontier outpost of gay life: not the center of an emergent gay community but a place where the outré could find a quiet loft or warehouse, take root and grow. This tour takes you through the various highlights of life along that frontier: the 1960s office of the

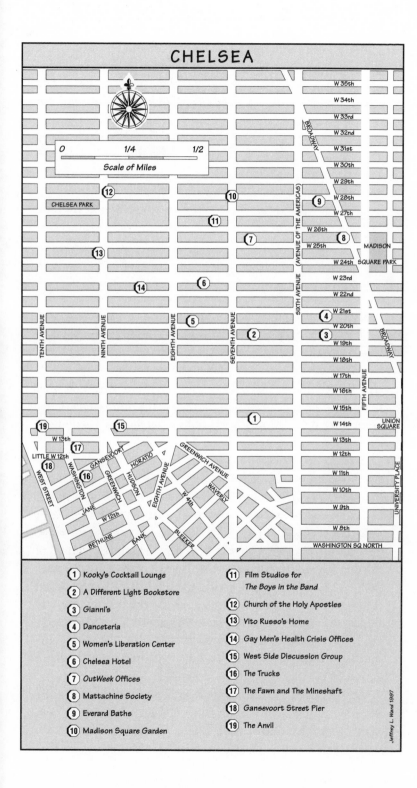

CHELSEA

① Kooky's Cocktail Lounge	⑪ Film Studios for *The Boys in the Band*
② A Different Light Bookstore	⑫ Church of the Holy Apostles
③ Gianni's	⑬ Vito Russo's Home
④ Danceteria	⑭ Gay Men's Health Crisis Offices
⑤ Women's Liberation Center	⑮ West Side Discussion Group
⑥ Chelsea Hotel	⑯ The Trucks
⑦ *OutWeek* Offices	⑰ The Fawn and The Mineshaft
⑧ Mattachine Society	⑱ Gansevoort Street Pier
⑨ Everard Baths	⑲ The Anvil
⑩ Madison Square Garden	

Jeffrey L. Ward 1997

Mattachine Society, the site of a World War I–and-beyond gay bathhouse, the offices from which *OutWeek* forced us to reconsider what it meant to be publicly gay in the 1980s, the waterfront cruise-and-sex-club strip from the 1970s, and the earliest home for the Gay Men's Health Crisis. Along the way, you'll also run into film historian **Vito Russo,** authors **William Burroughs** and **Herman Melville,** and composer **Ned Rorem.**

To get started, you can take almost any train to 14th Street. The 1/2/3/9 trains will place you smack on Seventh Avenue, but the F or the A/C/E trains will leave you only a block shy. You could even ride into Union Square on the 4/5/6 or N/R trains. (So many options!) Then we'll meet at Kooky's to see how Chelsea came into its own.

1. KOOKY'S COCKTAIL LOUNGE • 149 West 14th Street
between Sixth and Seventh Avenues

At the time of the Stonewall Uprising, there were only two lesbian bars operating in Manhattan: **Kooky's Cocktail Lounge,** which was in this building, and Gianni's, up on 19th Street, where we'll head in a minute. Kooky was the owner, unusual not for being straight—most gay-bar owners were— but for being a woman. Supposedly a former prostitute, Kooky had dyed, lacquered blond hair and a fondness for pink crinoline dresses; but appearances aside, she was rather a tough. She would frequently grab a woman's glass and shove the drink up to her mouth, shouting, "Drink up, drink up! This ain't a church, you know! You want to spend all your time talking, go to a church and talk in the pew." Then she would tell the bartender that the woman was ordering another drink; if the woman balked, Kooky would taunt her with her ubiquitous cigarette and have the bouncers help her find the sidewalk.

When some Gay Liberation Front women tried to hand out fliers about an upcoming women's dance, Kooky had her bouncers kick them out. When they hung around outside, she sent the bouncers out after them. GLF headquarters were just a block away on the corner of Sixth Avenue and 14th Street, and it was felt that Kooky feared the competition that liberation groups presented. (Some of the dance organizers suspected that she sent a couple of guys over to harass the women at the dance.) In the summer of 1971, women from the GLF, the Gay Activists Alliance, and the Daughters of Bilitis picketed Kooky's for their "exploitative policies," chanting, "Kooky's gonna crumble." But Kooky's was one of only two places lesbians had for themselves, and so it did not crumble quickly.

Follow Seventh Avenue up to 19th Street and hang a right.

2. A DIFFERENT LIGHT BOOKSTORE
- **151 West 19th Street**
  between Sixth and Seventh Avenues

Before catching up with the other half of 1969 lesbian nightlife, a quick but essential detour: though located here only since 1994, this **A Different Light Bookstore** forms part of one of the largest gay and lesbian bookselling operations in the country. The chain's flagship store opened its doors in Los Angeles back in 1979, founded by **Norman Laurila** with a silent partner. From there the two set up shops in the West Village (in 1983) and San Francisco (in 1986). Back in the 1970s, Laurila told me recently, starting a gay bookstore was hardly a high-yield economic venture; instead it was a political act, "based on political ideals, and certainly inspired by gay liberation." His take-home "pay" was all of $600 a month.

While Laurila insists that the store still runs as "a labor of love," business has clearly picked up. Just in terms of square footage, this store is the largest gay and lesbian bookstore in the country, with 3,500 square feet devoted to 15,000 titles. Additionally, they offer some 250 events a year, including readers' groups, writing workshops, book signings, and movie screenings. Importantly, the existence of stores like Laurila's, the Oscar Wilde in the Village, and Lambda Rising in Washington, D.C., profoundly transformed the book publishing industry. Mainstream publishers came to recognize that there was both a demand and a marketplace for gay literature, and they began to put money into publishing gay writers. The gamble that booksellers like Laurila took paid off in returns to the community as a whole. Hey, you don't hear me complaining.

Head east on 19th Street to get a sense of what the women's bar circuit was like in 1970.

3. GIANNI'S • 53 West 19th Street
between Fifth and Sixth Avenues

Although now a swanky publishing-house lunch spot, for at least forty years this building served as the home for one lesbian bar or another. (It certainly hasn't lost that feeling entirely.) Although the bar itself went through several name changes (and presumably several managements), it always catered to the women's crowd and anchored this stretch of 19th Street as a kind of permanent lesbian outpost. Its oldest—and longest—identity was as **Gianni's,** a bar open in the 1950s, if not before, and remaining open through the beginning of gay liberation. (This was Kooky's other half.) In the 1970s it recast itself, first as Casa Maria, then, briefly, as the Silhouette; in 1980, it became Ariel's and remained open throughout the decade.

Mind you, through all those years Chelsea wasn't just bustling with lesbians day and night, keeping the cash registers ringing. For one thing, it was far from legal to run a bar for lesbians. Even in 1970, the official bar policy was to operate as a straight men's bar during the daytime. Then, after eight P.M., the owner, a man, raised the prices. This by and large drove the men away without explicitly kicking them out, and allowed the women a bit of exclusive, if expensive, privacy.

Although usually successful, it was a policy with obvious pitfalls; it certainly failed to maintain a clear separation between the two clienteles. One evening in January 1970, for instance, two women were dancing when three or four men came into the bar. They followed one of the women into the bathroom and grabbed her. Her girlfriend came in and told the men to leave her alone. One fellow simply turned around and decked her, and then the men left and for a long time no one did anything. Finally, a group of women ran out into the street, intending to chase the men down; all but one of them gave up the idea—and the one who didn't was beaten up by the men.

The Gay Liberation Front, led by **Martha Shelley,** brought a protest group of forty women here. They complained about the lack of safety at the bar and the take-what-you-can-get attitude of the management. And though they made a point of dancing together before leaving—just to show that they could—there was little that they could accomplish: as gay men and women had learned over and over, as mere patrons they had no power. They needed to run their own bars and clubs and dances. The GLF held its first lesbian dance three months later. (It was that dance that Kooky tried to disrupt.)

For more about the GLF, see the West Village tour.

Walk east to Fifth Avenue, turn left, and then left again on 21st Street.

4. DANCETERIA · 30 West 21st Street
between Fifth and Sixth Avenues

Now **Danceteria** was not a gay-only hangout, but this 1980s dance club was operated principally by **Jim Fouratt,** a recurring figure in the life of New York's gay community. Active in the 1960s Caffe Cino theater scene, Fouratt was outside the Stonewall Inn the night the rioting began. He became a founder of the Gay Liberation Front and later helped to establish both the Lesbian and Gay Community Services Center and ACT UP.

But professionally, Fouratt's focus lay in clubs and music. Danceteria was his first major venture. It came to life with a sputter, first opening up shop on 37th Street in the summer of 1980. It didn't last, and in 1982 Fouratt and a partner tried again. This time they were successful, and Danceteria became a hip and exciting dance club, rock stage, and performance space. The entertainment ranged from X to the Go-Go's. There were three dance floors here (up on the tenth, eleventh, and twelfth floors, actually), a video lounge, video games, a restaurant (Club Sandwich), bars, and a stage. There were Wednesday-night Art Attacks with musical performances by Philip Glass or Diamanda Galas. And it was here that sounds like the Beastie Boys and Run-DMC first broke into the mainstream.

It was also here, in 1982, that a little (or a lot) of blond ambition finally paid off. Sweet Ms. **Madonna** Ciccone, decked out in torn clothes, oodles of baubles, and tons of makeup, made a point of befriending DJ Mark Kamins, requesting songs from him and dancing in front of his booth when he played them. That way, when she finally asked him to play a four-track demo tape of her song "Everybody" at the club, he was willing. That spring, a Sire records talent scout heard the song and took the dare, sweeping Madonna up and into the rest of our ears and faces.

Follow 21st Street west to Seventh Avenue, then scoot down to 20th and turn right.

5. WOMEN'S LIBERATION CENTER
- **243 West 20th Street**
  between Seventh and Eighth Avenues

In 1972, the Gay Activists Alliance, *the* gay political group of the time, set up a women's committee to address lesbian-specific issues. As the year progressed, though, the GAA women became increasingly tired of having to negotiate special times for their events and dances. Committee members began to think that gay women had to be separate, had to find their own identity. By 1973, they splintered off and set up operations here as the Lesbian Feminist Liberation, and then added a Lesbian Switchboard as well. Founder **Jean O'Leary** recalled that "just as gay people have had to become visible in society, lesbians had to become visible within the gay community, as well as in the larger society."

In so doing, they were following the lead of the Daughters of Bilitis, a San Francisco–based women's organization that had set itself up in the 1950s alongside, but separate from, the male-dominated Mattachine Society. DOB, discussed more in the Midtown tour, arranged lectures from psychiatrists, picnics, and "Gab 'n' Java" sessions with discussion topics like "How to Make Your Lesbian Marriage Work" and "Should

Lesbians Wear Skirts?" For a time, DOB actually shared space here in the Women's Firehouse.

By 1973, though, most organized lesbians were presenting their agenda a little bit more radically. LFL had an array of committees devoted to media concerns, finances, sports, and politics. And their discussions covered topics like "Overcoming Sexual Fears," "Politics in the Bedroom," and "So What's a Cute Dyke Anyway?" Mind you, LFL didn't consider itself as entirely separate from the larger male-dominated gay groups, and in 1976 LFL member **Joanne Passarao** was elected the first woman president of New York's Gay Activists Alliance. But at the same time, there was an increasingly clear impression that lesbian concerns were not always allied with "mainstream" gay issues. As O'Leary explained it, LFL was formed by "those of us who finally tired of talking about reforming a society with Gay males who know no other way of fighting our shared oppression than to attack the system through tired and ineffectual male politics. . . . We realized that Gay politics will never cut deep enough to eliminate the sexism in a totally sexist society and that for us to be freed as gay people would still leave us oppressed as women."

But operating at the intersection of gay liberation and feminism was not always a comfortable position. During the summer of '73, O'Leary and others had an angry shouting match at the Gay Pride Rally, where LFL members criticized the politics of drag queens. "We support the right of every person to dress in the way that she or he wishes," their leaflet read, "but we are opposed to the exploitation of women by men for entertainment or profit." And the next summer, LFL simply organized a separate lesbian rally for Gay Pride weekend. The continued existence of separate men's and women's rallies and marches is a legacy of those early struggles.

Wander up Seventh Avenue and make a left on 23rd Street.

6. CHELSEA HOTEL • 222 West 23rd Street
between Seventh and Eighth Avenues

Opened in 1884 as apartments, by 1905 the **Chelsea** had been converted to a residential hotel. (It was the first New York apartment building to have twelve stories, as well as the first with a penthouse.) The Chelsea has 400 rooms, 3-foot-thick walls, a reputation as "the world's most tolerant, non-expendable, third-rate hotel," and an artistic, not to mention gay, lineage that's hard to beat: **Tennessee Williams** lived here for a bit, as did **Mary McCarthy,** and composers **Ned Rorem** and **Virgil Thomson** (actually Thomson lived here for ages); **Larry Rivers** painted here, **Arthur C. Clarke** (ooh, didn't know about *him*, did you?) wrote *2001* while living on the tenth floor; and **William Burroughs** wrote *Naked Lunch* here; **Robert Mapplethorpe** and Patti Smith shared housekeeping here for some time, fashion designer **Charles James** stayed here, as did **Janis Joplin** (read *Going Down with Janis*) when she was in town, and **Andy Warhol** used it as a setting for *Chelsea Girls.* Even **Lance Loud,** who came out in that uniquely American way, on television, in PBS's portrait *An American Family*, spent many a night here. And that's just a beginning. (Check yourself in and add to the list.)

It's hard to choose among so many of our illustrious forebears. Perhaps this time we could defer to the serious-music folks. (Once in a while you have to, or they won't let you near the jukebox.) One, Virgil Thomson, deserves mention in part because of the genealogy he suggests. Thomson, born in Kansas City in 1896, was a child prodigy, performing professionally on the piano by the age of 12. After studying at Harvard, he went off to Paris to train with Nadia Boulanger and eventually decided that if he was going to starve as a composer, he "preferred to do it where the food is good" and settled there. Boulanger's trainees, mind you, included some of the American music world's brightest lights, as well as our own, and they came to be a bit of a community unto themselves: fellows like **Aaron Copland, Marc Blitzstein,** and **Leonard Bernstein,** to name a few. In Paris, Thomson became friends with **Gertrude Stein** (at a certain point you begin to wonder, who didn't?), and together they wrote two operas, including one called *The Mother of Us All* about **Susan B. Anthony.** He wrote all kinds of music, but after returning to the U.S. and settling all but permanently here in the Chelsea, he became most noted as a music critic.

Ned Rorem, on the other hand, has come to be recognized as one of the century's outstanding modern composers. Born in Indiana in 1923, he came to New York to study music at Juilliard and eventually ended up working with both Copland and Thomson. By 1958 he had written music for **Tennessee Williams**'s play *Suddenly Last Summer* and had been approached, he wrote, by **William Inge,** Williams's more depressive counterpart. Inge apparently wanted his assistance with "a libretto about a sodomite undertaker who is required to embalm, on stage, the person dearest to his heart." Rorem has also earned a reputation as an unabashed diarist, publishing volume after volume as the years have progressed. In the spring of 1955, he captured some of the details of gay New York life, where the new slang included "goof" and "flip," and the new craze was a kind of "male impersonation" that entailed "affecting leather and dungarees (male symbols, it seems)." Such a poser, wrote Rorem, "attends S. & M. meetings (i.e., sado-masochist or slave-master) where truly gory doings are rumored. Yet, when I question [fellow composer] **Bill Flanagan** about the details, the Third Avenue bartender, overhearing, intrudes: 'Don't kid yourself—they just hit each other with a lot of wet Kleenex!' "

Let me sneak in one last resident for a little spice. **William Burroughs,** one of the most dangerous geniuses of our century, was born in St. Louis in 1910, the grandson of the inventor of the adding machine. Those are the most mundane details about him. He loved one woman in his life and many men; the woman, he married and then, tragically, killed in a drunken stunt in Mexico. But her death, he has said, inspired him to write—it "brought me into contact with the invader, the Ugly Spirit and maneuvered me into a lifelong struggle, in which I have had no choice except to write my way out." Burroughs has not only written: his art has ranged from films to shotgun paintings. And his mind, vision, and style made him a guru to beat writers **Jack Kerouac** (whom **Gore Vidal** claims to have had sex with in this very hotel) and **Allen Ginsberg.** (For a while Burroughs was deeply in love with Ginsberg.) His visions are indeed extraordinary, whether they be the man with the talking anus in *Naked Lunch* or the aromatic Popsicles in *Cities of the Red Night* that smell like "the hyacinth smell of young hard-ons, a whiff of school toilets, locker rooms and jock straps, rectal mucus and summer feet." *Naked Lunch*, by the way, was banned in Boston in 1959 when it was first published.

Spin around for a quick second. See that beautiful YMCA across the street? A gay arts note: **Keith Haring** spent his first two nights ever in New York City there. (By the third night, he'd made a friend and moved in with him . . .)

Trundle up Seventh Avenue and head right on 25th Street.

7. OutWeek Offices • 159 West 25th Street
between Sixth and Seventh Avenues

Though short-lived (and truth be told, few magazines are not) *OutWeek* magazine set the gay world on its ear: its weekly publication marked the beginning of a newly energized wave of gay journalism. Started in the summer of 1989, it captured the activist dynamism of ACT UP and expanded it to broader gay concerns. Cofounder **Michelangelo Signorile** felt that the magazine "infused a generation of activists in New York with their weekly fix of anger, wrapped in a slick, sometimes irreverent, always media-savvy package. Even if you hated it, the magazine was a must read every morning at City Hall, in the media, and even among the most conservative types in the gay movement."

Perhaps most famously, in the summer of 1989, it introduced us to "outing"—the much-debated practice of publishing the names of famous but closeted gay men and women. Twice that summer, under an unspecified column called "Peek-a-Boo," *OutWeek* published a list of names. Who was on it? Well, lots of the usual suspects: that singer and her two actresses (despite her marriage to that skinny singing boy), for instance, or those kids from the movie *Grease*.

By 1990, especially in Signorile's columns and articles, outing was no longer a simple printing of names, and it was beginning to have repercussions. In March of that year, shortly after **Malcolm Forbes**'s death, Signorile, fearful that Forbes would be remembered simply as **Elizabeth Taylor**'s alleged lover, put together a lengthy article on his life which focused in particular on Forbes's tendency to sexually harass his male employees. From there, the politics of the closet and privacy spun out of the pages of *OutWeek* and into the pages of other gay journals and even the mainstream media. Gay people were no longer just dropping hints about **David Geffen** or **k. d. lang;** people in and out of the gay community were debating what it meant that **Pete Williams,** Defense Department spokesman during the Gulf War and a gay man, was representing an organization that refused to allow gay men and women to serve. There was pressure and soul-searching anxiety, but there was also opportunity. It is in large part due to the kind of discussion that *OutWeek* instigated that for so many public figures the veil has recently dropped, the closet door swung open. Olympic diving champion **Greg Louganis,** for instance, whose name appeared on the initial "Peek-a-Boo" list, has since performed on New York's gay theater stage, spoken in the media about being gay and HIV-positive, and published the story of his difficult life in a revealing autobiography.

OutWeek folded at the start of the 1990s, but several staffers went on to assist in the creation of the hugely successful monthly magazine *Out.* Certainly, their broader legacy remains with us.

Follow 25th Street east to Broadway and make a left.

8. MATTACHINE SOCIETY • 1133 Broadway, fourth floor
on the southwest corner of 26th Street

From 1965 to 1968, the New York Mattachine Society, the premier homophile and gay rights organization, maintained an office here. Founded in Los Angeles in 1950, the society started a New York branch in 1955 (you can read about it in the Midtown tour). Although the office here was open only weekday evenings and Saturday afternoons, its presence demonstrated that the society was no longer a kind of monthly club. It was here as a community fixture, organizing meetings with clergy as well as publishing articles on what to do if arrested or "How to Handle a Federal Interrogation."

These were crucial years of transition for Mattachine. In April 1965, two major homosexual rights demonstrations were staged. The first, organized in Washington, D.C., by Mattachine firebrand **Frank Kameny** (a Queens-born fellow), put homosexual picketers in suits and dresses out in front of the

White House. Their signs declared, "15 Million U.S. Homosexuals Protest Federal Treatment" and "U.S. Claims No Second-Class Citizens: What About Homosexuals?" The following day, twenty-nine New York protesters picketed in front of the United Nations buildings, protesting reports that the Cuban government was rounding up gay men and women and putting them in labor camps. While not the first gay rights pickets in the country, these were impressively visible and strategic.

The following year, conversations with the mayor led to an order to stop police entrapment. Also in 1966, Mattachine coordinated a sip-in at **Julius'** bar (described in the West Village tour) to challenge the state's law that prohibited serving drinks to homosexuals—and won that battle. The city government was no longer refusing to hire homosexuals, and the New York ACLU was finally handling their cases. Mattachine was making the kind of steady headway they had always hoped for.

But at the same time a new visibility and sense of daring were infusing their protests and protesters. Certainly men and women were starting to "come out" in unprecedented fashion. And Mattachine, conservative in its heart, was placed in a not entirely comfortable position. In a 1965 newsletter editorial urging Mattachine members to write letters to editors when they read homophobic articles, the staff simultaneously asked "that you try as hard as possible, *before* writing your letters, to analyze each situation thoroughly enough so that you can tell whether or not the original article was justified in its complaints." Be prudent, they seemed to be saying. Be on the offensive, but move slowly.

Prudence, ultimately, was not the tactic gay liberation chose. In the wake of the Stonewall Uprising, Mattachine tried to maintain a middle ground, one that condemned the raid but acknowledged the legitimate safety concerns at the bar. A middle ground, though, was no longer on the agenda. When energized young protesters tried to work through Mattachine to channel their energy, excited about "gay power" and a "gay liberation movement," older Mattachine members simply thought that while "the words were new to us, the substance was not." But what *was* also new was the style. For while the ultimate goals of Mattachine and the subsequent Gay Liberation Front or Gay Activists Alliance may not have been so different, the means to achieving those ends were: the days of patience were over.

Head up to 28th Street and turn left.

9. EVERARD BATHS • 38 West 28th Street
between Broadway and Sixth Avenue

From the serious to the sublime: the "Ever Hard," one of our more legendary bathhouses, and even more of an institution than Mattachine. The building that once stood here is now gone, though you can recognize it in the photograph. It was originally a church, but James Everard, part businessman-brewer, part politician, converted it to a bathhouse in 1888. It launched no advertising campaigns, but by the First World War its clientele was predominantly gay and soon famous as far away as Europe. Both a centerpiece of gay life and an icon of it, the Everard boasted a clientele as diverse as the gay community itself. And with the Mattachine Society offices so conveniently around the corner in the 1960s and some of the earliest gay discos just blocks away in the 1970s, there was always a steady stream of customers. (At some hour the discos would close; the Everard would not.)

Although when it opened, the Everard was considered the classiest of bathhouses, by the 1960s and '70s one of its fundamental attractions was its seediness. One patron in the 1970s described it as "sort of like Dante's Inferno. . . . They cleaned it up a couple of years ago and the patrons got upset and disoriented. So it wasn't long before it was filthy again. The fetid smell of the steam room in the old days, though, had its own kind of hairy and hoary sexuality that was sort of a turn on." And a younger fellow contrasted it with the Club Baths in the East Village "with all those pretty boys sitting around, most of who I knew and certainly wasn't interested in. And it was just so clean and sparkly there—you were afraid you might cum on the carpet or something, you know?" Really! But while a little mess wasn't frowned on at the Everard, talking was. One reg-

The Everard Baths in 1932.

ular remembered that conversation drew "stern looks of disapproval from the other patrons, deeply offended that so trivial a pursuit as *talk* was impinging on the high seriousness of *sex*."

Early one morning just before Memorial Day of 1977, a smoldering mattress set off a fire here. Two hundred firemen and 31 trucks came to fight it, but the sprinkler system didn't work and the fire crews were not enough. Six people had jumped from the windows, and twenty were rescued by ladders, but nine men were killed and seven critically injured; and the bathhouse was largely destroyed.

Follow 28th Street west to Seventh Avenue.

10. MADISON SQUARE GARDEN
• **Seventh Avenue and 28th Street**

Surprise! Madison Square Garden is *not* at this corner. It's not really a *pretty* place and hardly worth walking the extra blocks just to look it square in the face. If you look uptown to your right four blocks, you can make out its monolithic facade on the west side of the street, with its milling crowds and display board out front. (Pennsylvania Station—where people catch the train out to Fire Island—operates underneath it just to add to the confusion.) I do, though, want to share a couple of favorite Garden notes.

Now, the Garden has both a sports arena and a theater. On the theater side, the Garden has played host to folks like **Elton John**—in a 1976 three-hour spectacle that saw him adorned as both the Statue of Liberty and Uncle Sam—and **Barbra Streisand.** Less remembered today, the San Francisco–based singer **Sylvester** performed there in October 1980. Sylvester began his career singing in drag and, like Elton, toyed with various looks, sometimes wearing earrings, fringed cowboy clothes, or long corn-rowed hair pulled into a ponytail. But it was his voice and music that raised the world and set it in motion. Some of his songs—"Dance (Disco Heat)," "You Make Me Feel Mighty Real," "I Need Somebody Tonight," "Body Strong"—remain classic emblems of what disco fever was all about. (The theater also hosted the body-building competition for the Gay Games in 1994. I was there: very swoony.)

The sports arena, as far as I'm concerned, belongs to only one person: **Martina Navratilova.** Sure the Knicks play there now and again, but it was there that Martina all but created the Virginia Slims tennis tournament. For much of the 1980s and '90s, Martina was the dominant force in women's tennis. As a young girl, she has said, her first crush was on her math teacher, also an athlete. "I would find myself staring at her, trailing after her, just finding any excuse to watch her play sports or listen to her talk." Later in her life, she had a long relationship with author **Rita Mae Brown.** And when she retired from tennis in 1995, she did it at the Garden.

Head down Seventh Avenue and make a right on 26th Street.

11. FILM STUDIOS FOR *THE BOYS IN THE BAND*
  • **221 West 26th Street**
  between Seventh and Eighth Avenues

Here's the story, in case you don't remember it: Michael throws a party for Harold, hosting not only their diversely gay friends but also Alan, an old college friend whose marriage (and sexuality) seem to be on the rocks, as well as the birthday present *de grâce*, a mindless hustler. There is singing, humor, and then, for the ultimate in painful party entertainment, a yucky game of telephoning your greatest love and declaring your affections.

The play, by **Mart Crowley,** grew out of a playwrights' workshop started by **Edward Albee,** among others. It was hardly the first New York show to have a gay character, but it was the first to take some version of gay life for granted, and it inspired gay theater pieces all over town. It ran for two and a half years, from April 1968 to September 1970. **Rudolf Nureyev** saw it (apparently sitting on a male friend's lap because he couldn't get a seat); *Look* magazine featured it on the cover. Its reception from the gay community was mixed, though, and as its run wore on, the audiences were increasingly straight. One gay newsletter noted in the winter of 1969 that "as more time goes on, more Homosexuals decide they don't like the play and more Heterosexuals decide they do like it (possibly because *Boys* reassures the audience that Homosexuals are indeed the sick, depraved and guilt-ridden lot they are pictured as)."

Nevertheless, in the midst of that run, in that fabulous summer of '69, here in what is now the home of Chelsea TV (but was once Adolph Zukor's Famous Players Studios) *The Boys* became a movie. Crowley told a *New York Times* reporter that summer that he had gotten pitched by the big studios, but their "responses . . . were pretty much what I expected them to be." After grinning slyly, he explained: "Immediately at lunch they would start talking about the title tune." Crowley ended up with director William Friedkin, whose most significant accomplishment at the time was having directed Sonny and Cher's first film, *Good Times.* (Okay, that's a *slight* exaggeration: he had also recently completed the artful *Night They Raided Minsky's.*) But *Boys* the movie was a big enough success that Friedkin went on to direct not only *The Exorcist* but also the next decade's mainstream film about homosexual life (with an equally unpleasant perspective), *Cruising.* Success for Crowley meant that by 1980, he was a producer for television's *Hart to Hart.* Go, Mart!

Follow 26th west to Eighth Avenue, then scoot up to 28th Street and turn left.

12. CHURCH OF THE HOLY APOSTLES
corner of 28th Street and Ninth Avenue

Father Robert Weeks, the pastor here, was instrumental in laying the groundwork for the swelling of gay activism and support that occurred at the end of the 1960s. Weeks coordinated, in the fall of 1967, a gathering of ninety regional Episcopalian priests which put forth one of the first religious declarations that homosexuality was morally neutral. Weeks also privately blessed several gay marriages, and when **Diego Vinales,** a young gay Argentinean man, was critically injured in the 1970 raid of the Snake Pit, Weeks prayed at his bedside. (See more in the West Village tour.) The West Side Discussion Group, an essentially gay social group that dated back well into the 1950s, met here for many years; and both the Gay Activists Alliance and the Gay Liberation Front met here during their fledgling months. In May 1969, NYU and Columbia's gay student groups took over the social hall for the First New York City All-College Gay Mixer.

Additionally, in July of 1970, Weeks began turning the church over on Sunday afternoons to **Father Robert Clements** and his Church of the Beloved Disciple. Clements started his church with the same spirit that moved **Troy Perry** to open the Metropolitan Community Church in Los Angeles, hoping to create a religious home for a congregation that was primarily, though not exclusively, gay. Said Clements at the time, "We hope that people rejected in the past by other churches will find this a church that accepts them." Clements's afternoon services thinned the crowds out a bit on Sunday mornings, but later in the day the pews were packed.

Walk down to the corner of 24th Street.

13. VITO RUSSO'S HOME
- **401 West 24th Street, Apartment 1**
at Ninth Avenue

Born just after the Second World War and raised in East Harlem, **Vito Russo** devoted most of his adult life to gay activism and the gay community, and especially to examining the role of homosexuality in the movies. Only twenty-two years old the weekend of the Stonewall Uprising, Russo spent much of that Friday at Judy Garland's funeral and then, walking home, stumbled upon the crowd in front of the bar and climbed into a tree in Sheridan Square and watched. His own activism wasn't really sparked, though, until the Snake Pit raid in 1970, and then he started getting involved with the Gay Activists Alliance, especially running their weekly film nights. "Every film I've shown," he said at the time, "I had seen before with a straight audience. It's a new experience watching a gay audience reaction. They pick up on things that straight audiences miss—an innuendo, the direction, the way a scene is played. It also seems like gay audiences are always pulling for

the underdogs, which may have something to do with our own persecution as homosexuals."

Russo was doing graduate work in film at NYU and working in the film department at the Museum of Modern Art at the time. In 1973, he started researching the ways gays and lesbians have been depicted in film. Initially, the research spawned a traveling lecture, but eight years later, and after talking to eighteen publishers, Russo got a book published. *The Celluloid Closet* was released to an acclaim that has continued to this day, and most recently, under **Lily Tomlin**'s stewardship, the book was itself made into a film.

Arnie Kantrowitz remembered Russo as "a firefly" who raced from GAA meetings to movie screenings to writing. He adored Judy Garland: his brown eyes "brightened with fervor" at the mere mention of her name, and he had pictures of her in every room of his apartment, including the bathroom. He was a man of passion, with a sharp tongue, exploding once, "We're not 'girls,' lady; we're men who fuck each other, and you'd better get used to it!" But, as Kantrowitz recalled, "his tears were quick when he was hurt, his smile radiant when he was pleased." Russo died of complications from AIDS in November 1990.

Follow Ninth Avenue down to 22nd Street and hang left.

14. GAY MEN'S HEALTH CRISIS OFFICES
- **318 West 22nd Street**
  between Eighth and Ninth Avenues

In the summer of 1981, the *New York Times* published its first article about a "rare cancer" that was infecting gay men. One month later, **Larry Kramer** and some friends invited eighty men to meet in Kramer's apartment with an NYU doctor to discuss this "cancer." It was a tense, frightening, and sometimes hostile meeting, but, as one attendee reported, "each man swallowed his panic and found himself shocked into action." Their action created the **Gay Men's Health Crisis.** The organization was formally established in the beginning of

Young Vito Russo at a Gay Activists Alliance street fair in June 1971.

1982; its founders were Kramer, **Edmund White, Lawrence Mass, Nathan Fain, Paul Popham,** and **Paul Rapoport.**

When they were looking for office space, **Mel Cheren,** who owns this building (now the Colonial House Inn) and was renting out rooms for short-term stays, told them they could use the second and third floors. They remained here for two years and took over three-quarters of the building before moving into their own offices farther east. In the early years, they focused on getting research done on the disease. Before the organization was even fully chartered, they had raised $11,000—soliciting outside of discos and bars—for a Kaposi's Sarcoma Fund at the NYU Medical Center, and $50,000 that they distributed to individual doctors.

Increasingly, their efforts broadened to include client care. As one early volunteer recalled, "We started out just to find out who was supposed to be dealing with the problems [of people with AIDS]. Then we realized no one was: it would have to be us." They set up a twenty-four-hour information hot line, and **Rodger McFarlane,** the first executive director, worked to establish the now well-known "buddy system," which eventually offered support not only to clients but to lovers, friends, and family.

By now GMHC is the largest AIDS service organization in the country, with an annual budget that exceeds $20 million and more than two thousand active volunteers. By the end of 1992, they had helped fourteen thousand AIDS sufferers and were receiving between one hundred and two hundred new clients a month (let alone eighty thousand phone calls on their hot line). Their AIDS Walks and Dance-a-thons have raised millions of dollars and have become as institutionalized as the organization itself. In the intervening years, they have received their fair share of criticism—from founder Kramer, from ACT UP, from women and communities of color. Nevertheless, in 1981, GMHC organizers began asking questions that no one else was asking, they began providing answers even when answers barely existed, and they began the daunting and dismaying project of trying to strip away the homophobic and moralizing language that quickly came to surround the disease.

Turn right on Eighth Avenue and head down to 14th Street.

15. WEST SIDE DISCUSSION GROUP • 348 West 14th Street
between Eighth and Ninth Avenues

In the mid-1950s, the New York Mattachine Society established neighborhood discussion groups for people to talk and
socialize in private homes. The one on the West Side, though,
quickly became too large to meet in private homes or even to
stay part of Mattachine. In 1956, the WSDG became a separate organization and started meeting in a variety of places,
including Father Robert Weeks's Church of the Holy Apostles.
By 1970, 125 people were coming to their Wednesday-night
meetings, which were followed by a social hour featuring sodas
and jukebox dancing. By 1972, the WSDG had set up shop
here and 250 people were attending. According to one regular,
the crowds were wild: "There are campy queens, yummy
butches, Afroed blacks, groovy hippies, yarmulked Jews, mini-
skirted secretaries, Joe College types, all simply itching for
humpy you to grace our portals with your presence." Discussion topics in 1974 included "What Is Homosexuality?," "The
Sexual Revolution," "Gay Couples Counseling," and "The
Gay Drug Addict." By then, though, in addition to discussions,
the WSDG was having pot luck dinners with square dancing,
movie screenings, Saturday-night dance parties, even door-
prize raffles of passes to the East Village **Club Baths.** The
organization lasted well into the 1980s, although by then they
had moved down into the West Village proper, and their discussions had become more explicit, with topics like "Masturba-
tion" ("No, honey, you've got your hand all wrong!"), "Positive
Body Image: The Key to Successful Cruising" ("Repeat after
me: I *am* beautiful!"), and "Single Again" (same course, different title).

*Make a left on Ninth Avenue for two blocks, and then turn right
on Gansevoort out of the crazy cobblestone intersection. Follow
Gansevoort west one block (passing the sensational Restaurant
Florent as you go).*

16. THE TRUCKS
southwest corner of Gansevoort and Washington Streets

We're pushing the boundaries of Chelsea here. Truth be told, we've entered the nether world of wholesale food markets that has existed at the waterfront edge of the city for decades. These days, the marketing is almost exclusively in meat, carcasses rolling in and out in the early hours of the day. But back at the start of the century you could walk in the wee hours from where you are now, down along Washington or Greenwich or Hudson Street through a mile and a half of warehouses crammed with foods: coffee and tea and sugar and spices and fruits and vegetables. This was what it took to feed the city of millions. Those markets are largely gone, faded in the second half of the century. But the sensual memories of that vast Tenderloin and the men who worked there lingered. Indeed, under the heady spell of gay liberation, they became the fantasies of the men who came to prowl the old waterfront and warehouses.

In the months following Stonewall, places with names like the Zoo and the Department Store and the Glory Hole began springing up in this area, places where sex, for the first time since the 1920s, really, returned to the club scene. To borrow a phrase from **Arthur Bell,** "those joints taught us cruising needn't be staring at a guy's crotch in a mirror when you can grab it." One bar reviewer at the time noted that when the Zoo first opened that year, they were revolutionary enough to show porn flicks on the wall, "getting everyone so horny, they pole-vaulted into that dark back room where the orgy was always in progress. It seemed as if we were all on another planet."

Even more than for club life, though, this area became notorious for truck life. For years, all along this stretch of Washington Street, the trucks that by day brought fresh slabs of meat to a hungry city sat out here all night allegedly empty. In fact they were filled with reveling men hungry to put their own meat to finer uses. This was New York's meat packing district, where the daytime name was earned at night. (Snap! Snap!)

The precise locus of the activity shifted over the years, when new housing was built or truck parking areas were changed. But wherever the trucks were, after posturing and posing all night, men would ditch the bars and head for the pitch-black anonymity of the trucks. In 1970, **John Rechy** described his own wandering in the dark mist of Washington Street. "I move into the maze formed by parked trucks. The sound of feet on discarded beer cans jangles the darkness. In the aisles between the trucks outlines wait for a sexual connection. A man has followed me. We jump into the back of one of the trucks abandoned for the night. Sighs stir its heavy darkness. We move into another truck. We go through the motions. . . ."

Walk up Washington a block to Little West 12th Street.

17. THE FAWN AND THE MINESHAFT
• **835 Washington Street**
on the northeast corner of Little West 12th Street

Despite the explosion of clubs in the years right after Stonewall, the Zoo and the Glory Hole were not the first places to show up here. Early in the 1960s, there had been a men's dance club near here called the **Fawn.** It operated on the weekends only, and although it primarily catered to men, when the police closed it in 1963, their investigators reported they had also found women dancing with women. When the investigators filed their report, they also noted that there was a back room for which admission was charged. What went on back there? What do I know? Poker, I would imagine. . . .

Perhaps the epitome of the new waterfront scene was in this pink building. Opened in October 1976 and closed in November 1985 (with a padlock and a "public nuisance" notice), for nine years the **Mineshaft** reigned as the ultimate gay sex club. There was as strict a dress code as at the finest gentlemen's clubs in the city: NO to cologne, suits, ties, jackets, disco drag, makeup, designer sweaters, rugby shirts, parkas, and *especially* Lacoste shirts; YES to western gear, leather motorcycle outfits, Levi's, T-shirts, tank tops, official-looking uniforms, plaid shirts, rugged work pants, cutoffs, gym wear, jock straps, and plain old sweat. (It was the Village People's dress code to a T.) And there was a body-beautiful bouncer in leather at the door, enforcing the dress code, sniffing the would-be clientele. The genius of the code, by the way, was that if you came in the wrong outfit, you could always take it off at the door.

The Mineshaft created its own culture, with tenets like "The man in his uniform is a man to behold for his manly beauty." And there were special nights here: a body painting contest; a Winter Watersports Olympics; and a Brando film night, where "all men who show an uncut dick at the door will be granted free entry and a drink for keeping his manliness left untouched." (Heck, buy 'em two drinks.)

Inside, the first room was unassuming enough: a couple of bars, pool tables, and a jukebox. But then, in the second room, the playground combined what **Edmund White** termed "the props of passion, an arena for experiment, a stimulating darkness." Oh, and silence: the rules specifically stated, "Keep your damn mouth shut when playing in the playground." There were private cubicles along one wall, and a flimsy free-standing wall with glory holes cut into it. And there were slings with men suspended in them, feet in the air, butts to the wind, and you name it inside. (There was also lots of Crisco around.) From there, two staircases led down to the still-darker cold cement vaults, where at the very least, you could find, say, naked men sitting in bathtubs waiting for . . . well, suffice it to say that the Mineshaft was the first club in the city to herald spring's arrival with an April Showers Pee Party.

Someone once asked me if from the perspective of today and the reality of AIDS, we couldn't cast back judgment and blame on places like the Mineshaft. There seems to be a certain irony in knowing, say, that in 1983, they were hosting a casino night here to benefit the Gay Men's Health Crisis. But that judgment is too easy, and it wipes away all the pleasure and all the unimaginable fantasy that came to life here. While we can regret the eventual turn of events, we can't blame people for their ignorance; indeed, we do better to admire them for their ardor and pursuit of a dream.

Follow Little West 12th Street out to the West Side Highway.

18. GANSEVOORT STREET PIER
seen from the intersection of Little West 12th and West Streets

Though most of the original piers are now gone—allowed to decay—the overflow from the trucks often poured into the dark, rickety piers that dangled out over the water. Throughout the night quiet, and occasionally dangerous, rounds of hide-and-seek (-and-seek-and-seek) filled these vast spaces.

It's impossible to know just how far back men started playing on the piers. A hint, though, might lie in the fact that more than a century ago, the pier out ahead of you, the Gansevoort Street Pier (curiously at the end of the street with the same name), was under the stewardship for many a year of **Herman Melville.** Now if you remember anything from English class, you remember that Melville, who lived from 1819 to 1891, wrote a lot about ships—sailing ships, whaling ships, you name it. For some of that, he drew on his own experiences at sea. But he also served nineteen years as the customs officer here at the Gansevoort Street Pier. (Peter Gansevoort, a general in the American Revolution, was Melville's grandfather, so Melville had some useful connections.)

Melville did marry (and have a number of children), but it seems that home was not where his passions lay: they lay at sea, among sailors. He exchanged a few emotional letters with Nathaniel Hawthorne ("Your heart beats in my ribs and mine in yours"), but even more, his stories reverberate with profound moments of loving intimacy between men. Try, for instance, one such between hero Ishmael and fellow sailor Queequeg, who are forced to share a bed in *Moby-Dick.* They fast become "bosom friends," lying together, chatting, napping, Queequeg all the while "now and then affectionately throwing his brown tattooed legs over mine." Sweet, no? Not to mention the barely hidden metaphor when, out at sea, the ship's crew has slaughtered a whale and are draining its spermaceti. Ishmael's task—one he does with indescribable pleasure—is to squeeze out the lumps in huge vats of spermaceti. By mistake, though, he occasionally squeezes his co-workers' hands. Soon, "such an abounding, affectionate, friendly, loving feeling did this avocation beget; that at last I was continually squeezing their hands, and looking up into their eyes sentimentally; as much as to say,—Oh! my dear fellow beings, why should we longer cherish any social acerbities, or know the slightest ill-humor or envy! Come; let us squeeze hands all round; nay, let us all squeeze ourselves into each other; let us squeeze ourselves universally into the very milk and sperm of kindness." A bit over the top for even the nineteenth century, but that is life on the gay frontier: a little risky, potentially sticky, but likely full of abounding affection and loving feeling.

Make a sharp right and walk up Tenth Avenue two blocks.

19. THE ANVIL • 500 West 14th Street
on the southwest corner of Tenth Avenue

The **Anvil** (which is now the Liberty Inn), took those feelings and did more than squeeze. Open in the heyday of gay liberation, this club's main room had a burlesque runway next to a disco floor where, in its heyday, go-go boys did anything from dancing to having sex and swinging from trapezes. There was also a basement level, and well, in the basement the fun wasn't the exclusive domain of the go-go boys, and there wasn't much dancing. In a matter-of-fact report, after a 1975 Christmas-time raid, the police described how one man, "Norman, wearing nothing but a black mask, a leather belt, and a leather apparatus on his genitals, was swung by chains from the ceiling as he was stripped and"—well, you can imagine. The police also made note of two nude bartenders, two similarly clad dancers, and "a darkened kitchen" where "individuals took turns performing private homosexual acts 'for no charge.' " As if!

Among the go-go dancers here was one **Felipe Rose**. **Jacques Morali** said that he first spotted Rose here, but saw him again at another club, where Felipe was in full Indian drag dancing next to some fellow in a cowboy outfit. Inspiration struck. Morali and some friends wrote a few songs, which they hired a singer to record while Felipe danced. Officially, there was no group, but the album that came out got popular fast and people began demanding performances. Morali put an ad in the *Village Voice* to hire performers, and by 1978 the cast was all assembled—Motorcycle Man, Indian (Felipe), Soldier, Leather Man, Construction Worker, Cowboy—and in the studio recording "Macho Man." The **Village People** were truly born. "Macho Man" raced up the charts, followed by "YMCA" and "In the Navy." Inspiration can come from anywhere!

If you knew anything about gay life, or if you read the paper even, you could have known that the Village People were gay. Morali came out about both himself and the group in a *Rolling Stone* interview in the fall of 1978. Somehow, though, the fact eluded most of the country. And to straight audiences, Morali insisted, "The Village People don't look like queens, they look like boys. And the straight guys in America want to get the macho look." Oh yeah, and touch and feel. Frontier living just has irresistible appeal.

The New Dynamic Electric Force: Gab 'n' Java in Midtown

Midtown Manhattan, like much of New York, is rather neurotic. By day, it is a center of business, of suits and ties, of literary lunches and financial pursuits. At night, the lights come up in Times Square, the marquees shine along Broadway, and culture and entertainment (and that's *all* kinds of entertainment) hold sway. Broadway has earned the name "the Great White Way," and Times Square, "the Crossroads of the World," and beneath the bright lights, in the white heat of the action, it does feel as if everyone is here.

Novelist **John Rechy**'s description of emerging into the Times Square of 1963 seems as vividly accurate today as it was then:

> From the thundering underground—the maze of the New York subways—the world pours into Times Square. Like lost souls emerging from the purgatory of the trains (dark rattling tunnels, smelly pornographic toilets, newsstands futilely splashing the subterranean gray-depths with unreal magazine colors), the newyork faces push into the air: spilling into 42nd Street and Broadway—a scattered defeated army. And the world of that street bursts like a rocket into a shattered phosphorescent world. Giant signs—Bigger! Than! Life!—blink off and on. And a great hungry sign groping luridly at the darkness screams: F*A*S*C*I*N*A*T*I*O*N.

Looking west on 42nd Street in the early 1930s.

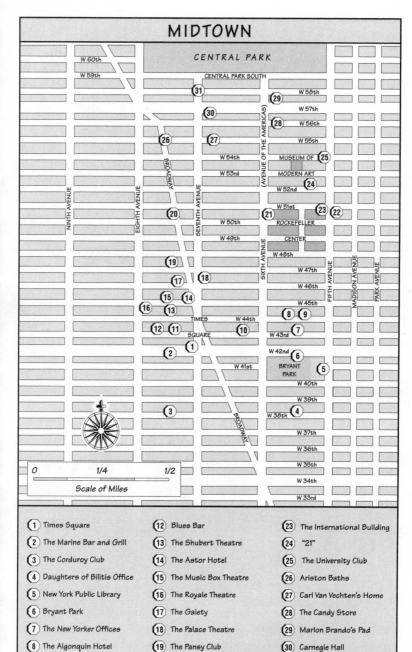

MIDTOWN

CENTRAL PARK

CENTRAL PARK SOUTH

Scale of Miles

0   1/4   1/2

1. Times Square
2. The Marine Bar and Grill
3. The Corduroy Club
4. Daughters of Bilitis Office
5. New York Public Library
6. Bryant Park
7. The New Yorker Offices
8. The Algonquin Hotel
9. The Iroquois Hotel
10. Mattachine Society
11. The New Apollo Theatre
12. Blues Bar
13. The Shubert Theatre
14. The Astor Hotel
15. The Music Box Theatre
16. The Royale Theatre
17. The Gaiety
18. The Palace Theatre
19. The Pansy Club
20. The Winter Garden Theatre
21. Radio City Music Hall
22. St. Patrick's Cathedral
23. The International Building
24. "21"
25. The University Club
26. Ariston Baths
27. Carl Van Vechten's Home
28. The Candy Store
29. Marlon Brando's Pad
30. Carnegie Hall
31. The Venice Theatre

Jeffrey L. Ward 1997

Certainly to the degree that gay and lesbian lives have been involved in those cultural endeavors (which seems disproportionately true in the theater world), this part of town, from the chorus boys to the Times Square hustlers to the *New Yorker* writers, has always had a gay presence.

This tour steps off in Times Square itself. (There's a stop on the 1/2/3/9 trains as well as the N and R, but 42nd Street is easily reached by almost any train in the city, and then you can walk to the square.) From there, it wanders over to the early digs of the Daughters of Bilitis and the Mattachine Society, stops by the New York Public Library, and then begins the culture climb, trudging through the places that made **James Dean, Leonard Bernstein,** and even **Liberace** famous. At the end you'll find that you, too, have made it to Carnegie Hall.

Strategic note: Through lots of Midtown, there are little passageways and lobbies that you can sneak through to get from one block to the next without going out to the avenues. Where I can, I'll point them out for you, but keep a lookout, okay?

Onward and upward.

1. TIMES SQUARE
• Seventh Avenue, Broadway, and 42nd Street

In early 1950, one scribe wrote that **Times Square** was like "a riddled beauty who has squandered her loveliness and knows it will never come back. She sits on a bar stool in a soiled satin dress, strings of blondined hair brushing the messy makeup on her cheeks, her hand shaking as she gets the drinks to her face. That's about all you can say about her now. She gets the drinks to her face." Perhaps the description will seem as apt to you today as it was then. Perhaps, though, you will see both the vitality and the beauty that persist.

Always and forever, Times Square, which officially stretches up to 45th Street, was the place for action. Friendly, unfriendly; safe, unsafe—who's to say? But well back before the Second World War, the area east and west of the square, and especially the intersection of Eighth Avenue and 42nd Street, was *the* place for a pickup, usually a hustler. **Donald Vining, Tennessee Williams, David Wojnarowicz, Montgomery Clift—** they all tramped here looking for action. Clift, sad to say, was

The Crossroads of the World, Times Square today.

even arrested for soliciting a young hustler here shortly after he had received an Oscar nomination for *The Search*.

In the 1920s, this area, which already had a busy female prostitution trade, became the central spot in the city for male hustlers. Different types of hustlers over the next two decades staked out their territories. According to historian George Chauncey, the area along 42nd Street between Fifth and Eighth Avenues became the domain of effeminate "fairy prostitutes," while the well-dressed, "straight-acting" hustlers worked along Fifth Avenue itself. In the 1930s, burlesque came to 42nd Street, bringing strippers and barkers, and then men's bars and restaurants. To match, a new kind of hustler arrived, a tougher-seeming "rough trade." The tough boys—as well as the sailors and soldiers that flooded through during the Second World War—came to dominate 42nd between Seventh and Eighth Avenues, while the swish scene moved east, to the other side of Sixth Avenue.

Perhaps no other writer has captured the hustler experience as powerfully and dramatically as **John Rechy.** In his 1963 novel, *City of Night*, he told the tale of a young man who arrived in New York, alone and uncertain, and discovered the possibility of hustling. A merchant marine he met at the YMCA suggested it to him, and the idea "acted on me like a narcotic that makes me crave it." He lingered in the square one night, like the other young men he saw, milling, waiting.

And then a gray-haired middle-aged man, hat tilted to the side, walked by with a "dont-give-a-damn walk" and said, "I'll give you ten, and I dont give a damn for you." The young man followed the older.

"What did you say?" I asked.

He looks at me steadily: "Was I wrong?" he asks me, but hes looking at me smiling confidently.

"I just asked what you said."

"You heard me," he says, without looking at me now, completely sure now . . . "Well, for chrissake, you wanna come or not?"

"Yes."

"Then come on, we're getting wet."

That world has opened its door, and I walk in.

Historic note: Rechy's novel was published by a mainstream publisher, Grove Press, in 1963. And Grove actually placed a photo of real Times Square hustlers on the cover—using a gay image to sell the book and target a gay audience. Pretty radical in those days.

Of course, Times Square cruising was hardly only about economics. **Tennessee Williams** wrote in his memoirs about cruising the area and making "very abrupt and candid overtures" to groups of sailors and GIs. He half-expected to be slaughtered on the spot, but Williams's bluntness instead earned him success: "They would stare at me for a moment in astonishment, burst into laughter, huddle for a brief conference, and, as often as not, would accept the solicitation." And there's a fascinating—and surprisingly early—account of an evening's prowl in **Charles Henri Ford** and **Parker Tyler**'s rather surrealist 1933 novel, *The Young and Evil*. A chapter aptly called "Cruise" finds the heroes wandering Broadway with big eyes when "a torso passed with a head" (I did say "surrealist.") They're captivated—"What did I see?" "It wasn't fate"—and then mesmerized when the man with the body passes again. One of them slows down, turns around, and begins pursuit. Friend Frederick seems shocked, but friend Karel simply mutters, "He's got his own key," and carries on.

Head west on 42nd a few steps.

2. THE MARINE BAR AND GRILL • 228 West 42nd Street
between Seventh and Eighth Avenues

Dame Forty-second is being remade these days, lifted and tucked and generally reconstructed. It's hard to know exactly which buildings will be standing when they're done. But back in the 1930s, the **Marine Bar** operated at this site directly across from the colonnaded building and was one of the most famous and notorious of our Times Square bars. It was exactly the kind of place that attracted the newer, rougher scene. Sailors and hustlers were frequent habitués, and the working boys used to line up out here on the street, waiting to be invited in. Those who could afford their own drink went inside to prowl the room. The Marine Bar replaced the still more notorious Barrel House, a similarly styled bar which had operated across the street until the police shut it down.

Take either Seventh or Eighth Avenue down to 38th Street.

3. THE CORDUROY CLUB • 240 West 38th Street
between Seventh and Eighth Avenues

Skip ahead a couple of decades to the late, if still pre-Stonewall, 1960s, and the community-minded gay men and lesbians were coming here. This was a private, three-story club that provided social outlets for the older homophile community: dances, card parties, movies, plays, and dinners—an alternative to a culture that increasingly centered its activities around bars. With its membership rolls topping a thousand in 1968, **Craig Rodwell**'s *Hymnal* described the Corduroy as "probably the only legitimate private club in New York City." When the East Coast gay rights groups gathered in New York in 1968—the Daughters of Bilitis, the Mattachine Society, the Student Homophile League, and the West Side Discussion Group, to name a few—half of their conference was held here.

Head east toward Fifth Avenue.

4. DAUGHTERS OF BILITIS OFFICE
- **27 West 38th Street, fourth floor**
between Fifth and Sixth Avenues

The years following the Second World War were complicated ones for gay men and lesbians. As historian **Allan Bérubé** has vividly documented, the war and its aftermath brought untold numbers of gay men and lesbians together for the first time ever, initially in the military and then in the country's larger cities. The possibility emerged of crafting full and complex subcultures, as well as community organizations. At the same time, however, the 1950s saw widespread persecution of homosexuals, and not just at bars and in park arrests. The shadow of Joe McCarthy's witch hunts reached out to homosexuals as well as communists, and there were sweeping, well-publicized purges of homosexuals from the State Department.

Nevertheless, the 1950s witnessed the courageous, even audacious, birth of what came to be called the homophile movement—the earliest widespread American homosexual rights movement, embodied in organizations like the Mattachine Society, SIR, ONE, and the **Daughters of Bilitis.** DOB, the nation's first lesbian organization, started in San Francisco in 1955. Initially, it formed as a social group in an effort to give middle-class lesbians an alternative to the gay bar scene. According to the founding members, Bilitis was a contemporary of **Sappho,** the great lesbian poet of ancient Greece; what's more, they thought the name "Daughters of Bilitis" sounded like a women's lodge, akin to the Daughters of the American Revolution, and if need be, could easily be explained away "as a women's group studying early Greek poetry."

For all the years of its existence (and DOB, in some form, lasted well into the 1970s), the women of DOB hosted social events, and the New York branch, founded by **Barbara Gittings** in 1958, frequently used the Corduroy Club, where you just were, as a setting. There were dances and candlelight dinners, game nights and sing-ins. And of course, there were the Gab 'n' Java get-togethers, the staple DOB event. At all DOB meetings, someone always greeted the guests at the door, saying, "I'm ———. Who are you? You don't have to give me your real name, not even your real first name." Initially, the gab sessions were fairly general discussions about homosexuality.

As Gittings later recalled, these meetings "allowed gays to come and hear about 'those' people, presumably without being identified themselves." By the late 1960s, though, the Gab 'n' Java topics were a bit narrower, even a little explicit, with titles like "The Meaning of Love" and "Is Sex Necessary in a Lesbian Relationship?" (I wonder what they decided. . . .)

For many years, the DOB political agenda was very much an integrationist one: working to fit into society. The four-part DOB statement of purpose included "advocating a mode of dress and behavior acceptable to society." (Translation: skirts, no pants, and quit sticking that cigarette behind your ear!) One early issue of the *Ladder*, the DOB newsletter and magazine, carried the no-nonsense message from the president that "our organization has already converted a few to remembering that they are women first and a butch or fem secondly. . . . There is a place for them in society, but only if they wish to make it so."

Mind you, as unpolitical as that sounds today, at the time it was radical enough to get the DOB infiltrated by the government and have files maintained by both the CIA and the FBI. But as the truly revolutionary 1960s rolled across the nation, Gittings, her partner **Kay Tobin,** and others became increasingly critical of the assimilationist position. They felt that DOB sold lesbians short as a class. In 1962, Gittings was named editor of the *Ladder* and began making it more militant, but by 1966 she was ousted. (Gittings later helped lead the campaigns against the American Psychiatric Association to depathologize homosexuality, and to open up academia to gay literature and gay studies. Tobin went on to help found the Gay Activists Alliance in 1969.)

By the spring of 1973, hardly a vestige of DOB's old self remained. They had joined ranks with the newer radical lesbian feminism, and their new publication, *ComingOutRage*, had essays on "Dyke Separatism" and "What Is Sisterhood?" and was strident in its tone: "Rage is contagious / in the coming out stage / We are outrageous / in our coming out rage." They even laid into Joan Baez and thumbed their noses at Carole King's lyrics ("Where you lead I will follow"). This was a long way from pants and skirts, and there was no going back.

Follow 38th Street out to Fifth Avenue and make a left.

5. NEW YORK PUBLIC LIBRARY
- **Fifth Avenue between 40th and 42nd Streets**

This was one of **James Baldwin**'s favorite retreats in the city. His discovery of the library marked a dramatic broadening of his young intellectual horizons and expectations. Built near the turn of the century, it has been the birthplace of many an American novel and research project (for instance, Betty Friedan's *Feminine Mystique*), including much of this one. Also, since 1992, these steps have been the gathering point for the Irish Lesbian and Gay Organization as it protests its repeated exclusion from New York's annual St. Patrick's Day Parade.

I have to admit it is also one of *my* favorite places in the city, and, nudge that I am, I almost always make people go inside. It's worth visiting not just for its grandeur—although it *is* pretty swell—but also to appreciate its space and imagine the tides of humanity that have washed through. Picture Audrey H. tracking down George P.'s book in *Breakfast at Tiffany's*. Consider how many coming-outs have been accompanied and guided by old copies of **Radclyffe Hall** and **Donald Webster Cory,** or by *Surprising Myself* and *The Object of My Affection*. This library contains the archives of the International Gay Information Collection, an outstandingly varied array of gay and lesbian periodicals, personal papers, leaflets, books, and films from the world over. And during the 1994 summer-long celebration of the twenty-fifth anniversary of the Stonewall Uprising and the Gay Games, this library hosted an elaborate and extensive display of gay New York history, called "Becoming Visible: The Legacy of Stonewall."

One of my most treasured discoveries during this project is a book, preserved in one of the special collections upstairs, that **Walt Whitman** himself literally made, binding and all. It's a compilation (not a reprint) of the actual letters that soldiers from the Civil War wrote to the poet. Whitman, who spent much of the war nursing soldiers in Washington, D.C., later wrote, "I believe no men ever loved each other as I and some of these poor wounded, sick and dying men loved each other." These letters are their testimony. In one indicative set of careful correspondence, a man wrote on behalf of his sick brother, **Caleb Babit.** Caleb's illness seemed unremitting, but,

wrote his brother, he "wishes he could see you and tries to gratify himself by looking at your portraits which he has out five or six times during the day." Eventually, Caleb himself wrote, though only weakly. He said that Whitman's "letters have been of more value to me than you can imagine. It was not only the words that was written that don me the good but to know that they came from the bottom of the heart of a *true* and sympathizing friend." Indeed.

Step inside for a moment and explore.

Walk to the back of the library on 42nd Street.

6. BRYANT PARK
- **Sixth Avenue between 40th and 42nd Streets**

Bryant Park, tucked behind the library, merits attention for a bundle of reasons, starting with how wonderful it is to find a pretty place in the middle of the grimy old city. You can get a coffee here, a sandwich, a lemonade, just sit for a minute. Secondly, there's a terrific little statue of **Gertrude Stein** tucked up at the eastern end of the park (one of the few statues of a woman in the city), which is well worth tracking down. Third, for the more pop-literary-minded, if you read Caleb Carr's *The Alienist*, you remember the final dramatic scene that occurred on the high walls of the reservoir: that reservoir stood here, where the park and library now are, before the turn of the century. And then for the smut-minded, there's just a bit more from the history of cruising for you to relish. It seems in the 1920s and '30s, the park was widely known as a "fairies'" hangout, and there was a steady circulation between the park and an Automat across 42nd Street that was also a pretty busy place. In the 1940s, the mayor had the park closed at night to try to "clean it up," although who knows just how effective that was. In the 1960s, **John Rechy**'s eager young hustler watched the nightly dance as "shadowy figures" with "male-hungry looks" would disappear behind a statue and then emerge, "after a few frantic moments, from opposite directions: intimate nameless strangers joined for one gasping

New York Public Library.

brief space of time." Cleaning up Bryant Park has remained a continual municipal project.

If you exit the park at the eastern end in the center of the block, you can walk to 43rd Street, through either the lobby of the swooping Grace Building or the City University passageway next door. Or try an avenue.

7. *THE NEW YORKER* OFFICES • 25 West 43rd Street
between Fifth and Sixth Avenues

Up until quite recently, this esteemed magazine of culture and letters resided here, occupying most of the top floors of the building. (Their offices are now just across 43rd.) *The New Yorker*'s history, stretching back some seventy years, includes surprising pockets of gay writing: two of its founding contributors back in the 1920s were **Alexander Woollcott** and **Janet Flanner,** and since then it has introduced much of the world to **Truman Capote** and **John Cheever** as well as **David Leavitt** and **Ethan Mordden.** Essayist Brendan Gill remembered the young Capote "sweeping through the corridors of the magazine in a black opera cape, his long golden hair falling to his shoulders: an apparition that put one in mind of **Oscar Wilde** in Nevada, in his velvet and lilies." Mordden, on the other hand, takes proud credit for being the first to pen the word "cock"—at least with *that* connotation—into the magazine's pages.

Janet Flanner, writing under the name Genet, was the magazine's Paris correspondent for some fifty years. She began her reports in October 1925, just a few months after the magazine was founded, and wrote steadily into the 1970s, becoming the ultimate chronicler of the American in Paris. (Even after so many years abroad, Flanner still insisted that she was American: "The idea that I've become French would be ludicrous and impertinent," she told an interviewer. "I don't believe one shifts one's breed easily. The first twenty years of one's life stamp one, don't you think so?")

Born in Indianapolis in 1892, Flanner had wanted to be a writer since the age of five. Her chronicles, which she said were about "what catches my sense of what is true, important and dramatic," were admired as much for their historical insight as for their style and dazzle, and offered a window on Europe as it fêted its way through the 1920s and '30s, and then dug its way out after the Second World War. During the war, Flanner stayed in New York, where she struck up a "passionate friendship" with former actress and broadcaster **Natalia Danesi Murray.** Separated near the war's end as each returned to her international pursuits, Flanner wrote Murray, "Darling, I miss you simply terribly; that's the truth. I've been knocked to one side, like a piece of furniture which has lost its place in the home by your departure. There is no time sense left, no point in getting up, no fun in breakfast, no excitement at the end of the afternoon with your voice shouting up the stairs or demanding a cocktailino or my answering eccolino. . . ."

Despite such a legacy, the magazine did not race to embrace gay liberation. While a 1994 issue did show a gay wedding on the cover, even as late as 1979 a *Christopher Street* magazine ad was rejected for being "gay advertising." Nevertheless, in the summer of 1970, the magazine did run a charming "Talk of the Town" story on the first Gay Pride Parade. After describing the parade and the displays with *New Yorker*ly insight—at one point noting the activist dachshund with the sign "Me Too"—the writer described the Gay-In in Central Park. The writer noted that as people gathered and applauded for the marchers just arriving, "one boy climbed on another's shoulders. A third boy looked on approvingly and said, 'You've got the grooviest sign in the parade.' " Sweet, no?

Walk through the lobby of the old New Yorker *building.*

8. THE ALGONQUIN HOTEL • 31 West 44th Street
between Fifth and Sixth Avenues

With such easy access to the *New Yorker* offices across the street, the *New York Times* offices a few blocks over, and various Ivy League university clubs in any direction, the Algonquin became the much-celebrated home of the infamous Round Table, watering hole for New York's witty martini literati in the 1930s and '40s. Regular drinkers here included not only *The New Yorker*'s founding editor, Harold Ross, but his and our critic **Alexander Woollcott,** trenchant wit Dorothy Parker (married to gay writer **Alan Campbell,** with whom she wrote the original *A Star is Born*), actress **Tallulah Bankhead,** and George S. Kaufman. It was here, for instance, that Parker and her wit-nemesis Clare Boothe Luce first generated these phrases, which have no doubt spilled out of your sweet little mouth at some catty moment: Parker and Luce were leaving at the same time. Luce, allowing Parker to step ahead, said, "Age before beauty." And as she passed, Parker muttered, "Pearls before swine," thank you very much. Bankhead used to hang out here so much with three pansexual actress friends (**Estelle Winwood, Eva Le Gallienne,** and **Blyth Daly**) that they came to be called "the Four Horsemen of the Algonquin."

For years the Algonquin was considered a swanky hotel in its own right, and regular guests have included **Noël Coward, Tennessee Williams, Gore Vidal, Thornton Wilder,** and **John Osborne. Gertrude Stein** and **Alice B. Toklas** stayed here during Stein's 1934 lecture tour. And many others—a young actor you are about to meet who lived next door at the Iroquois, the struggling writers who lived across the street at the Paramount—have used the Algonquin address and lobby to impress editors and directors.

Walk east a few steps.

9. THE IROQUOIS HOTEL • 27 West 44th Street
between Fifth and Sixth Avenues

Born James Byron in Marion, Ohio, the young man who moved into room 82 here was destined to burn his way into America's heart as a young sensitive rebel, but not quite a giant. (Hey, who thinks I should be writing game-show questions? Or better yet, talk-show introductions?) Okay, okay. **James Dean** shared room 82 with William Bast (who later went on to produce TV's *The Colbys*). At the time, in early 1952, Dean was a guinea pig testing out stunts for the producers of the game show *Beat the Clock.* This was already his second home in New York: he first took up residence in the fall of 1951 at the West Side Y, one of those enormous residential

YMCAs built in the 1930s that became famous as gay retreats. Dean himself became well-known in gay circles for his penchant for leather bars and for having his lovers burn him with their cigarettes; somewhere along the way, it is said, he even picked up the *nom de nuit* of "the human ashtray." Of his sexuality, Dean once said, "Well, I'm certainly not going through life with one hand tied behind my back."

Two *Rebel* notes: When Dean began to back out of the filming of *Rebel Without a Cause*, the alternate who was lined up was **Tab Hunter.** Either way, they seemed to want a queer boy for the job.

Late in his sadly abbreviated life, the actor **Sal Mineo** commented that during the filming of *Rebel*, for which he was all of fifteen years old, he "was in incredible awe of [Dean]. I was fascinated by him. I think it was sexual to an extent, but I had no idea or any understanding of affection between men. I really gave him hero worship, and I recognized later what it was, but the feeling then was that I couldn't wait to just get near him. . . . It was only years later that I understood I was incredibly in love with him." You and half the world, Sal.

Head west and pick up 43rd Street off Sixth Avenue.

10. Mattachine Society • 108 West 43rd Street
between Sixth and Seventh Avenues

Harry Hay, together with **Chuck Rowland, Rudi Gernreich,** and a handful of others, founded the **Mattachine Society** in Los Angeles in 1950. There is record of a Society for Human Rights in Chicago in the '20s, and there were various rumblings in the years after the Second World War, including a Veterans Benevolent Association here in New York and a group of Los Angeles men who gathered as Bachelors for Wallace in support of Progressive candidate Henry Wallace in the 1948 presidential campaign. Mattachine, though, was the first homosexual rights organization formed in this country that really held and grew, with chapters forming around the country. Not that it didn't have its in-fighting and organizational troubles, folding shortly after getting started and then starting up again a couple of years later. But Mattachine provided the

organizational foundation on which much of the modern liberation movement was built.

Hay, as a struggling young actor, had been essentially
seduced into the Los Angeles Communist Party by sometime
lover **Will Geer** (Grandpa Walton to you and me). And
though it was many years (and a wife and family) later before
Hay and a handful of other former Party members decided to
form Mattachine, the group initially had the same underground flavor. The name itself was derived from the Italian
term for medieval court jesters, individuals who were both
truth tellers and mask wearers. Hay recalls that the group initially hosted public discussions of Alfred Kinsey's just-
published and much-celebrated volume on male sexuality,
focusing special attention on the chapter on homosexuality.
Though nearly everyone came in male-female couples, Hay
and his compatriots would circulate during the discussion,
keeping an eye out for the extra-attentive listeners. After the
discussion, those individuals might be invited out to dinner,
felt out for genuine interest, and then told about the group
behind the discussions.

A chapter formed in New York in December 1955, founded
by **Sam Morford,** an industrial psychiatrist, and **Tony
Segura,** a research chemist. The first meeting had five people
in attendance and took place in the old Diplomat Hotel,
which used to stand here. For several years after that, they met
monthly at the Avalon Studios, one block west at 220 West
43rd. Their meetings often consisted of a lecture or a discussion, usually coordinated around some psychiatric or religious
expert and with a topic like "Ten Myths About Homosexuality." The group also began to provide assistance for gay men
and women arrested in bar raids.

Mattachine, like Daughters of Bilitis, was formed in times
of great conformity and repression, and their attitude about
the proper place for homosexuality, and the founding goals for
the organization, were very much a reflection of those years.
The group's first newsletter posed the question whether Mattachine was "an organization of homosexuals." The answer:
"Emphatically *NO*. . . . This is *NOT* an organization attempting to create a 'homosexual society' but rather an organization
seeking the integration of the homosexual as a responsible and
acceptable citizen in the community. The society will not

tolerate use of itself or its name for any subversive political activity or reprehensible conduct." Mind you, though, integration wasn't simply a passive or assimilationist ideal. Mattachine was committed to research and education that would "dispel false ideas about human sexuality" and move toward liberation.

By the end of the 1960s, and especially in the years surrounding the Stonewall Uprising, the conservative stream of the Mattachine ethic came under heavy criticism for not being radical or activist enough; indeed, in 1969 and '70 the organization itself was superseded by the Gay Liberation Front and Gay Activists Alliance. (There's more on that in the Chelsea tour.) Nevertheless, Mattachine was the crucial cell from which all those activities were able to form. The Washington, D.C., chapter, under the leadership of Queens-born **Frank Kameny,** was fighting the federal government's hiring procedures in the 1960s. And it was quite literally at Mattachine offices that the incipient gay community met the weekend of Stonewall to plan the response that marked the birth of the new liberation movement.

Head west on 43rd Street.

11. THE NEW APOLLO THEATRE • 234 West 43rd Street
between Seventh and Eighth Avenues

At the moment, this stretch of the street is being redone, and it's hard to know what will be standing when the dust settles. But in mid-November 1977, a tragic tale of gay love and life in Nazi Germany opened here at what was then the New Apollo. *Bent,* by **Martin Sherman,** told the story of two gay men taken to a concentration camp, where they eventually find love, but not freedom. The stage was held by David Dukes and Richard Gere (starting one of many rounds of rumors which never quite seem to die). The *New York Times* named it one of the year's ten best plays, and a reviewer there described it as "strong material; strong performing; dramatic blows do not often strike with this force." It was the Broadway debut for Dukes and David Marshall Grant (who went on to star in *Angels in America* on Broadway). *Newsweek,* meanwhile, applauded Gere's courage in taking the part.

In London the production of *Bent* starred our own **Sir Ian McKellen.** There is much that is a pleasure to say about our shining knight, one of the English language's finest actors. He has been stunning theatergoers for years, whether it be in his Tony-award-winning portrayal of Salieri in Broadway's *Amadeus* or in his one-man show *Acting Shakespeare*, which toured the country. In recent years, he's come out publicly (at the age of forty-nine and with prodding from *Tales of the City* author **Armistead Maupin**) and become an activist for changing antigay British laws. In the 1994 summer of Stonewall 25, McKellen graced New York with another one-man show, called *A Knight Out*, full of gay theater and thoughts on gay activism and gay living. Asked once if he encouraged other actors to come out, McKellen said that he has spoken with a number of actors about it, largely "because nobody ever asked me to come out. Nobody! . . . I wish they'd all come out. They don't have to make a great thing about it. They don't have to start activating like I've done. They could just say they're gay, and that could be it, and they can get on with their job."

Head west a few more steps.

12. BLUES BAR • 264 West 43rd Street
between Seventh and Eighth Avenues

As too many of us can attest, antigay discrimination in this city or any other didn't end after Stonewall or even the passage of local civil rights ordinances. Last I checked, nobody was doing business at this address, but in the late 1970s and early '80s the **Blues Bar** was a gay bar popular with black men. One night in September 1982, twenty uniformed policemen descended into the bar, their guns bared, shouting, "This is a mother-fucking raid! Every faggot to the rear!" There was no legal justification for the raid, but twelve people were hurt, and the property damages by the police totaled $30,000. At some point, one cop apparently shot his gun into the floor, shouting, "These are faggot suppositories! Next time I'll put 'em up your ass the right way!" The following night, New York's gay community marched in protest, but nine days later the cops raided again. They entered with their guns drawn, kicked one man, and announced, "We broke in last time and got headlines in the *Voice*. We're going to get headlines again." Protesters returned the following week, one thousand strong, and their outrage was echoed by demonstrators in San Francisco. Outrage, though, does not undo the past.

Walk up Eighth to 44th Street and turn right.

13. THE SHUBERT THEATRE • 225 West 44th Street
between Seventh and Eighth Avenues

Ah, the **Shubert**—a name that represents a legacy of theatrical success. And no success was greater here than **Michael Bennett**'s *A Chorus Line*, which arrived in 1975 and held sway on this stage for fifteen years—establishing a record in Broadway history, and supporting the financing of other theatrical ventures around the city. Truly "one singular sensation"! The show was conceived, directed, and choreographed by Bennett, who earlier had choreographed such shows as *Company* and *Follies* and later developed *Dreamgirls*. He died of AIDS-related illnesses in 1987, at the age of forty-four.

The truth of *Chorus Line* was made evident when Richard Attenborough held, appropriately enough, an open casting call for his film version of the show one street up at the Royale Theatre. A line started forming well before seven A.M., and ultimately close to two thousand auditioners appeared, head shots and resumes in hand. Half were rejected on sight; the other half actually got to perform. Only three hundred of those were even chosen to be seen again. And this for a show where a cast of seventeen is itself winnowed down to eight for the actual chorus line. You can almost hear them: "God, I hope I get it. I hope I get it. How many people does he need? . . ."

Head east to Seventh Avenue and make a left.

14. THE ASTOR HOTEL
   • **Northwest corner of Seventh Avenue and 45th Street**

Just a quick note: The hotel is, sadly, gone, but not only was the **Astor** the site of many a drag ball in the 1920s, the elegant bar that functioned there since 1904 was, like the Oak Room in the Plaza Hotel, a legendary men's pickup bar for much of the century. Popular since the 1910s, it became especially so during the Second World War, when it had a national reputation among gay servicemen as a place to hook up with a local civilian. It had a black, oval-shaped bar, and the gay customers congregated on one side, the straight ones on the other. The management allowed the gay men to gather as long as they weren't too "obvious" in their behavior.

   Gore Vidal, for one, remembers that in the war years, day or night, hundreds of men would pack themselves in, six deep, for a go in the Astor waters. Interestingly, Vidal also remembers that Alfred Kinsey used the mezzanine there as a kind of office, interviewing men about their sex lives for his then-astounding *Sexual Behavior in the Human Male* (which gave us the handy six-point Kinsey scale as well as the figure that 10 percent of all men are predominantly homosexual). Vidal also imagines that "it was by observing the easy trafficking at the Astor that [Kinsey] figured out what was obvious to most of us, though as yet undreamed of by American society at large: Perfectly 'normal' young men, placed outside the usual round of family and work, will run riot with each other." Riot indeed!

Turn west on 45th Street.

15. THE MUSIC BOX THEATRE   • **239 West 45th Street**
   between Seventh and Eighth Avenues

In the 1940s, this theater was venue to **Tennessee Williams's** *Summer and Smoke.* It didn't do so well here, actually, but an eventual revival down in the Village with a young Geraldine Page—then sewing buttons to make a living—made both her and the play huge hits. In the 1950s, however, **William Inge's** great plays, *Picnic, Bus Stop,* and *The Dark at the Top of the Stairs,* all were performed here to great acclaim. Inge was a young journalist in St. Louis in the 1940s when he met Williams and Williams inspired him to write. He dedicated *Dark at the Top of the Stairs* to Williams, and for much of the fifties, their plays were considered among the best the American theater had to offer. Inge, about whom more is said in the Upper West Side tour, eventually won both a Pulitzer and an Oscar, but he never achieved a clear sense of accomplishment or happiness; he committed suicide at the age of sixty.

One addition: In 1989 **Tom Hulce,** who came out well after his enormous success in the film *Amadeus,* opened here in *A Few Good Men,* before Tom Cruise (whom we've heard *nothing* about) made the movie version.

Cross the street.

16. THE ROYALE THEATRE • 242 West 45th Street
between Seventh and Eighth Avenues

Here, on February 1, 1954, Broadway saw the premiere of **André Gide**'s *The Immoralist,* a tale of desert love. That night in the role of Bachir—the North African houseboy and one of Broadway's first positively homosexualized characters: a young **James Dean.** On opening night, Dean did two things: curtseyed for his curtain call (snap, snap!) and gave notice. Elia Kazan had screen-tested him for *East of Eden* during the show's previews, and within two weeks Dean was off to begin a spectacular and brief Hollywood career.

A few years later, in 1961, this stage held the debut of **Tennessee Williams**'s *The Night of the Iguana,* which brought **Bette Davis** back to the Broadway stage, and began the period of her career that included squaring off with **Joan Crawford** in *What Ever Happened to Baby Jane?* (Talk about icons!) Davis, you'll be happy to know, once said of gay men that "a more artistic, appreciative group of people for the arts does not exist. And conceited as it may sound, I think a great deal of it has to do with their approval of my work, the seriousness of my work. They are more knowledgeable, more loving of the arts. They make the average male look stupid." (If she were still around, I'd hire her as my publicist.)

Backtrack along 45th Street and scoot through the Marriott to 46th.

17. THE GAIETY • 201 West 46th Street
just east of Seventh Avenue

This is just the sort of thing a kid like me could get in trouble for (though more from Mom than from the publisher). I have to say, though, I do it with the best of intentions—I swear. First off, I think it's important to appreciate low culture as well as high, right? Don't want to be accused of being a snob. But secondly, in the heyday of gay liberation, there was a way in which a strip club, which is what the **Gaiety** was, was indicative much more of the spirit of liberation than of something seedy.

Take, for instance, a 1976 description of the Gaiety burlesque showboys in *Man Alive!*, the gay man's rag of choice back then. The writer spent a fair amount of time just discussing the musical choices (lots from the soul charts) and dance technique (some dynamite footwork) of the performers. There's a kind of jubilant artistic appreciation, although equal recognition that "some of the all-time favorites obviously have endeared themselves via their large personalities rather than dancing ability." ("Personalities"?) Nevertheless, what he envisioned was a kind of love fest: "Since salaries are decidedly modest, one concludes that a good share of Gaiety and Ramrod peelers do it either as a lark or as a labor of love. It would be hard to find a more adoring audience. The real aficionados return week after week and many of them come back three or four times to see the same show!" Nothing sleazy or embarrassed about it—just stars and their fans. Now run upstairs, and I'll meet you back here in . . . Just kidding!

Head back out to the Avenue and make a quick left on Broadway.

18. THE PALACE THEATRE • 1564 Broadway
between 46th and 47th Streets

Before vaudeville gave up the ghost in the 1930s, everyone on the variety circuit, and I mean everyone, had performed at the **Palace:** from Fred Astaire to Jack Benny (one of the most celebrated of campy performers), Sophie Tucker, even Houdini.

Then in the 1950s (and on into the 1970s) the Palace became committed to huge, splashy one-person gala shows. **Judy Garland** made one of her stunning comeback runs here, performing nineteen weeks beginning in October of 1951; **Danny Kaye** did fourteen weeks. And the international **Josephine Baker,** the **Divine Miss M.,** and the astonishing **Miss Ross** all performed here as well.

But in the summer of 1983, and for the following four-plus years, the boards at the Palace were pounded nightly by a male couple and a bevy of drag queen beauties. *La Cage aux Folles,* a musical version of a much-adapted French show (most recently screenplayed into *The Birdcage* with Robin Williams and the brilliant **Nathan Lane**), had been crafted by a three-generation team of gay men: directed by **Arthur Laurents,** adapted by **Harvey Fierstein** (fresh from *Torch Song Trilogy*), and set to music by **Jerry Herman.** (As for multigenerational gay artistic efforts, Herman's *Hello, Dolly!*, which ran for 2,844 shows in its first run, was based on a play by, yep, closeted **Thornton Wilder.** Wilder, it seems, was rather a prude; **Samuel Steward,** who had an on-and-off affair with him, wrote that Wilder had sex "almost as if he were looking the other way" and that for him "the act itself was quite literally unspeakable." Hmm, may be time to reread *Our Town.*)

Aaaanyway, Herman said recently that when *La Cage* opened, "we didn't know what to expect from the audience. Arthur, Harvey, and I stood in back of the last row. There was a gray-haired straight couple sitting there. By the time 'Song on the Sand' started—a man singing a love song to another man—we thought, 'This is the moment! We'll be stoned or accepted.' That older couple leaned their heads together and held hands. The three of us just started to cry."

You remember the story: Lovely couple—Georges, the proprietor of the Cage club, and Albin, his leading drag queen. Somewhere along the way, it seems, Georges has had a hetero liaison (it happens). His son is going to get married, and the future father-in-law, a crusading homophobe, wants to meet Dad. Albin's disappearance now seems temporarily necessary (or so Georges thinks), and as Act One closes Albin sings that brilliant song of pride and protest, "I Am What I Am," insisting,

> *It's my world*
> *That I want to have a little pride in*
> *My world*
> *And it's not a place I have to hide in.*

(For God's sake, if you don't know the words, go out and learn them!)

The show was surrounded with loads of splash and rumor. The opening-party guest list included Angela Lansbury, Mikhail Baryshnikov, **Michael Bennett,** Beverly Sills, Elaine Stritch, and Steve Lawrence. For a while the story was that **Danny Kaye** had turned down the lead, but that now that it was such a big hit, he was trying to get the part of Albin in the London production. Similarly, **Rock Hudson** was allegedly vying for the part of Georges. More impressive than all of that, though, each of the three collaborators won a Tony for the show.

Scoot up a block.

19. THE PANSY CLUB • 204 West 48th Street
at the southwest corner of Broadway

Although it's been all but forgotten now, at the start of the 1930s, as vaudeville and prosperity were closing up shop, there was a craze in straight culture for the "pansies": effeminate, almost-drag-queen, gay male performers. While that excitement can be linked to any number of sources—too much Prohibition, an ugly President (Herbert Hoover), basic good taste—it is clear that a good sixty years before **RuPaul** started telling us all to work and boys like Patrick Swayze decided even they could give drag a try (as if!), pansy performers like **Jean Malin** and **Karyl Norman** were the rage of the night-club set, even getting profiled in the papers. For a brief moment, pansies were widely represented in the cabarets and clubs in the Village and Times Square areas.

Jimmy Durante, in a book he wrote about New York night-clubs, talked about the Club Abbey, where Malin, a large fellow, was master of ceremonies, and what a gas it was there, how everybody always seemed "hopped up." Gypsy Markof sat on the piano, "her feet resting on the keys while she plays . . . Jean Malin, the master of ceremonies, *ad-libs* and tenors: 'I'm a Gigolo.' . . . There's nothing extraordinary about that, is there? The band plays and people prance. They do that everywhere. But they seem to enjoy it more." What kept them so happy? Well, according to historian George Chauncey, Malin simply took the campy gay wit from the Village and brought it uptown, to what was one of the poshest clubs in the city.

At this spot, just from 1930 to 1931, stood another such venue, the **Pansy Club.** Hosted by Karyl Norman, a nationally famous female impersonator known as "the Creole Fashion Plate," the Pansy presented a nightly show which featured, according to the advertisement, "a bevy of beautiful girls in 'something different' entitled 'Pansies on Parade.'" Mind you, the city's embrace shouldn't be overemphasized. One nightlife critic recalled the "vogue of the female impersonator" as an era that "caused little except a faint nausea, and the police, with their traditional hatred of the intermediate sex, kept their nightsticks poised."

As it was, the end of the pansy craze seemed to be triggered by a huge gunfight that broke out one night early in January 1931 at the Club Abbey. The club's boss, Dutch Schultz, went into hiding, the club was shut down, and the police went on a pansy crackdown, letting their nightsticks fly. But both Malin and Norman went off to Hollywood, where they were also prominently featured in nightclubs. Sadly, Malin died soon thereafter, only twenty-five, when his car careened off a pier and into the Pacific Ocean. And the pansy rage didn't really return until—well, welcome to the 1990s!

Head up Broadway two more blocks.

20. THE WINTER GARDEN THEATRE • 1634 Broadway
between 50th and 51st Streets

By this point, you should have the sense that oodles of gay lore could be milked from any of the theaters along here. (I'm drafting a petition to have Broadway officially renamed "the

Great Gay Way.") But just to give you one more taste, take the **Winter Garden.** In the 1930s **Vincente Minnelli,** Liza's dad and hardly a model heterosexual, put on his production of *At Home Abroad* here, starring **Ethel Waters** (about whom you can read in the Harlem tour). Later on, a revival of the *Ziegfeld Follies* featured **Josephine Baker** (along with Bob Hope and Eve Arden). *West Side Story* debuted here, created by—and how's this for lineage?—author **Arthur Laurents,** director/choreographer **Jerome Robbins,** composer **Leonard Bernstein,** and lyricist **Stephen Sondheim!** Four gay men craft one of the greatest of Broadway's shows: What is that? Coincidence? *Funny Girl* featured **Barbra** here, and **Jerry Herman**'s *Mame* ran for 1,508 shows here, putting Angela Lansbury as Mame and Bea Arthur as her friend Vera together on stage to sing the show stopper "Bosom Buddies"! Even after that, when it was just *Cats, Cats,* and more *Cats* for eons, judging from what you know of chorus boys and girls, you can imagine how many of our tribe put food on the table from that endless extravaganza. Got the picture?

*Okay, let's leave Broadway for now. Walk east to Sixth Avenue along either 50th or 51st Street. If you take 51st, you can pause at the plaza on the north side of the street, outside the PaineWebber Building. It was designed—tables, chairs, benches, and planters—by sculptor **Scott Burton** in the mid-1980s before he died of AIDS. It's a swell place to rest your tootsies.*

21. RADIO CITY MUSIC HALL
- **Sixth Avenue between 50th and 51st Streets**

My God, who *hasn't* performed here? Who's your favorite superstar singer? Yes, they had a show here. I saw **k. d. lang** here. (Loved her!) **Johnny Mathis** performed here. Did you know that he came out in June 1982? As hard as it is to believe, even **Madonna** gave it up here. And did I mention the Rockettes? Higher, kick higher, damn it!

For this moment, though, we observe most of all that the dazzling golden sunburst stage of **Radio City** was the site of

Radio City Music Hall today.

the last performance of the extravagant piano genius **Liberace,** just after Halloween 1986. Born in 1919, just outside of Milwaukee, Walter Liberace was a far cry from the fur-caped, jewel-encrusted superstar that he would become: he spoke too fast to be understood, and he was shunned for being a sissy—not exactly popular. He started playing piano when he was four, though, and that was his ticket to glory. It wasn't always easy. At one point in his childhood, Liberace had a hangnail which got infected and led to blood poisoning. His doctor wanted to amputate the finger, but his mother refused. Instead she gave him a Polish cure which involved, among other things, immersing his arm in boiling water. It worked: he kept the finger, he had a career, he was eternally grateful. (It's true: Liberace—or Lee, as friends would call him—was famous for his gratitude to and fondness for his mother. But he obviously had good reason.)

Those of you with a more twisted bent might appreciate **John Waters**'s description of the beatific pianist as "the personification of everything I believe in pushed to the nth degree. He'd be perfect for a horror film. There was even a rumor in the gossip columns (hotly denied) that he was signed to play the lead in the sequel to *The Texas Chainsaw Massacre.* . . . Picture him chasing Drew Barrymore across a swamp with a buzzing chainsaw and you can envision a mega hit of staggering proportions." His last shows here were indeed such a hit: fifty-six of them in three weeks, entertaining three hundred thousand and setting Radio City records. The shows, which ran two and a half hours, began with Liberace flying onstage and included four cars, six costume changes, and a waltz with one lucky lady from the audience. Oh, and Gershwin, Chopin, and Strauss were thrown in for good measure.

Three months later Liberace died of AIDS-related causes and no doubt some exhaustion. He is buried in a grave site just outside of the city that is flanked by two trees shaped like his trademark candelabras.

Follow 50th east to Fifth Avenue.

22. St. Patrick's Cathedral
- **Fifth Avenue between 50th and 51st Streets**

This center of Roman Catholic faith—as well as of enormous power and authority—has long been the focus of one gay activity or another. On the day that the Gay Pride Parade passes along Fifth Avenue, no matter what year, these intersections are the setting of continuous confrontation, as religious hecklers shout their condemnations at the marchers, who return their volleys with wit, style, and passion. And since the early 1970s, when gay activists began making their protests angrier and more visible, the cathedral has frequently been chosen as a site of action.

The most infamous confrontation here occurred one Sunday morning in December 1989. After months of planning and debating, ACT UP scheduled a large demonstration and invited the media to attend, which they did in full force. A crowd of five thousand gathered outside in near zero-degree weather, crying chants like "You say 'Don't fuck,' we say 'Fuck you!' " Inside, when Cardinal O'Connor started his Sunday sermon, several ACT UP members began their protest. According to former CBS news producer and ACT UP member **Ann Northrop,** "the idea to go inside was to raise the ante," but the plan was for a dignified protest, one modeled on protests that nuns had staged in the very same cathedral. And when the cardinal began speaking, a number of protesters simply lay down silently in the aisles, while several handcuffed themselves to the pews, and a group rose toward the rear to read a statement attacking the church's homophobic position. Things, though, quickly heated up.

Thanks to ACT UP's advance planning, the cardinal was hardly caught off guard. Shortly before the mass began, the cathedral had been cleared and the police had brought through bomb-sniffing dogs. And by the start of the service, once the congregation had been readmitted, the cathedral was packed. According to Northrop, "you could tell that most of the parishioners were there itching for a fight." The initial calm erupted into chaos. One protester stood on a pew and started screaming, "You're a murderer! You're a murderer!" Parishioners started yelling back, and other ACT UP members joined the shouting match. The police quickly moved in with stretchers and started carrying protesters out.

But some of the protesters had gone down the aisle to receive communion and either made direct statements to the cardinal or, in one case, crumbled the communion wafer and let the pieces drop to the ground. That last act, according to Northrop, "became the trigger that turned this into a worldwide event," and piled heaps of criticism onto ACT UP both from within and outside of the gay community.

"It is not our goal to be liked," Northrop recently told me. "We're not out there to be popular. We're there to get the issues confronted." And attacking the church was part of a broader and never-ending campaign to defeat the homophobia-inspired lethargy that has paralyzed the response to AIDS. Northrop relayed an anecdote from a friend's suburban mother: Before the St. Patrick's demonstration the mom's neighbors viewed gay people as "weak pansies." Afterward, "they thought gay people were strong and angry. That did it for me. If a couple of housewives in suburban Connecticut could get that, then I'm doing this every week." That day, before the media's watchful eye, 111 protesters were arrested, but it was the Church that stood condemned.

Gore Vidal, for one, recalls that when the cathedral was occupied by **Francis Cardinal Spellman** in the 1940s and '50s, the gay spirit moved rather differently here, was even welcomed. (In some circles the cardinal was nicknamed "Thelma" Spellman.) Vidal says that a mutual Catholic friend of his and the cardinal's kept him posted on the cardinal's manner of, uh, blessing the newest shows in town *and* their chorus boys. The friend would also accompany the cardinal, out of his gown, for a bit of frolic with a variety of youths at the house of a "procurer"—and then the cardinal would redon his robes and "head back to the palace." The irony of it all!

Cross the Avenue.

23. THE INTERNATIONAL BUILDING • 630 Fifth Avenue
between 50th and 51st Streets

The building across from the cathedral, where Atlas holds the world on his shoulders (and don't we all know how that feels?), was the 1970 home of the New York Republican State Committee. This was back when a Republican named Rockefeller (Nelson) was governor, and a new election was looming. But 1970 was also the year that gay activism really began to make a name for itself. (Check out the West Village tour!) The leaders of the Gay Activists Alliance requested discussion time with Rockefeller, and repeatedly he failed to acknowledge their requests. The GAA folks decided that perhaps they weren't being clear enough. One afternoon in June, just a few days shy of the one-year anniversary of Stonewall, eight or nine activists entered the premises to demand that Rockefeller cease his "crime of silence." Not being immediately ushered into anyone's office, let alone Rockefeller's, the GAA members made themselves at home in the reception area while a picket line demonstrated outside the building, shouting, chanting, holding hands, and kissing. The media arrived and snapped some footage, but five o'clock rolled around with only the communiqué that state officials in Albany were being sent the GAA demands; the GAA refused to leave. At six-thirty, the Republican Party state chairman agreed to meet with one GAA representative at the airport; he refused to allow a media person to attend, though, and his offer was rejected. Around seven, the police arrived and informed the protesters that they could leave or be arrested: five stayed and were arrested. They were the first gay protesters ever arrested for a gay issue. One of them, GAA president **Jim Owles,** went on to make an unsuccessful bid for New York City Council.

Follow Fifth up to 52nd Street and make a quick left.

24. "21" • 21 West 52nd Street

Okay, a quick self-indulgent moment (as if this were the first): Opened in the 1930s as a speakeasy called Jack and Charlie's, "21" became one of *the* New York clubs, a must stop on the celebrity night-out circuit. (**Joan Crawford**'s table was upstairs in the main dining room, just left of the entrance.) Noted here in part because, well, it's here in *All About Eve* (come on, you love that movie) where Karen Richards has a lunch date with Margo Channing (you know, **Ms. Davis**) and bumps into Addison DeWitt, the manipulative theater critic who, surprisingly enough, has in tow none other than the incomparable Eve Harrington. Good stuff.

Also, however, "21" affords the chance to remember **Paul Monette,** the poet, essayist, screenwriter, and activist. Monette, who lived most of his life in New England and Los Angeles, came increasingly into the public eye first with his deeply moving memoir *Borrowed Time*, about loving and then losing his partner, **Roger Horowitz,** to AIDS. The painful story of his own coming out, *Becoming a Man*, later won the National Book Award. In one of his last essays, Monette described dining in "21"—at Robert Benchley's booth, "a spitball's throw from the downstairs bar"—with Horowitz and **Gertrude Macy,** an older lesbian he became friends with in the 1970s. Macy, who had been lover and assistant to **Katharine Cornell,** one of the divas of the American theater, regaled Monette with stories of **Garbo** and **Coward** and **Dietrich** and the Lunts, and the false marriages and overstuffed closets of the theater world. She even inspired him to write a play about it, which *nearly* got produced and nearly starred Donald Sutherland. Both Monette and Macy have since died, she a good ten years before him, he certainly all too soon. But in their friendship and exchanges lie the web of community and history and tradition.

Make a left on Fifth Avenue and head uptown two blocks.

25. THE UNIVERSITY CLUB • 1 West 54th Street

Time for a romance break outside the **University Club.**

F. O. Matthiessen was one of the century's great literary scholars; **Russell Cheney,** one of the nation's more successful, if less well-known, artists. They lived apart for much of the time, but because of that they left behind some wonderful engaging, introspective love letters. In their letters, they were "Rat" (Cheney) and "Devil" (Matthiessen). They met on a trans-Atlantic crossing in the summer of 1923 on a ship called *Paris.* Matthiessen later wrote to a friend of how they fell into an easy intimacy, talking about anything and everything, except for sex. Matthiessen remembered both that he wanted to bring it up, and that he was scared to. Finally at two A.M. in Matthiessen's cabin, Cheney was eating a pear and Matthiessen announced "in a voice that attempted to maintain its usual pass the bread, please conversational tone" that "I know it won't make any difference to our friendship, but there's one thing I've got to tell you: before [his senior year at Yale] I was sexually inverted. Of course I've controlled it since. . . ." Cheney stopped chewing. This wasn't your typical new-friend-on-the-boat announcement in those days. "Then," wrote Matthiessen, "in a far away voice I had never heard came the answer: 'My God, feller, you've turned me upside down. I'm that way too.'"

The end of the trip found them back in the cabin, sitting and talking, and eventually lying down together, but closer. They remained dressed, but there was an electric tension whenever they brushed against each other. "Many hours we lay there, saying little, but feeling the steady, warm throb of the body at our side. About dawn Rat turned and with full red lips kissed me fully on the lips. The very tips of my fingers tingled with the new dynamic electric force."

Over the next thirty years, they wrote each other some 3,100 letters—1,600,000 words. Their correspondence kept them vivid and present for each other even as distance did not. One April morning in 1925 Cheney wrote to Matthiessen from here at the University Club, where he often stayed in the city. "My own Pic" ("Piccolo" was another nickname), "It is 6:30 A.M., the sun is streaming in the window, and I have been lying here a half hour or so with you at my side talking things over. The first thing when I wake it seems so always, you are right here, the long night together, and I bury my head in the pillow again, saying somewhere away inside me—hello Pic, Pic, and lie there close to you. . . ."

Head west to Broadway and then up to 55th Street.

26. ARISTON BATHS · 1732 Broadway
on the northeast corner of 55th Street

Although the apartment building that stood on this corner at the turn of the century is gone, the one on the southeast corner should give you a clear idea of what it looked like. And anyway, it's not the building we're interested in; it's the basement. Nearly one hundred years ago, the **Ariston** ran a bathhouse there with an active gay clientele.

According to historian George Chauncey, a man entered from 55th Street and then, after paying a dollar and turning in his valuables, was given a changing room and a sheet to wear. The Ariston offered massages, manicures, a cafe, and a swimming pool, as well as steam room, sauna, etc. But the focus, it seems (and this was 1903), was pretty much a free-for-all, with sex in the dressing rooms, dormitory rooms, and cooling rooms.

Sadly, Chauncey knows all of this because of a 1903 police raid that involved several hours of observation and resulted in fifty-two detentions and twenty-six arrests. The raid itself attracted a crowd, so that the fifty-two men who were eventually released here were still forced to walk past a hooting and jeering mob. The twenty-six others hardly fared better. One fellow, a fifty-three-year-old Irish pantryman, was reported by police to have had nine sexual partners in the course of the evening; he was sentenced to twenty years in the state penitentiary. Two of his partners were given seven years and two months, and a third was sentenced to four years.

If you feel like it, you might want to take a peak at a more recent sin dive, **Studio 54,** *the fabulous discothèque from the late 1970s and early 1980s, where regulars ranged from* **Truman Capote** *and* **Liza Minnelli** *to* **Halston, Andy Warhol,** *and* **Roy Cohn.** *(He was the club's much-needed attorney.) It's at 254 West 54th, over by Eighth Avenue. Otherwise, scoot east across Seventh.*

27. CARL VAN VECHTEN'S HOME • 150 West 55th Street
between Sixth and Seventh Avenues

The Harlem Renaissance, perhaps like most noted artistic movements or moments, was generated by the confluence of two things: a community of young, talented, committed artists gathering together and the attentions, financial and critical, of the outside world. **Carl Van Vechten,** born in 1880, was one of *the* essential promoters of that movement from the 1920s into the mid-1930s, generating both popular interest and financial support. A tall, blond Iowan, Van Vechten cast himself as the ultimate urbane, witty Manhattanite, knowledgeable about music and art. Although he arrived in New York in 1906, it wasn't until 1924 that he got introduced, really, into black circles. Shortly thereafter, though, the apartment that he shared here with his vagabond wife, **Fania Marinoff,** was soon dubbed the "midtown branch of the NAACP." Van Vechten developed a lifelong friendship with **Langston Hughes,** sharing counsel and criticism, as well as strong friendships with **Zora Neale Hurston, Countee Cullen,** and **Ethel Waters.** (Read more about them in the Harlem tour.)

Van Vechten and Marinoff lived here for much of the 1920s and '30s, entertaining with famously fabulous parties. (Don't worry about the marriage business: perhaps his most famous line is "A thing of beauty is a boy forever," and she once got a good wallop for trying to make it with **Bessie Smith.**) At one such party here, George Gershwin tinkered on the piano, Theodore Dreiser sat brooding, Paul Robeson sang, and James Weldon Johnson read from *Go Down Death.* Langston Hughes met **Somerset Maugham** and Salvador Dali here and even saw **Rudolph Valentino** turned away at the door for having arrived well past the party's peak (Van Vechten didn't want him to think the party was poorly attended). On another occasion, Bessie Smith sang some blues, followed by Marguerite d'Alvarez, a singer with the Metropolitan Opera, who stood and sang an aria. Bessie, it seems, did not know d'Alvarez, but, liking what she had heard, went up to her when she was done and cried, "Don't let nobody tell you you can't sing!" These events were well attended indeed.

In 1926, Van Vechten published *Nigger Heaven*, the first novel about Harlem by a white person. Van Vechten's irony eluded many, who saw only a novel celebrating the worst qualities of African-American living, but the book did succeed in dramatically increasing the attention the rest of the world was paying to Harlem. Van Vechten was also a great correspondent, writing to all the significant figures of his day: **Mabel Dodge Luhan,** H. L. Mencken, Theodore Dreiser, and Upton Sinclair. And he wrote with flourish. He signed his letters with send-offs like "Purple parrots to you" and "Best butter dolphins to you!"

His greatest correspondence was with his dearest friend, **Gertrude Stein.** Indeed it was Van Vechten who introduced Stein's work to American audiences. (He also inspired the rediscovery of **Herman Melville.**) At a certain point, he, she, and **Alice Toklas** became a family of sorts, nicknaming each other Baby Woojums (Gertrude), Mama Woojums (Alice), and Papa Woojums (Carl). In December of 1934, after Alice and Gertrude were shown around Chicago by playwright **Thornton Wilder** (who generously included a police tour in the visit), Carl wrote "Dearest Gertrudy" warning, "Thornton Wilder has got me down with jealousy. Don't go and like him BETTER, PLEASE!"

By the way, Van Vechten's line about boys and beauty actually appears as the letterhead on the stationery of one of his characters, a duke. Describing an opera production he's involved with, the duke says, "I have no friends, only people that amuse me, and people that I sleep with. . . . The people that amuse me are all in the play. . . . The theater isn't big enough to hold the others." I love that!

Head east across Sixth and walk uptown a block.

28. THE CANDY STORE • 44 West 56th Street
between Fifth and Sixth Avenues

Just in passing: A gay bar here dated back to 1966. Post-Stonewall bar critics remembered it as a place of cigarette-smoking sophistication, the kind of place where it was important to drop names, travel stories, and acquisitions. It was also the kind of place where if you dropped a little money, younger cuties were there specifically to pick it up. One hipster critic, **John Hunter,** said in his 1970 bar guide that the **Candy Store** was known "as a Wrinkle Room, and not without reason." But someone else remembers its winding staircase and crystal chandelier, and "ho . . . how the queens love to sweep down that staircase."

Follow Sixth Avenue uptown one block.

29. MARLON BRANDO'S PAD • 53 West 57th Street
between Fifth and Sixth Avenues

Although **Marlon** himself was born in Omaha, Nebraska, in 1924, the Brando clan was well ensconced in Manhattan by the 1940s, with Mom and two sisters living on the Upper West Side. In 1949, having opened on Broadway the previous year in **Tennessee Williams**'s *A Streetcar Named Desire*, Marlon shared a two-room apartment here with the actor **Wally Cox.** This was his home base, and from here he went back and forth to Hollywood for the filming of *The Men*, *Streetcar*, and *Viva Zapata!* At the time, Brando was studying yoga, boxing, and fencing and had a pet raccoon. He and Cox used to travel around town on motorcycles, but their home was a haven for actors, intellectuals, and various characters.

Oft described as bisexual, Brando has said that "like a large number of men, I have had homosexual experiences and I am not ashamed. Homosexuality is so much in fashion it no longer makes news." (You can read more about Brando and his life-long friendship with **James Baldwin** in the West Village tour.)

Okay, one block west.

30. CARNEGIE HALL • 150 West 57th Street
at Seventh Avenue

My grandmother's favorite joke: How do you get to **Carnegie Hall?** . . . Practice, practice, practice. (You would have loved her.)

Built in 1891, this bastion of music history became a show-place for some of the world's and our own, great musical talents. Its opening was graced by **Peter Ilich Tchaikovsky,** the tragic composer of *The Nutcracker* and *Swan Lake*, who had abandoned his wife and their sexless marriage. Here young **Leonard Bernstein** conducted and **Marlene Dietrich** sang. In 1961, **Judy Garland** marked an enormous comeback here with a concert that would become a live double album, and in 1972 newly proclaimed bisexual **David Bowie** received a standing ovation from a sold-out crowd after a concert that including his kissing and simulating a blow job with his lead guitarist. (Bowie later explained that "the whole bisexual chic, which I'm credited with originating, started six years ago as an answer to an impertinent interviewer about my sex life. . . . I'm not a leader of the gay liberation movement or anything like that. But I have nothing to hide. It's in my music. I like men. I like Black girls, I can be 100 different people in 100 different scenes." I wonder if he could play modest.) Ten years later, **Cris Williamson** and **Meg Christian** played here, and in recent years the **Gay Men's Chorus of New York** have been regular performers.

Two stories: Bernstein actually made his dramatic conducting debut here with the New York Philharmonic in a classic understudy move. It was a November afternoon in 1943. The guest conductor, Bruno Walter, had fallen ill, and the principal conductor was out of town: Bernstein, the assistant conductor, without benefit of rehearsal, and anxiously awake most of the night before, stepped in. As the New York *Daily News* described the understudy task: "Like a shoestring catch in the centerfield—make it and you're a hero. Muff it and you're a dope." Bernstein, that day, made it. With neither a baton nor formal attire—he wore a simple suit—Bernstein seemed to shape the music with his bare hands, and astounded both the audience and the critics.

Above and around the hall itself are the Carnegie Studios, which at different times provided homes to Bernstein, **Brando, Isadora Duncan,** even space for dance lessons for a young Rita Hayworth. And if you turn around for a second: kitty-corner, at 205 West 57th Street, is the Osborne, home for Bernstein while he wrote the score to *West Side Story*.

Head up Seventh Avenue to 58th Street.

31. THE VENICE THEATRE
  • **northwest corner of Seventh Avenue and 58th Street**

Though **Marc Blitzstein's** life ended tragically with his murder, for a while he seemed blessed, and certainly this tale from his earlier days is a heart-warmer. Gather round. Blitzstein was a young Philadelphia-born composer who studied with our own **Aaron Copland** and became dear friends with

Leonard Bernstein. In the course of his career, he crafted the English version of Weill's *Threepenny Opera*, which ran off Broadway for years, and an operatic version of *The Little Foxes* called *Regina*. But in 1937, when Blitzstein was thirty-two, he and a young Orson Welles and John Houseman joined forces with the Federal government's Works Progress Administration to put on Blitzstein's opera, *The Cradle Will Rock*.

The opera was set in the Depression and told the tale of Steeltown, U.S.A., caught in a struggle between city bosses and union politics. That very spring and summer, though, real steelworker strikes were rocking the country, and the day before the show's mid-June opening, the government (this is before the NEA, mind you) decided not just to pull their backing but to confiscate the sets, costumes, and music. When Welles and Houseman insisted the show would still go up, the WPA persuaded Actors' Equity and the orchestral union to forbid their members from performing and, just to be certain, sent twelve guards to secure the Maxine Elliott Theatre, where they were set to perform.

Welles, Houseman, and Blitzstein, however, were determined. They spent the next day, the day of the scheduled opening, in a scramble, trying to find an alternate theater. Someone found a piano that could be rented for five dollars and a truck and driver that would take it anywhere. Then, with only an hour to spare, they discovered that the Venice Theatre (which used to stand here on the east side of the avenue) was available. The piano was sent off to the theater, and the audience, which had already begun to gather, was directed uptown.

By nine, the theater was packed. All of the 1,742 seats were taken, and countless more crammed into the aisles. Just a little behind schedule, Welles stepped onstage to set the scene for the opening, and then the curtain rose: Blitzstein and the piano sat alone onstage. He began to play the overture and slowly described to the audience the missing sets and backdrops. Warming up, he had launched into the first act and first aria—the song of a young woman broke and alone on the street—when he was interrupted by a timid echo from the audience. The actress, barred from the stage by her union, stood in her box on the second tier and, in a frightened voice, began to sing her part from there. When it was time for the next character to join the young woman, the actor cast in the role rose on cue from his seat in the orchestra section and sang up to her. And so it went for the rest of the evening. With only Blitzstein sanctioned to appear on stage, and without anyone knowing what the repercussions of their actions would be (for their unions or for their careers), the entire show was performed, improvised, created that night from the seats of the audience, scene after scene after scene. The applause, it is said, lasted an hour.

Sometimes the incredible does happen.

Several years later, Blitzstein was killed by three young men he had been carousing with in Martinique. They turned on him, beat him, and robbed him in an alley. He was taken to the hospital and seemed to be in stable condition, but he died the next day. Before he died, though, he had contributed to the legacy of gay music. It seems young Bernstein, neither famous nor yet friends with Blitzstein, saw the New York production of *Cradle* and decided to stage a version of it at Harvard. Blitzstein himself attended, and, as Bernstein later recalled, after the performance the two men "walked, all afternoon, by the Charles River. Now that image leaps up in my mind: Marc lying on the banks of the Charles, talking, talking, bequeathing to me his knowledge, insight, warmth, endlessly." Perhaps they were lovers, certainly close friends. But in such moments and such relationships the torch passes along.

Beyond the Bird Circuit: Gay Lives on the Upper East Side

In a straight, if seedy, 1948 guide to the city called *New York: Confidential!* two know-it-all journalists described the Upper East Side as "a Manhattan melange of money and beauty, prodigality and banality, with haunts and hangouts of every description." In the years following the Second World War, right in the heart of that melange, there was a circle of bars running up and down Third Avenue that defined the path of any gay man's night out. Whether those haunts or their patrons arrived first, the route, known as "the Bird Circuit," marked the border of an increasingly vibrant gay social world. Hardly a political hotbed, the Upper East Side was where gay men and women of all stripes came to live. And living, after all, is what gay people do best.

In talking about East Side life, even the far from tasteful *Confidential!* fellows referred to "the horde of homosexuals" who had adopted this side of town, noting the Third Avenue bars where, "drinking shoulder to shoulder, are jaded sons and daughters of the rich, Bohemians, musical comedy favorites, artists and newspapermen, fairies and Lesbians." And on the avenues, they wrote, "they parade with mincing steps in pairs and trios up both sides of the avenue. Some are blondined, some act 'masculine,' Negroes mix with white ones, all on the make for strangers." The good life, seen through any eyes, it seems, is still the good life.

What lies ahead is your chance to mince and parade with some of the East Side's finest. Indeed, this is the true Uptown, the world of Celebrity, Glamour, and Fortune. And if you

THE UPPER EAST SIDE

1. Subway Grating, or Getting in the Mood
2. Cole Porter's Home
3. Georgia O'Keeffe's Home
4. The Bird Circuit
5. Philip Johnson's Townhouse
6. Truman Capote's Home
7. Noël Coward's Home
8. Greta Garbo's Home
9. Anne Morgan's Home
10. The Beau Brummel
11. Charlotte Manson's Home
12. The Hotel Elysée
13. Tiffany and Co.
14. The Plaza Hotel
15. Danny Kaye's Home
16. Divine's Headquarters
17. Bloomingdale's
18. Montgomery Clift's Townhouse
19. Tallulah Bankhead's Townhouse
20. Mercedes de Acosta's Home
21. George Cukor's Childhood Block
22. Roy Cohn's Home
23. Halston Headquarters
24. Joan Crawford's Home
25. Frank E. Campbell Funeral Home
26. Marlene Dietrich's Home

Jeffrey L. Ward 1987

0   1/4   1/2

Scale of Miles

METROPOLITAN MUSEUM OF ART

WHITNEY MUSEUM

CENTRAL PARK

FIFTH AVENUE
MADISON AVENUE
PARK AVENUE
LEXINGTON AVENUE
THIRD AVENUE
SECOND AVENUE
FIRST AVENUE
YORK AVENUE

E 84th
E 83rd
E 82nd
E 81st
E 80th
E 79th
E 78th
E 77th
E 76th
E 75th
E 74th
E 73rd
E 72nd
E 71st
E 70th
E 69th
E 68th
E 67th
E 66th
E 65th
E 64th
E 63rd
E 62nd
E 61st
E 60th
CENTRAL PK SOUTH
E 59th
W 58th
E 57th
E 56th
E 55th
E 54th
E 53rd
E 52nd
E 51st
E 50th
E 49th
E 48th
E 47th
E 46th
E 45th
E 44th

SUTTON PLACE
BEEKMAN PL
FDR DRIVE
East River

don't mind a word of gossip, a little dish, a little up-close-and-personal (if you know what I mean), then honey, you've come to the right place, 'cause dishing is what made this side of town famous. Along the way, you'll not only cross the Bird Circuit, but you'll see the homes of some of our most legendary: **Truman Capote, Noël Coward, Divine, Greta Garbo, Marlene Dietrich,** and on and on to your heart's content. Slip on your sunglasses, grab your martini glass with one hand and cigarette holder with the other, and let's head uptown. (The 6 train will get you to the stepping-off point.)

1. SUBWAY GRATING, or GETTING IN THE MOOD
  • **Northwest corner of 52nd Street and Lexington Avenue**

All right now, this is important, historically speaking as well as for tour spirit. Northwest corner. Look familiar? How about if I tell you that there used to be a movie theater here, the Trans Lux? How about if I tell you that on a hot September evening in 1954, if you'd just seen *The Creature from the Black Lagoon* with, say, your neighbor whose family was away for the summer and who seemed to be suffering from some sort of seven-year itch, you might have stood out on the sidewalk for a minute, talking about the movie? Maybe you'd be over there near that grating; then maybe, just maybe, an underground train would roll by, sending a blast of hot vapors straight up, and you'd find yourself giggling, hair flying, skirt billowing, and saying, as a delicate **Marilyn Monroe** in a frolicking white dress did one night, "Oh, do you feel the breeze from the subway? Isn't it delicious?" Come on, say it. Relish that word, "delicious." But do try to hold your skirt down, a little at least. This is just supposed to be about warming up the spirit.

Walk down Lexington to 50th Street and make a right turn.

2. COLE PORTER'S HOME • 100 East 50th Street
  between Lexington and Park Avenues

Born in Peru, Indiana, in 1891, **Cole Porter** catapulted his way through Yale and into stardom, writing some of the wittiest, sexiest, most urbane songs we have—"I Get a Kick Out of You," "Begin the Beguine," "I Love Paris," even "Wunderbar." (Actually, at Yale they still sing some of the school songs he wrote.) Go home and listen to your *Red, Hot & Blue* album if you don't recognize the titles. And tell me what you make of his lyric "But if, baby, I'm the bottom, You're the top." Most impressive of all, though, Porter got **Cary Grant** to portray him in his bio-pic *Night and Day.* Go get 'em, Cole. Asked why he'd let Cary Grant play him in the movie when he could have been played by Fred Astaire, he said, "Would *you* turn down Cary Grant?"

Porter made his home here, on the forty-first floor of the private Waldorf-Astoria Towers, from 1935 to 1964. (If you cross Park Avenue you get the best view.) He and his wife, Linda, *both* lived there . . . in adjacent but separate apartments. He had a parquet floor imported from an old French chateau (all my friends from Indiana are that way) and also had acoustical mud put on the walls to deaden the sound of his piano. Frank Sinatra eventually took over Porter's apartment.

As for Linda, you'll be pleased to know that in 1910, at the ripe age of twenty-eight, she was considered to be one of the most beautiful women in America, and by the time she hit her forties, fashion magazines were calling her the loveliest in the world. She was a wealthy divorcée from an abusive marriage when she and Porter married; one biographer has suggested that this is one of the reasons she was happy to marry a man obviously homosexual. The press announced their marriage with the banner headline BOY WITH 1 MILLION WEDS GIRL WITH 2 MILLION!! She was famous for her taste, whether it was in furniture or in clothing. Women copied the fashion that she introduced of a simple black dress decorated with a single elaborate piece of jewelry. And since they shared many of the same tastes, she was able to guide Cole toward the *truly* luxurious living that he desired. He came to rely on her deeply.

When it came to men, Porter seemed more interested in sex than in romance, and loved to go cruising with his lifelong friend actor **Monty Woolley.** Porter's tastes ran toward the burly, unwashed truck-driver type, and he even seemed to savor paying for the excitement. There's also a rumor that he had a bit of a fling with Jackie O's father, "Black" Jack Bouvier. Sadly, a riding accident in 1937 crushed both his legs and left

Outside the Waldorf-Astoria, Cole Porter's former home, today.

him with only limited mobility; two decades later one of his legs was amputated. He died a recluse in October 1964. As a writer, though, Porter managed to recast sex and lust, and filled the air with the buzz of romance. He left us with phrases we use to this day, like "I've got you under my skin," or "You do something to me." They are our very words of love.

Walk south on Lexington.

3. GEORGIA O'KEEFFE'S HOME • 525 Lexington Avenue
between 48th and 49th Streets

From the mid-1920s to the mid-'30s, before she went west to paint the desert and horse skulls, this building was home to **Georgia O'Keeffe** and her husband, photographer Alfred Stieglitz. Born in 1887 on a farm in Wisconsin, O'Keeffe studied art in Chicago and New York. Stieglitz saw her work and, against her wishes, exhibited her charcoal drawings and watercolor sketches at his 291 Gallery, the premier gallery in the 1910s for new young artists. Although he was many years her senior, the two married in 1924 and moved into suite 3003 of this building (then the Hotel Shelton, now Halloran House).

They lived here for ten years. Their living room sat on the corner, facing north and east; with its view of the city skyline it served as her studio.

Both Stieglitz and O'Keeffe are said to have dallied in New York's adventurous sexual life, and O'Keeffe's biographers have noted lesbian love affairs throughout her life. Muralist Diego Rivera reported that O'Keeffe and his wife, painter **Frida Kahlo,** had a liaison. O'Keeffe is thought to have discovered more lesbian love across the country, though, when she visited and eventually settled in New Mexico. Actually, Santa Fe and Taos in the 1920s and '30s were thought to be lesbian meccas—no doubt in some small part thanks to **Mabel Dodge Luhan,** who tried to get everyone she knew to relocate out there. (More about her in the West Village tour.) The theater set in those days even referred to a woman who had taken up the life as having "gone Santa Fe."

It was certainly Luhan who initially begged O'Keeffe to come to Taos in 1929. (Just so you know, the community of successfully wooed artists ranged from D. H. Lawrence to Ansel Adams.) On one night, at least, Luhan even managed to lure O'Keeffe into bed with her. Whatever the temptations, they were enough for O'Keeffe, and after Stieglitz died in 1946, she settled there, living out her years on Ghost Ranch until 1986.

Walk east a block to Third Avenue.

4. THE BIRD CIRCUIT
  • **Corner of Third Avenue and 50th Street**

In the wake of the Second World War, Third Avenue was *the* Strip, the Avenue, the place to see and be seen if you were gay. As is often the case with gay neighborhoods, Third Avenue was considered fairly borderline: it was close to the jewels of Fifth Avenue, but still at a remove. It had an elevated train running its length, lowering the rents as well as the visibility. But in the war years and after, gay men moved into the railroad flats that were east of the avenue, forming a large presence. There was a house at 405 East 50-something that was referred to simply as "Four Out of Five" because of the high percentage of gay men living there.

And of course, like moths and flames, the bars opened up here. Third Avenue, stretching down into the Forties and up into the Sixties, became a night-out circuit. The bars had names like the Golden Cockerel and the Yellow Cockatoo and the Wishbone (hence the nickname "Bird Circuit"). They were places where camp burgeoned and took hold, and everyone became she and Miss So-and-So. Mostly these places, and even the buildings they were in, are long gone, but just to give you an idea. . . . The Swan Club stood at 780 Third Avenue, on the corner of 48th Street. Across the avenue, on 50th Street, was Red's. Red's had been a speakeasy since the twenties, and as the Second World War approached, it became increasingly popular with gay men, an absolute must on any night out. Down at 45th Street there was a place called the Golden Pheasant, and the Blue Parrot was just up the street at 162 East 52nd Street.

The Parrot is actually remembered as a bar for the gentleman homosexual who liked his liquor and knew his old show tunes (although I didn't know show tunes were already old by then). But that was the flavor in this neighborhood, a certain gentlemanly campiness, even gentlemanly cruising. One writer recalled the technique as "the mirror game": puff on your cigarette and glance at his crotch in the mirror; if he returns the favor (via the mirror, that is), send him a drink. It sounds like very little, but one fellow years later recalled the Parrot as "an excellent cruising spot." It had a narrow front aisle along the bar, and then a "large square back room, dimly lit with blue lights (whence the name), and though there was no 'orgy' element in the modern sense, there was a good deal of freedom of conversation, quick propositions, etc." And for an added twist, General Eisenhower, before becoming President, had his office above it.

Practically anywhere you looked along here, there was a gay hideaway. And while the avenue was no Christopher Street, it certainly was busy. In for a drink, out for a stroll; in for another, back on the prowl. As long as you didn't spill your drink on your blouse or twist off your heel in a grate, there was plenty up here to keep you happy. And as Mae West used to say, "Too much of a good thing . . . can be wonderful."

Walk up Third to 52nd Street and turn right.

5. PHILIP JOHNSON'S TOWNHOUSE • 242 East 52nd Street
between Second and Third Avenues

This 1950 townhouse was designed by architect **Philip Johnson,** and though it's hardly his most famous structure, he lived here for several years after its construction. Born in the summer of 1906 into a wealthy family, Johnson went to Harvard but studied no architecture. The decision to be an architect came later, after graduating, while curating architectural exhibitions, and working with a friend who was the director of the then new Museum of Modern Art. Even then, the path wasn't simple: Johnson repeatedly failed the New York state architectural licensing exam.

Eventually, he succeeded. He became a crony of the Rockefellers and the Astors as well as **Andy Warhol** and **Truman Capote.** (Actually, he wore spectacles with round black frames much like Capote's, though Johnson's were designed as copies of those worn by Le Corbusier, his architectural idol.) While he didn't begin professional practice until 1946, his architectural hand can now be seen all over the city: he designed both the sculpture garden and two additions for MOMA; the New York State Theater at Lincoln Center is his work, as is the former AT&T building (now Sony-owned) on Madison Avenue and 55th Street. (If you look up, you can probably see it: it's an icon of postmodern architecture with its Chippendale pediment—meaning it looks like a circle was cut out of the rooftop—and was both panned and praised as a display of arrogance and extravagance.)

One of Johnson's most acclaimed works is his Glass House in New Canaan, Connecticut, which was completed in 1949. The all-but-invisible home quickly became the subject of international fascination, with people from all over the world coming to study its glass joints and wonder about anyone's ability to live in an open room with no curtains and all-glass walls. Living there late in his life, Johnson rattled off his own list of grievances: "Everything goes wrong. The heat goes off, something fell down and knocked out the pump. The water pressure goes out." But with a sigh and then a smile, he added, "How can I tell you how wonderful it is to wake up in the middle of the night and all I can see is Chinese fog and the tops to trees?" Or in the winter when it snowed, he'd turn off all the indoor lights, turn on the outdoor ones, and with the snow coming down, he said, "you feel as if you're going up, up, like an elevator."

A tip from the design master: Johnson once noted that the "improvement of sex" is one of an architect's main objectives. Recognizing that, he suggested building domed ceilings and installing pink reflector lights on theatrical dimmers. See, now you just have to figure out how to dome your ceiling.

Walk east on 52nd to First Avenue, turn right, head downtown three blocks, and then turn left onto Mitchell Place, just shy of 49th Street.

6. TRUMAN CAPOTE'S HOME • 870 United Nations Plaza
officially First Avenue between 48th and 49th Streets, but seen from Mitchell Place, between First and Beekman Place

Looking down at **Truman Capote**'s home is oddly appropriate. Capote stood five foot three, and in his lifetime he was as much caricatured as embraced for his charm, his grace, his size, his lisp, and the high pitch of his voice. **Gore Vidal,** ever temperate and kind, said he couldn't read Capote's work—"I'm a diabetic"—and suggested he had "the mind of a Kansas housewife: likes gossip and gets all shuddery when she thinks about boys murdering boys." Vidal and Capote, you should know, were a dramatic cross between friends and competitors (a libel lawsuit did trade hands for a bit), and James Michener used to tell this story: On a cross-country trip, Truman made his driver take them to a rural library and wait while he ran in. First time it happened, Michener said nothing. "Next time I asked, 'Truman, what in the hell are you doing in these libraries?' and he explained with childish delight: 'Checking the card catalogs. In this one, Mailer had seven cards. Vidal had eight. But I had eleven.' " That's how it was.

Capote published his first novel, *Other Voices, Other Rooms*, in 1948, at the age of twenty-four; he was quickly heralded as the next boy genius. Equally well received was *In Cold Blood*, which appeared in 1966. Just before its publication, Capote moved into this enormous complex, in an apartment on the twenty-second floor which Gloria Steinem described as "a dusty plush 'best parlor' in the South, seen through the eyes of Vuillard, and suspended twenty stories above Manhattan."

Capote characterized himself as a slow but diligent writer, working from four-thirty or five in the morning until about noon. (He didn't always work here. He and his lover **Jack Dunphy,** a dancer, also had houses next door to each other out on Long Island.) He was extremely possessive of his writing, and claimed that he would sit on his work at least a year before he would consider publishing it. Even then he wouldn't simply send it out for consideration. Instead, he would select the venue himself. "Shall I publish it in *The New Yorker?* If so, I call up Mr. Shawn and I say, 'I've got something for you. But I want to have lunch with you to talk about it because I'm not about to let anybody see anything of mine until they've already taken it.' " He sat for so long on his last work, *Answered Prayers,* that only a portion of it was ever published.

Capote was also a bit notorious for stirring things up, both with his writing and with his more prolific gossip. (Vidal sued him for close to a million dollars, and when the selection of *Answered Prayers* did appear, one socialite, Ann Woodward, actually committed suicide.) A frequent subject in **Andy Warhol**'s *Interview* magazine, Capote was asked once if he saw himself as a "dangerous friend." "Well," he said, "I'll answer your question this way: I feel that all a writer has is his own experience. Mmm? I mean that's all a writer has to write about—what he see and hears and what not. If you happen to capture my imagination for some reason and I decide to write about you and you don't like what I wrote about you, which is entirely possible, then yes, I'm a dangerous writer." Capote, though, didn't hide himself from the public eye, undergoing a very public facelift in 1981 and, the year before, declaring, "I'm an alcoholic. I'm a drug addict. I'm homosexual. I'm a genius."

My favorite Capote story is the charming anecdote of his being in a crowded bar with **Tennessee Williams** when a woman came over to their table. She pulled up her shirt and asked, handing him an eyebrow pencil, that he autograph her navel in a circle, like numbers on a clock. Capote said, "Oh no, forget that," but Tennessee insisted, saying, "Oh, now, go on, go ahead." So he did it. This little exchange had caused things in the bar to quiet down a bit, enough so that everyone could tell that, when the woman went back to her table, her husband was enraged. "He was drunk as all get-out," Capote later explained, "and he got up from the table and came over and he had the eyebrow pencil in his hand. He looked at me with infinite hatred, handed me the eyebrow pencil, unzipped his fly, and hauled out his equipment. By this point there was a dead, total silence in the whole bar. Everybody was looking. And he said, 'Since you're autographing everything, how'd you like to autograph *this?*' There was a pause . . . and I said, 'Well, I don't know if I can autograph it, but perhaps I could initial it.' "

Walk east the half-block to the start of Beekman Place.

7. Noël Coward's Home • 1 Beekman Place
at Mitchell Place

The humbly born British playwright and actor **Noël Coward** skyrocketed to fame and fortune in the mid-1920s when his plays took over Broadway and London's West End. He lived here in 1933 while *Private Lives*, one of his classics, was still playing on Broadway.

Born in 1899 (close enough to Christmas to be called Noël), Coward first arrived in New York by ship in the spring of 1921. The city, he later wrote, "rose out of the sea to greet us. It was a breathless June morning, and wads of cotton-wool smoke lay motionless among the high towers. The Statue of Liberty seemed insignificant but the harbour was glorious. There will always be a stinging enchantment for me in this arrival. Even now, when I know it so well in every aspect, my heart jumps a little." Success came to Coward by 1924, when he wrote and starred in *The Vortex*, a gleefully flippant play which cast Coward as the dandy and involved drugs, homosexuals, and mother fixations. It contained his signature bitchy conversations with exchanges like: "Oh, my God, look at that lamp shade!" "I gave it to her last Christmas." "Wasn't that naughty of you?" In 1933, his show *Design for Living* even featured a ménage à trois.

Coward worked hard to keep his sex life private, extremely concerned about the effect it would have on his career and reputation. He carried on public affairs with friends **Marlene**

Dietrich and Gertrude Lawrence and cast himself, both in his plays and out, as a cad and a bachelor. He speculated in his journal once with amusement that after his death, "there will be books proving conclusively that I was homosexual and books proving equally conclusively that I was not. . . . *What* a pity I shan't be here to enjoy them!"

But he did, in his life, not only have an affair with **Prince George,** the youngest son of King George V, but two long-lasting love affairs, with **Jack Wilson** and **Graham Payn.** The first took place here, with Wilson, a New Jersey-born businessman who saw Coward perform in *The Vortex* in London, went backstage to meet him and pursued him almost as soon as Coward settled in New York. (It wasn't a difficult pursuit: Coward had seen Wilson over the footlights and had played nearly exclusively to him.) Wilson was stunning, with a sharp wit, and the two were for a time rather inseparable. Coward wrote the song "Mad About the Boy" after meeting him. Their affair became complicated as Wilson gave up his own business dealings to become Coward's business manager—a task that, between drinks, he seems to have rather bungled. But though their romance eventually ended, their friendship did not, and both men went on to greater achievements, Wilson himself becoming a successful theater director and producer. After the Second World War, Coward met Graham Payn, an actor, and they remained a couple until Coward's death—by then he was Sir Noël Coward—in 1973.

Across the way, at number 2, **Greta Garbo** kept a six-room apartment in the 1930s that was her home away from Hollywood. (The apartment would later belong to Antoine de Saint-Exupéry, the French pilot and writer who left us *The Little Prince*.) But more about Garbo at the other end of the street. . . .

Walk uptown to the dead end at 51st and scoot around either corner to 52nd.

8. GRETA GARBO'S HOME • 450 East 52nd Street
at the East River

For the secrets this building has held, it deserves to be a legend unto itself, especially in the gay world. (And I didn't even know there *were* secrets in the gay world.) Known as the **Campanile,** it was built in the 1920s, from brick, with Gothic arches and leaded glass windows. It is most famously associated with **Greta Garbo.** She lived here on the ninth floor until her death in 1990. Born Greta Louisa Gustafsson, Garbo dazzled the world first as a silent-film beauty. Later, with roles like Anna Christie and Ninotchka, with films like *Mata Hari* and *Grand Hotel,* and with moments like the final close-up in *Camille,* she became deeply etched in the gay consciousness. It is said that when Garbo was doing her close-ups, she asked that black screens be set up to enclose herself and the camera away from the gaze of the rest of the cast and crew. Otherwise, she could not take what she was doing seriously enough.

One critic, like many of her fans, reveled in the moment in a Garbo film when, finally, all reserve gone, "with a sound that was half sob, half ecstasy, she ran to the arms of her lover. At such moments, every man"—and equally, every woman in the audience—felt that he or she "alone was holding this exquisite woman, who, suddenly defenseless, revealed a depth of sexuality that would require a lifetime of delightful appeasement."

While living here, Garbo became as famous a recluse as she had been a film star, an occasional if haunting presence on the streets of the East Side. Indeed, she is remembered for saying "I want to be alone." Yet in her private life Garbo seems to have had complicated affairs ranging from **Mercedes de Acosta** (about whom you'll hear more) to **Cecil Beaton,** the gay British photographer and designer. (She even had an affair with a friend's husband, made more difficult by the fact that the couple also lived here in the Campanile.) Her affair with Beaton was ambiguous in its pleasures; Beaton, for instance, relished how she referred to herself as a young man, and he would then write her, "Dear Youth, Have you yet learnt how to use a razor? . . . Have you got to the age when you wear long pants & a dinner jacket in the evening? Has your voice started to break yet?" She, alternately, seemed to enjoy his dandyish, feminine nature.

The building was also home for a time to **Noël Coward** and, in the late 1920s and '30s, **Alexander Woollcott,** the sharp-tongued critic for the *New York Times* who was one of the founding voices of *The New Yorker.* Woollcott lived on the third floor here in an apartment his colleague in the battle of the scathing pens, Dorothy Parker, referred to as "Wit's End."

Entrance to the Campanile, Greta Garbo's New York retreat.

Return to First Avenue and head up to 57th Street and then east to Sutton Place.

9. ANNE MORGAN'S HOME • 3 Sutton Place
  just north of 57th Street

Anne Morgan was born in 1873, the youngest child of the infamous robber baron John Pierpont Morgan. (Imagine having a father named J. P.) Perhaps the fact that there was a squash court in their house gives you a sense of their family wealth. Or that when the family returned from a trans-Atlantic cruise, their yacht, the *Corsair*, came out to meet the ocean liner and escort them into the harbor. You wouldn't have it any other way, would you?

But Anne . . . Anne was a shy young woman, and it wasn't until well past her youth that she was brought out, by that marvelous agent, playwright, and impresario **Elizabeth Marbury.** Marbury, who lived for a time just up the street at 13 Sutton Place, wrote that "there was something pathetic about this splendid girl, full of vitality and eagerness, yet who, as the youngest of a large family, had never been allowed to grow up." Morgan, though, did grow up, joining forces with Marbury and others in 1903 to start the Colony Club, the first-ever women's social club in the city. It featured a pool, a roof garden, a squash court, and a smoking room (!) decorated by Marbury's companion, **Elsie de Wolfe.** (De Wolfe is considered by many to have been the nation's first professional interior designer.) Morgan also volunteered to inspect work conditions for women in factories. But she most gained prominence when, following World War I, she worked to restore France, organizing the American Friends for Devastated France, finding homes for fifty thousand, setting up clinics and orphanages, and distributing $5 million in food and medicine. In 1932, the grateful nation made her the first American woman ever to be a Commander of the Legion of Honor. Anne herself had a $3 million trust fund and said, "I believe in the true aristocracy . . . which realizes that it has inherited something magnificent, with the obligation to carry it on."

One of Anne's biggest projects was the renovation of the Villa Trianon in Versailles, which she performed along with de Wolfe and Marbury. Those two ladies were companions for some forty years, and though they both also lived up here on Sutton Place, their more famous home was down by Gramercy Park on the corner of Irving Place and 17th Street (122 East, to be exact). The two met in 1887, when de Wolfe was struggling to be an actress and Marbury was building up an influential theatrical agency. She came to represent people like George Bernard Shaw, J. M. Barrie, and **Oscar Wilde** in the U.S. market, but for a time she did her darnedest to promote de Wolfe as the most fashionable figure on Broadway. Their best success, though, was their house: they had fabulous salons and even hosted Wilde there during his American tour. Among de Wolfe's accomplishments were popularizing short white gloves, making it hip to tint gray hair blue, and inventing the Pink Lady cocktail. On her deathbed in 1950, it is said, she insisted, "They can't do this to me. I don't want to go."

A final note on the richness of the lesbian network. This house was photographed by **Berenice Abbott** in her encyclopedic photographic series *Changing New York*. Abbott's caption for the photo noted that "the basement contains the mechanical equipment of the house, including the elevator machinery. There is no necessity here for ice-man, furnace-man, ash-man and garbage-man, the most modern mechanical appliances . . . being installed." We get the picture, Berenice: no need for any men at all.

Head down to 56th Street and then west past Lexington.

10. THE BEAU BRUMMEL • 120 East 56th Street
between Lexington and Park Avenues

Just a note, as we're passing. The gay presence in this part of the city, while strong for much of the century, has gone through cycles, as has gay life all over. In the early 1960s, for instance, this bar catered to rather wealthy homosexual clientele during the lunch and early-afternoon hours. The management actually deflected any heterosexual attendance. Light cruising and even some quiet "petting" took place among patrons. Promptly at 7:00 P.M., though, the bartenders changed. And with this cue, the gay crowd dispersed. Soon, a straight crowd began arriving, and the management then reversed its filtering process. (By way of contrast, check out Kooky's Cocktail Lounge, which operated as a workingmen's bar by day and a women's club at night, in the Chelsea tour.)

Okay, west to Park Avenue and then down a few steps.

11. CHARLOTTE MASON'S HOME • 399 Park Avenue
at 55th Street

This luxury building, in a much different time and in a much different spirit, housed one of the benefactors of the Harlem Renaissance and the gay cultural spirit, **Charlotte Mason.** In the 1920s, the culture of Harlem—the music, the poetry, the nightclubs, the celebration—was a culture the world was eager to embrace. And many white people from downtown and all around were ready and willing to be patrons of those arts. In that spirit, Mrs. Mason befriended **Alain Locke,** a light-skinned homosexual professor from Howard University who published a literary anthology called *The New Negro*, which shone an international spotlight on the cultural events of Harlem. Locke brought young artists to meet Mason and she in turn made herself their patron. Mason did not give her money without strings: she expected to be written to almost daily, she expected to be addressed as "Godmother," and she expected that all expenses would be strictly accounted for. It was an arrangement most artists found draining and could sustain for only a few years. It is also said that Locke did not offer access to Mason entirely freely; he was known to expect, well, favors in return, for which he wasn't always entirely praised. (**Zora Neale Hurston** once referred to him as "a malicious little snit.") Nevertheless, through Locke and Mason's efforts, **Langston Hughes** was cared for while he wrote his first novel, **Claude McKay** was supported, and Hurston was able to do ethnographic research and stage a musical drama on Broadway. (See the Harlem tour for more about all these folks.)

Follow Park down to 54th Street and turn right.

12. TENNESSEE WILLIAMS'S HOME
• 56–60 East 54th Street
between Park and Madison Avenues

The Hotel Elysée gave frequent comfort to two of our greater lights, **Tallulah Bankhead** and **Tennessee Williams,** and it is especially with Williams that it was associated. The playwright, who had burst on the dramatic scene with *The Glass Menagerie* in 1945 and had gone on to write such dazzling works as *A Streetcar Named Desire*, *Cat on a Hot Tin Roof*, and *Orpheus Descending*, occupied a suite here from the mid-1970s until his death early in 1983. He actually died here, just shy of his seventy-second birthday. He was known to call the place "Hotel Easy Lay" in reference to a hustler bar around the block that seemed to keep him well cared for.

Born Thomas Williams in 1911, the writer grew up in and around Mississippi and St. Louis. His family life was far from simple: a drinking father, fighting parents and grandparents. In his childhood, he was devoted to his sister, Rose, who became increasingly mentally unstable—ultimately to the point of a lobotomy (then considered therapeutic) and lifelong institutionalization. With his success he was able permanently to care for her and his mother, and in many ways it his own family that comes to life in several of his plays.

Williams once wrote that "for love I make characters in plays. . . . After my morning's work"—and Williams wrote religiously every morning—"I have little to give but indifference to people." His close friend **Gore Vidal** has said that Williams's plays always began with a germ of true desire which, unfulfilled in reality, Williams would bring to life onstage in order to live out the fantasy. And according to Vidal, desire was something of which Williams had no short supply, counting his seductions on, well, many, many fingers; the two men, it seems, even shared lovers on occasion. Williams could also be deeply funny: after sitting in a bar listening to some tedious boy repeat yet again "Live and let live is my motto," Williams replied, with extreme courtesy, "Surely, in your situation, there is no alternative philosophy."

Williams did have three great loves in his life, all tragic. The last was **Frank Merlo,** a Brooklyn sailor with whom Williams lived from shortly after the Second World War until 1960. Two years later, Merlo died of lung cancer. Williams's career was at its peak, but when he died, Williams wrote, "I went to pieces. I retreated into a shell. I wouldn't speak to a living soul."

If you feel like wandering by, during the 1940s and '50s Williams lived in a brownstone at 235 East 58th Street. There he wrote *Summer and Smoke* and *The Rose Tattoo*. And there, so the story goes, Williams returned home one night to find his friends Vidal and **Truman Capote** (this is before the lawsuit) standing in his living room with a police officer. Apparently the scribes, a bit worse for having made the Third Avenue circuit, had decided they wanted to visit and were impatient for Williams to return. They found a window they could use and, as is only too easily imaginable from those two, were not entirely discreet in their cat-burglar efforts. They succeeded in entering but were soon greeted by the police officer, who had seen them go in. Williams, unflinching, had them arrested. (Well, not really, but it would have been funny.)

Head west to Fifth Avenue and turn right.

13. TIFFANY AND CO. • 727 Fifth Avenue
   at 57th Street

Almost not worth the mention, except for *Breakfast at Tiffany's*, written by our own **Truman Capote.** Picture Audrey—her hair piled high to show off that neck, gobs of pearls, black elbow-length gloves, and sunglasses—peering into the window. Take a peek yourself if you feel like it: it's a great place to dream of a different future or to have something engraved.

   In the 1920s, this structure was an apartment building and didn't have this elegant establishment downstairs. For a brief time, before heading off to Paris and an unimaginable wave of celebrity, **Cole Porter** and his wife, Linda, made their home here. But Tiffany's took the place over in the 1940s and hasn't let go since.

Walk uptown to 59th Street.

14. THE PLAZA HOTEL
   • **Southwest corner of Fifth Avenue and 59th Street**

While the exact future of the **Plaza** has wavered in recent years with the tide of the Trump fortune, this place has been a fixture of New York life—and rather grand New York life—for many a decade: its high teas and crenelated ceilings, its Palm

Court and Oak Room, its suites and sweeties. Go in and take a gander if you like, have a tea or a cocktail before going farther. Know that the guests here have ranged from the Fitzgeralds (F. Scott and Zelda—Zelda earned a reputation for herself by climbing around in the fountain) to **Marlene. Garbo** and **Cecil Beaton** carried on most of their affair here; and here too, it is said, FBI terror **J. Edgar Hoover** camped about in his red gown. And know that the Oak Room, mentioned in almost any guide or history you look at, has long been considered *the* spot for the discerning gentleman's—you know, of a certain set—discreet encounter.

But here's the real tale for us: On November 28, 1966 (myself, I was just the tiniest of baby-fat creatures at the time), **Truman Capote** threw a fabulous black-and-white masked ball here for his friend Katharine Graham, then the publisher of the *Washington Post* and *Newsweek*. In preparation, he drew up an intimate and select guest list of 540 high-society and literati types: from Old Blue Eyes (and his then-beloved, pre-Woody Mia), to **Marlene** and **Greta** (neither actually showed); **Paul Cadmus, James Baldwin,** and **Richard Avedon; Tallulah Bankhead** and Ted Kennedy; even the Duke and Duchess of Windsor. Somehow, though, the guest list was leaked to the press and published before the event, shocking and insulting the socialites who didn't make the cut. Hundreds of people left the city that weekend, as if to say, "What party? Didn't hear about it." Dear **Carson McCullers,** who did not appear on the list, threatened to give her own ball that night and invite Jackie O. Jackie, it turns out, attended no Manhattan functions that evening, but imagining some of those who did come here—**Andy Warhol,** Lauren Bacall, Bankhead, Lady Bird Johnson, Norman Mailer, and Arthur Schlessinger—all dancing and wearing little masks, it's enough to make you swoon. Later—much later—Capote was said to remark, "You know, I sit up at night aghast at the people I forgot to invite." Oh, Tru, how we only wished you meant it!

Cross the intersection both ways to the northeast corner of 59th Street.

15. DANNY KAYE'S HOME · 781 Fifth Avenue

Much of the most recent fuss about the Plaza was the concern that Mr. Trump would be turning some of it over to permanent residents as condominiums. And while this would have marked a new step for the Plaza, many of the hotels in the city for years have served as permanent residences of some kind or other.

Kitty-corner from the Plaza is the Sherry-Netherland, which, in its day, has housed Pia Zadora, **Diana Ross,** and our very own **Danny Kaye.** Born David Daniel Kaminsky early in the century, Danny was the youngest son of a dress designer and grew up in Brooklyn's East New York. He rose from cabaret performer in the Village to Broadway and Hollywood star. Forever he was the singing, dancing, charming, comic clown.

Kaye married Sylvia Fine when he was relatively young, and she became his chief writer and life partner. Nevertheless, to borrow **Donald Spoto**'s phrase, this onetime sidekick to somber Bing Crosby was "a dynamically aggressive homosexual," attached most famously to **Laurence Olivier.** The two actors had an affair of roughly ten years' standing, in the 1950s, when Olivier was married to Vivien Leigh. But who can blame old Larry? Who doesn't remember *Hans Christian Andersen, White Christmas,* or *The Court Jester* ("The pellet with the poison's in the vessel with the pestle, the chalice from the palace has the brew that is true") with a certain warmth?

You know, it used to be so simple to call someone gay. You did it, their career was over, you gloated. Now even our own historians are saying, "Ah, ah, ah—careful!" But when do you have enough proof? In *Confessions of an Actor,* Olivier writes, "I am prepared to believe that the sense of romance in those of our brother and sister who incline toward lovers of their own sex is heightened to a more blazing pitch than those who think of themselves as 'normal.' " Now what is that? Pure conjecture? Early rumors about Kaye and Olivier circulated when Larry and Vivien moved to L.A. for the filmings of *Carrie* and *Streetcar.* For a time they even rented a house next to the Kayes. At some point, Danny and Larry went to visit our favorite hostess, **Noël Coward,** in Jamaica (although they took Vivien along), and supposedly Danny appeared in drag at a costume party there. Most convincing for me? Danny's decision to star as Hans Christian Andersen. As **Moss Hart** told the story, Hans starts off smitten with the ballerina, but in the end, who does he go home with? His *buddy Peter.* 'Nuf said!

Before I forget, let me remind you that this intersection, since the beginning of the 1990s, has also been the stepping-off point for New York's annual **Gay Pride Parade.** Originally, the marches began in the Village and, taking over perhaps a lane of traffic, headed up Sixth Avenue to Central Park and the nearest open meadow for rally and relaxation. Eventually, though, the parade moved over to Fifth Avenue and headed down, so that celebration could take place along Christopher Street and in the heart of the West Village. If you look closely at the center of Fifth Avenue, at one of the intersections when traffic is stopped, or in the crosswalk as you're crossing the street, you should be able to see the Lavender Line that is painted each year to mark the path of the parade.

Follow Fifth down to 58th and then head east two blocks.

16. DIVINE'S HEADQUARTERS • 40 East 58th Street
   just west of Park Avenue

Born Harris Glenn Milstead, in Baltimore no less, this slip of a lass was headed for cultdom as soon as **John Waters,** a high-school friend, cast him to play Jackie O. in *Eat Your Makeup.* (**Divine** claimed that years later he and the real Jackie showed up at the same party. "We were wearing the same dress. We didn't talk, just glared at each other across the room.") Waters actually christened him "Divine," the name that ended up on his passport, because, the star said, he saw "that inside me was a divine person."

On the outside, Divine, who was based here in the mid-1980s, was equally splendid. His earliest drag creation, he said, involved a simple slip and a hat. (He recalled being chased across the lawn by his grandmother after she found him dressed in just that.) Eventually, the accouterments involved fright wigs, high-flying eyebrows, and unstinting quantities of eyeliner, eye shadow, and eyelash to create what one writer described as "a nuclear-powered caricature of 1960s working-class Baltimore women." The real advantages, he said, came later, such as when he went through customs at the airport: "They open my bag and see two tits staring up at them and they slam it closed. You could smuggle heroin in them."

With Waters's guidance, Divine ended up starring in films like *Pink Flamingos, Polyester,* and *Hairspray* (as Ricki Lake's mother!). *Pink Flamingos,* with its now-famous poop-popping scene, is the one that catapulted Divine to cult status, though he never lost his shy, retiring private persona. But "all of a sudden I was in this big social whirl. Andy Warhol's luncheons, meeting all these people. I really like it. People were like, 'AAAAAAgh' when they saw *me!* That was weird. But I never let it get to my head. Well, maybe a couple of times. But when it's all over you're still sitting there on the plane all alone going home." Divine, for much of his life, had a strained relationship with his parents, but his increasing success seemed to change that. A few years before his death in 1988, Divine said he'd recently asked his father if he was embarrassed by his career. His dad said, "At first I was, but I feel if I made as much money wearing a dress as you do, I'd wear dresses too."

Follow Park up to 59th Street and turn right.

17. BLOOMINGDALE'S • 1000 Third Avenue
between 59th and 60th Streets

Okay, fashionable set, listen up: this is a historic tour, not a shopping spree. We stop here for a quick reflection, nothing more. (Although if you do go in, tell them how you ended up here: maybe one of us can get a discount out of it. . . . Oh, and I'm an XL and look best in blue tones: think winter palette.)

Bloomie's gets a mention just as one of the gayest spaces in the city for as long as anyone can remember: shopping, cruising, you name it. Even back in the 1910s, when the store was on the other side of Lexington Avenue, the local train stop was a well-frequented cruising spot, and the saloon across the street was a popular gay hangout. And while historically the Bloomie's people seem to have resisted this association—they refused to have one of those opening shots for *Boys in the Band* filmed here—gay activists have frequently made the shop, its

workers and customers a primary leafleting target at the very least. In the summer of '69, when the *Band* boys were filming elsewhere, activists outraged by Stonewall and eager to take some very public action considered St. Patrick's Cathedral—seat of the Catholic archdiocese and source of much political power in the city—and Bloomingdale's as equally good primary targets. Neither won out right away, but the reasoning was "Boycott Bloomie's—they'd be out of business in two weeks!"

One hip 1970s guide to the city suggested that depending on who you're looking for, they could all be found on a Saturday evening at Bloomingdale's: bachelors in housewares, gay men in the bargain basement or the men's department, lesbians in linens, and the leather crowd near the wallets.

There is a story told about Mrs. Astor and Lady Montague visiting Bloomie's: Her Ladyship, huffy about all the milling gay men, says that all of them should be lined up against the wall and shot. To which Mrs. Astor replies, "My dear, in that case, we should have no opera, no ballet, no theatuh, and this place would be self-service."

Bloomie's chairman Marvin Traub has said, "Above all else, we sell image." And what image! Did you know that Bloomingdale's was the first to advertise the Pet Rock? (Does anyone even remember the Pet Rock?) Perhaps its appeal was put more accurately by one company VP, who said, "The in-store environment builds a crescendo of excitement in a store, gets the shopper turned on, and cultivates a powerful image." Whatever it is, it's been enough to bring in **Barbra, Jackie O.,** even the true queen of queens, Queen Elizabeth, to shop. Now it's your turn: go to work.

Follow Third Avenue up to 61st Street and turn right.

At Bloomingdale's, where customers look for more than flatware.

18. MONTGOMERY CLIFT'S TOWNHOUSE
- **217 East 61st Street**

between Second and Third Avenues

Here lived beauty, even after beauty was thought to have disappeared. This brownstone was legendary actor **Montgomery Clift**'s home for the last six years of his life. Monty started acting on the Broadway boards in 1935 when he was fourteen—performing onstage with the closeted **Lunts**—and appeared in his first film in 1948. Considered one of the great expressive actors of his generation—a counterpoint to Marlon Brando—he went on to star in *Red River, A Place in the Sun, Suddenly Last Summer, The Misfits,* and *From Here to Eternity.* (He was the one who'd lobbied hard for Frank Sinatra to get a role in that last film, the role that resuscitated Sinatra's fading career.)

Clift made his home here from 1960 to 1966. He had lived on the block since 1951, when he moved into a spacious duplex a few doors down at number 209. Clift's days became increasingly unhappy after a 1956 car wreck left him, *he* thought, terribly disfigured—though he was still cast to star in films. At his 209 residence he had a fourteen-foot medicine cabinet installed for all the "pain relievers" he began to use. When a fire forced him from that home in 1960, he moved here.

This home, originally a wedding present from Teddy Roosevelt to his own daughter, had four bedrooms, six bathrooms, six fireplaces, a garden, and a sixty-foot-long living room. It is said that the goings-on here became increasingly wild as Clift sought more and more solace in drugs and alcohol, and that he was especially hard hit by the 1963 deaths of his *Misfits* costars Clark Gable and **Marilyn Monroe.** Area residents recall that Clift frequently called out from his upstairs windows to men passing by on the streets, hoping to entice them in for an entertainment or two: no doubt he succeeded almost as often as he tried. **Jim Fouratt** remembers that once as a young man he got rather drunk and stood out here shouting "Monty! Monty!" He doesn't remember much else—except that he woke up in Clift's guest room and couldn't recall meeting the actor. Clift died here of a heart attack on July 23, 1966, at the age of forty-five.

Swing around the block.

19. TALLULAH BANKHEAD'S TOWNHOUSE
- **230 East 62nd Street**
between Second and Third Avenues

Born in Huntsville, Alabama, in 1903, actress **Tallulah Bankhead** was the toast of London in the 1920s and a flop in Hollywood in the 1930s. She returned to the Broadway stage at the end of the thirties and was wonderful as Regina Giddens in *The Little Foxes* (the part **Bette Davis** played in the movie) and as Sabina, the maid, in **Thornton Wilder**'s *The Skin of Our Teeth*. Bankhead described herself as "ambisextrous," and she had her way on both sides of the aisle. "My family warned me about sex, dahling," she said, "but they never mentioned a word about women." She lived here in the 1970s, late in her life, and, for a time, had twelve rooms, six fireplaces, a latticed garden and sycamore trees—as well as a healthy supply of the drugs and alcohol that were her staples.

Bankhead was hardly one for the timid gesture or understated comment. She declared once, "I can say 'shit,' dahling. I'm a lady," and then usually went on to state much more than that. Asked, for instance, if she thought Noël Coward was gay, she replied, "I wouldn't know, dahling, he's never sucked my cock." On another occasion, after smooching a young woman at a rather straight party, Bankhead borrowed the woman's astonished male date's hanky and wiped the smeared lipstick off the other woman's mouth. And once she ran into **Joan Crawford** on a train from New York City to Hollywood with Joan's then-hubby, Douglas Fairbanks, Jr. Quiet little Tallulah could only say, "Darling, you're divine. I've had an affair with your husband. You'll be next."

A final offering: "Sex?" she shouted in one group. "I'm bored with sex. What is it, after all? If you go down on a woman, you get a crick in your neck. If you go down on a man, you get lockjaw. And fucking just gives me claustrophobia." Yes, indeed, a lady.

Head east on 62nd Street, then up Second Avenue to 68th.

20. MERCEDES DE ACOSTA'S HOME • 315 East 68th Street
between First and Second Avenues

Born in 1893 in a strict New York Spanish Catholic family, **Mercedes de Acosta** became a writer of novels, plays, movies, and poetry. And though largely forgotten today, for a time in the 1930s and '40s de Acosta was a formidable social presence among the celebrity set. **Truman Capote** once thought up a game called "International Daisy Chain," where the goal was to try to link people through their history of sexual liaisons and use as few intervening beds as possible. (A genuine boy genius, no?) Mercedes, he decided, was the best card to hold. From her, one player remembers, "you could get to anyone—from **Cardinal Spellman** to the Duchess of Windsor." Her affairs included dancer **Isadora Duncan** and actresses **Eva Le Gallienne** and **Ona Munson** (Belle Watling in *Gone With the Wind*), not to mention both **Garbo** and **Dietrich**. As **Alice B. Toklas** said, "You can't dispose of Mercedes lightly: she has had the two most important women in the U.S." (Read on to get some of the more juicy tidbits.)

Walk west on 68th toward Third Avenue.

21. GEORGE CUKOR'S CHILDHOOD BLOCK
• 68th Street between Second and Third Avenues

This block gave birth to a filmmaker who, in the decades surrounding the Second World War, would come to dominate Hollywood with his vision and style. A chubby child in a family of Jewish immigrants, **George Cukor** grew up here just after the turn of the century. At that time, the subway that now runs beneath Lexington Avenue was a newly innovated elevated train that ran above Third Avenue itself, outside of the Cukors' first apartment. Eventually the family would move away from the train, though not off the block: Cukor cousins and aunts and grandparents had all settled on the same street.

Cukor went on to Hollywood and to direct some of the great romantic films of the 1930s, '40s, and '50s. His work included movies like **Judy Garland**'s *A Star Is Born*, *The Women*, *Born Yesterday*, *My Fair Lady*, and even some of *Gone*

With the Wind (although Clark Gable allegedly had "that fag" fired—in part, some have suggested, because Cukor knew that Gable's gigolo services had not been exclusively heterosexual in nature). Cukor also directed most of Katharine Hepburn's best films, including *Adam's Rib* and the ever-delightful *Philadelphia Story*. His ideas about moviemaking, much like a Spielberg's or a Coppola's, held sway in Hollywood in his time, but he also came to be known as "a woman's director," a phrase that both indicated his ability to work well with actors and actresses and may equally have been a slurring reference to his being gay.

But before all that, Cukor lived here with his folks, from his boyhood until well into his twenties. He wasn't much of a student and was forever sneaking away from school with his friends to go see a show, see **Isadora Duncan,** add to their autograph collections. At one point, he and friends were walk-on extras at the Metropolitan Opera. Eventually he became a theater director, and as a young man in the 1920s he developed one of the country's best summer-stock theater companies up in Rochester, New York. Soon thereafter he began directing on Broadway, including a stage adaptation of Fitzgerald's *The Great Gatsby*, and then quickly headed out to Hollywood, where he truly made a name for himself.

It seems there is no serious romance to report for George—mostly brief affairs and encounters, which occasionally yielded a screen appearance for some young man. He was, though, of the Hollywood scene that had infamous boy-filled Sunday pool parties, and for a time in LaLa Land, Cukor and **Cole Porter** rivaled each other in that regard. Above all, though, he gave us all a vision of romance for ourselves—often troubled, usually charming, always hopeful.

Continue walking west.

22. ROY COHN'S HOME • 39 East 68th Street
between Park and Madison Avenues

One of the most powerful closeted gay men of the century, and hardly the most pleasant, **Roy Cohn** was an attorney whose career rose to prominence with Senator Joseph McCarthy's communist witch hunts in the early 1950s. Those hunts turned not only against many of the nation's liberal thinkers but targeted its homosexuals as well. From then on, his role as a political and social powerbroker only grew—see **Tony Kushner**'s *Angels in America* to get a full sense.

This was Cohn's home before he died of AIDS-related illnesses in the summer of 1986, and he lived here with a maid and a cook—no long-term lover. It is said that he let the house slip into enormous disrepair, but an associate once described his bedroom as bulging with stuffed animals, and "froggies everywhere, froggies appliquéd on the bedspread and froggies all over the pillows, froggies here and froggies there and God! It was a riot. I can just see Roy propped up there. He probably had a nightshirt with froggies on it, and a nightcap!"

The secrets we carry!

Follow 68th Street west to Madison and turn right.

23. HALSTON HEADQUARTERS • 813 Madison Avenue
on the northeast corner of 68th Street

This one is for those of you who truly attend to fashion. **Roy Halston Frowick** was born in April 1932 in Des Moines. Dad was an accountant and Mom was good at crocheting afghans. (Go, Mom!) At the ripe age of thirteen, for Easter, young Roy gave his mother a homemade red hat and veil. As his brother Robert later told *Newsweek*, "We all wondered how the hell and why he did it! But it was a smash, and really flattered my mother." (Robert also told them that his little brother always wore great clothes and was surrounded by rich girls who would chauffeur him around in their convertibles.) His entree into fashion was in Chicago, where he opened his own shop as a hat designer, serving first Fran Allison (of *Kukla, Fran and Ollie*) but soon designing hats for Kim Novak, Shirley Booth, Gloria Swanson (ready for her close-up), and Deborah Kerr.

By the time he was twenty-five, Halston was ready for his close-up and came to New York. He soon found himself at Bergdorf's designing Jackie Kennedy's famous pillbox hat for the inauguration. In the city, he also discovered the world beyond hats and developed his own clothing line, with a shop in this building and a look that would be known as "casual chic": sweaters, wide-leg pants, longish shirt-dresses, and, for the signature touch, a sweater tied around the shoulders. (Preppydom, unite!) The ladies loved it, and Halston's client list grew to include **Elizabeth Taylor, Liza Minnelli,** Lauren Bacall, Ali MacGraw, Candice Bergen, and Bianca Jagger. His prestige as a designer grew, and by the late 1970s he himself was a fashion superstar, jet-setting around in his black turtleneck, showing up at Studio 54 and hanging out with **Andy Warhol.** The 1980s proved more difficult: in 1982 he signed on to design for J. C. Penney, which was not a success. In 1984 he failed in trying to buy back his designer name (which he'd sold in the mid-seventies to Norton Simon), and instead it ended up with Revlon. And then suddenly he was sick, and in 1990 he died out in San Francisco. Think of him, though, next time you tie that sweater around your neck and smile at yourself in the mirror.

Scoot up Madison and make a left on 70th Street.

24. JOAN CRAWFORD'S HOME • 2 East 70th Street
at Fifth Avenue

Here's one for the movie and Lypsinka lovers in the troop, old and young. (Hey, that's a scouting reference, not military, and that's *Girl* Scouts—I know what the Boy Scouts say.) After all that time beating the kids in L.A., **Joan Crawford** had to split town for a while. She married Al Steele—no, not a porn star; a soda jerk: he owned the Pepsi company. In the mid-1950s, they moved here. She took a sixteen-room apartment, knocked down a few walls, and *voilà:* eight rooms—none of which, daughter Christina has pointed out, was a guest room. After Steele died in 1959, she moved down a block and over two to 150 East 69th Street, but she didn't let go of her hold on the Pepsi Generation. Indeed, if Faye Dunaway is to be believed, she marched straight into that boardroom and declared, "Don't fuck with me, fellas!"

Crawford, by the way, was born Lucille LeSueur in 1908. She grew up in Oklahoma, where her stepfather ran a vaudeville theater, and by the age of seventeen she was dancing on

Broadway. In 1925 she went off to Hollywood, where she changed her name to Joan Crawford and quickly danced her way to stardom. She spent the next several decades developing a reputation for stealing scripts for upcoming films and then convincing producers that she was best for a given part; then she would pick her own director and demand that the dialogue be changed to suit her desire. (Among her lesser-known roles: after teaming up with **Bette Davis** in *Whatever Happened to Baby Jane?* in 1962, she went on to portray a nurse who used judo to keep mental patients at bay in *The Caretakers* and an ax murderess in *Strait Jacket!*)

You should know, Crawford was also among the folks who traveled up to sexually progressive Harlem in the 1920s heyday of the Harlem Renaissance. Well before careening through her four-marriage career she was a recognized regular at the Lafayette Theatre, where **Bessie Smith** frequently performed, and she traveled in a circle of fabulous and notorious bisexual women: indeed, she was considered to be one of them.

A parting image: In 1964, when she was living in her duplex down on 69th Street and flying around in private jets, she told a journalist, "I've always felt that if you're going to be a star you have to act like a star." And then she added, "I never go out unless I look like Joan Crawford, the star." Ah, Joan.

How're the gams? Little achy? Cut over to Madison and then hike uptown ten blocks: it's worth it, trust me.

25. Frank E. Campbell Funeral Home
- **1076 Madison Avenue**
  at 81st Street

A funeral home? you ask. All this for a funeral home? Honey, this ain't just any old funeral home. These people, the Frank E. Campbell people, they've done us well. Right here in this home, they've laid to rest our very own beautiful **Mont-gomery Clift** and our dear **Judy Holliday,** even your newest friend, the legendary bisexual Hanger Mistress, **Joan Craw-ford.** And these same people, when they were across town on Broadway and 66th, gave last respects to our dear **Rudy Valentino.** (If memory serves, author **John Preston** used to tell a story of a friend who kept a hair from the living, uh, privates of Valentino at the foot of his bed, encased in glass and displayed by pinpoint spotlights; it was the last thing he saw each night before falling asleep.)

But here, from that Stonewall summer of 1969, one name especially calls out to us: Judy, Judy, Judy. **Judy Garland** died in London that June, after several attempts at suicide. She was found in her bathroom, collapsed on the toilet, too many substances competing in her body. Her daughter **Liza** arranged for her to be brought here and made plans for the service—yellow and white flowers, a eulogy from Mickey Rooney, and a white casket lined with blue velvet and covered with glass. Before the plane carrying her body even touched down at New York's Kennedy Airport, fans began lining up here for the viewing. Some twenty-two thousand people filed past for a final visit, waiting in a line that stretched across 81st Street onto Fifth Avenue and into Central Park, many of them the gay men who had embraced the voice, spirit, and struggle of the legendary Miss Garland: they kept the parlor open through the night.

The funeral was held on June 27th. Those who attended included Ray Bolger, Lauren Bacall, Jack Benny, **Cary Grant,** Katharine Hepburn, Burt Lancaster, Dean Martin, Lana Turner, and sweet **Vito Russo.** In the end, Rooney was too distraught to deliver the eulogy, and instead it was offered by James Mason. The service closed with the gatherers singing the "Battle Hymn of the Republic"; it was the song Judy had sung on her 1963 television special, grieving for a fallen President. That very same night, the Stonewall Inn was raided, and the rioting in the West Village began.

Follow Madison up to 84th Street, then head right to Park Avenue.

26. MARLENE DIETRICH'S HOME • 993 Park Avenue
at 84th Street

Christened Maria Magdalene in Berlin in 1901, **Marlene Dietrich** spent her childhood committed to studying the violin. An injury to her wrist prompted her to turn to the stage, though, and then to the movies. Her screen potential was first tapped by Josef von Sternberg in *The Blue Angel* in 1930, and she was quickly signed by Paramount to compete with **Greta Garbo** (with the thought that with her legs, Dietrich had the edge). She rode a wave of stardom in films like *Blonde Venus* (1932) and *Destry Rides Again* (1939). During the Second World War she worked hard both to entertain U.S. troops and to make anti-Nazi propaganda, and after the war she developed a nightclub act that evolved into a one-woman show which she took from Vegas all the way to Tel Aviv before her death in 1992.

She once told an interviewer, "In Europe it doesn't matter if you're a man or a woman. We make love with anyone we find attractive." And when she was attracted, it seems she could be ardent in her pursuit. Among her many liaisons, her affair with writer **Mercedes de Acosta** (whom you've only just met) remains vivid. Having spied de Acosta one evening in Hollywood with **Cecil Beaton,** Dietrich went to her house the next day laden with white roses. Although shy at first, she finally took de Acosta's hand and explained, "I hope you will forgive me. I noticed you last night in the theater and wanted to meet you. I know very few people in Hollywood and no one who could introduce us, so I just found out where you live and I came myself." When Mercedes tried to strike up a conversation about movies, Dietrich said, "Oh, let's not talk about pictures. . . . Last evening when I looked at you I felt you were very sad. I am sad, too. I am sad and lonely. . . . You are the first person here to whom I have felt drawn. Unconventional as it may seem, I came to see you because I just could not help myself."

For a year thereafter, they had a passionate affair, in which Dietrich smothered de Acosta with flowers, gifts, letters, and telegrams. Her first telegram read: "My room is a white dream. It will be hard to leave Hollywood now that I know you."

It wasn't all pure romantic passion with Dietrich, however. One friend, the playwright Samuel Taylor (he wrote *Sabrina Fair*), remembered her as equally avid about sex. Not that she herself so exuded sexuality; rather, she was "fascinated by sex, all kinds, everybody's. She could have written a book to challenge Krafft-Ebing [the sexologist] if she had just dictated what she knew." Perhaps one of you can take up the task.

Across the Fruited Plains:
The Mix of the Upper West Side

The Upper West Side didn't really come to life until well into
the second half of the nineteenth century. Before that, it was
mostly farms and summer homes. But the Ninth Avenue
el(evated) train arrived in the 1870s, which meant that people
could live here and commute to Midtown. In the 1880s, one
adventurous visionary built the Dakota, and the city government even started to grade and level the streets. Soon enough,
following the Dakota's lead, more large, luxurious apartment
buildings began to appear along Central Park West, and the
city's gentry began to move up here. Even today, that mon-
eyed presence remains (try getting an apartment on Central
Park West), but so do a wide variety of other economic and
ethnic groups that gathered here during this century, as well as
the runoff from the arts communities of the theater district
and Lincoln Center and from all those intellectuals up at
Columbia University.

That pooling of communities has been a powerful incentive
for lesbian and gay living, and this neighborhood has been—
and remains—a home for a real cross-section of our tribe.
Indeed, the Upper West Side has been one of the richer
neighborhoods for sustaining the diversity of the gay community. It has certainly provided venues for our cultural products,
at Lincoln Center and Off Broadway theaters. But the chorus
boys and composers have met offstage here as well, at turn-of-
the-century bathhouses, at the "coffee and yak-yak" cafes of
the 1920s and '30s, even out along the hidden rambles and

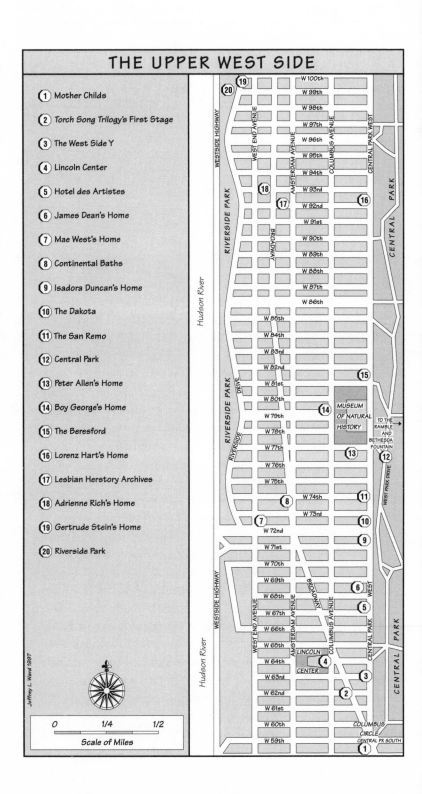

THE UPPER WEST SIDE

1. Mother Childs
2. Torch Song Trilogy's First Stage
3. The West Side Y
4. Lincoln Center
5. Hotel des Artistes
6. James Dean's Home
7. Mae West's Home
8. Continental Baths
9. Isadora Duncan's Home
10. The Dakota
11. The San Remo
12. Central Park
13. Peter Allen's Home
14. Boy George's Home
15. The Beresford
16. Lorenz Hart's Home
17. Lesbian Herstory Archives
18. Adrienne Rich's Home
19. Gertrude Stein's Home
20. Riverside Park

Jeffrey L. Ward 1997

0   1/4   1/2

Scale of Miles

"fruited plains" of Central Park. And many of our finest figures have settled up here to live.

The tour that follows starts off at Columbus Circle (where
you can pick up the A/C, the B/D, or the 1/9 trains) and
weaves its way up to 100th Street. It leaps among the diversity,
from coffee-shop cruisers and top-drawer celebrities like **Mae
West, Rock Hudson,** and **Rudolph Valentino** to Central
Park pickups, political activists like **Harvey Milk,** and writers
like **Gertrude Stein.** You'll even see where **Bette Midler** first
won her way into the hearts of gay men, and where lesbian historians first began to gather the artifacts of our history. It's a
wide array, but we're all of that, as they say, and a bag of chips.

1. MOTHER CHILDS · 300 West 59th Street
at the southwest corner of Eighth Avenue and Columbus Circle

In the 1920s and '30s, gay life in New York set up its own Cafe
Society (imagine letting all those Parisians get the lead),
although truth be told it was more of a *cafeteria* society. Like
the famed Horn & Hardart Automats, Childs was one of the
preeminent cafeteria chains that started opening around town
and many a Childs shop became a playpen for freewheeling
gay and camp festivities late into the night.

The Childs on Columbus Circle came to be known as
Mother Childs (you can imagine why), and here the worlds of
the theater, Times Square, and Central Park cruisers would
gather, mix, and mingle. A North Dakota man who moved to
the city in 1922 recalled Mother Childs as "a meeting place for
gays" where they would "sit and have coffee and yak-yak and
talk till three and four and five o'clock in the morning. . . . I was
always there with friends, that was the social thing to do." The
park benches across the street from the cafeteria also apparently
became a rather active pickup spot, and to this day those along
Central Park West have carried the tradition proudly. (Future
San Francisco supervisor **Harvey Milk** and bookstore owner
and activist **Craig Rodwell** met each other there in the early
1960s and carried on a passionate, if brief, affair.)

Follow the west side of Broadway up to 62nd Street.

2. Torch Song Trilogy's First Stage
- **36 West 62nd Street**
at Broadway

John Glines's theater production company has become one of the essential gay theater producers in the city. Beginning with small shows for two dollars way downtown at the American Thread Company building in TriBeCa (at 260 West Broadway), the Glines supported dance shows, poetry readings, and original plays. Initially, Glines's goal was to create a "space for my brothers and sisters to express their attitudes toward the gay experience." Even early on, however, his company was able to provide a platform for a whole new explosion in gay theater. They introduced writer **Richard Hall** and the Radical Lesbian Feminist Terrorist Comedy Group and produced staged readings of new one-acts by **Harvey Fierstein, Arthur Laurents,** and **Jane Chambers.** (Chambers also developed her award-winning play *Last Summer at Bluefish Cove* through the Glines.) They even organized the first-ever All American Gay Arts Festival, which brought in Theater Rhinoceros from San Francisco and had readings by **Quentin Crisp, Jonathan Katz, John Rechy,** and **Edmund White.**

In the Richard Allen Arts Center, which used to stand here, the Glines produced the original full three-part production of *Torch Song Trilogy: The International Stud, Fugue in a Nursery,* and *Widows and Children First!* The show, which had developed in stages at La Mama in the East Village, opened here in October 1980. **Harvey Fierstein,** the author, played Arnold; Matthew Broderick was David, the adopted son; and Estelle Getty (yes, the Golden Girl herself) was Mrs. Beckoff, Arnold's mother. Tickets were ten dollars for the four-hour show.

Fierstein once wrote ecstatically of all the folks who came to see the show as it moved from here to the Village to the Helen Hayes, a proper Broadway theater: Cher, Leonard Nimoy, Bea Arthur, Carol Channing, and **Rip Taylor.** "But the best, my most never-fading memory is of Ethel Merman. She popped back after the show, with her niece, silencing the most callous of stagehands. 'What did you think of the show, Miss Merman?' I croaked. She glared at me as only Merman could and bellowed back, 'I thought it was a piece of shit, but the rest of the audience laughed and cried, so what the fuck do I know?' " How sweet, Miss Merman; happily, the Tony Awards and Hollywood disagreed.

Make a left on Central Park West to 63rd Street.

3. THE WEST SIDE Y • 5 West 63rd Street
between Central Park West and Broadway

What is it the Village People said about young men and "no need to feel down"? Late in the previous century, the New York Young Men's Christian Association began to be concerned about all those lost single fellows newly swept up in the urban workforce, living alone or in boardinghouses. Just imagine a city filled with hordes of men, done with their day's work and with nothing to do but commingle and look for trouble, and you can understand their concern. They began to build activity centers, hoping to provide a moral framework in an otherwise immoral world. As one writer pointed out in 1872, the Y not only offered "many inducements to young men" but recruited as well, sending "members forth into the haunts of suffering and vice, and endeavor[ing] to win back those who have gone astray from the paths of virtue, and to alleviate the misery of those who are in distress."

By the turn of the century, when 25 percent of New York's adult men were unmarried, they had more than activities to offer. The YMCA began building dormitories, and by World War I, well, the recruitment system had changed. Let's just say that the new Y dorms had enough of a reputation as centers of gay social life that when a sailor in Irving Berlin's World War I show, *Yip, Yip, Yaphank*, commented on having several friends at the YMCA, he got a knowing laugh.

In 1930, the YMCA built this building and another large structure down on 34th Street, and these hotels quickly became well-known gay residential centers. And it wasn't just folks from out of town who took a room here; lots of local men would check in for the weekend—mind you, for the community feeling as much as the titillating encounters. According to George Chauncey, gay men used to say that "the letters Y-M-C-A stood for 'Why I'm So Gay.' " One

fellow who made this Y his first New York residence: young
James Dean.

All right now. Out into the streets and get your arms in the
air—"You're better off at the Y-M—"

*Head back west and cross first Broadway and then Columbus
Avenue.*

4. LINCOLN CENTER
*stretching from 62nd Street and Columbus Avenue to 66th Street and
Broadway*

Too much important culture, gay and otherwise, has appeared
here for me to make light of it. (Believe me: I've racked my
brains trying to think how!) If you care about opera or ballet,
theater or symphony, in the last thirty years most of the greats
have appeared in one of these halls. I'll take two from the
legions—**Benjamin Britten** and **Aaron Copland**—but there
truly is an extraordinary gay legacy to be considered here.
Why, the Metropolitan Opera House was even opened with
the world premiere of a **Samuel Barber** opera, *Antony and
Cleopatra*, and its most successful premiere in recent years was
John Corigliano's *Ghosts of Versailles*, with a libretto by
William Hoffman. Impressive stuff! But before I dive head-
long into music history, and the rest of you start napping, let
me point out that the classical music scene could offer pretty
racy action. Standing room at the original Metropolitan
Opera House at Broadway and Thirty-ninth Street (this one
dates back only to 1966) was said to be quite a busy place.
Even an observer back in 1929 pointed out that it was notoriously full of "young men mostly of outlandish origin or with
long fair hair." And while some of those young men were there
only for the music, a number stayed otherwise entertained
during those long operas. Standing room at the Met certainly
provided young **Harvey Milk** with some of his earliest sexual
encounters. According to **Randy Shilts,** there were jokes even
fifty years ago about how the standees had zippers on the front
and the back of their pants, and how you could never tell if the
bravos were louder than "the sound of the flies going up."
Rumor has it that things aren't too quiet in this house either.

Now, to our musicians:

Composers both, Britten and Copland are compelling not only for the music they wrote but for how they seemed to build gay community out of the fabric of their lives. Britten, perhaps best known as an opera composer, frequently collaborated with other gay artists to produce homoerotically tinged work. He worked repeatedly with **W. H. Auden** (his first opera was written with Auden and was about Paul Bunyan), put music to the words of **E. M. Forster** and **Michelangelo,** and made theater of the stories of **Henry James, Herman Melville,** and **Thomas Mann.** Born in England, Britten came to this country in 1939 with his lover, the tenor **Peter Pears.** Increasingly as he composed, his operas were written around a central role for Pears. One of his great successes was the opera *Peter Grimes,* which told the story of an introverted fisherman shunned and persecuted by his community after one and then another of his apprentices mysteriously die. Pears played Grimes, and Britten hinted at a homoerotic relationship between Grimes and the apprentices. Similarly, Pears played Captain Vere in Britten's adaptation of Melville's *Billy Budd,* a deeply homoerotic story, for which Forster (along with Eric Crozier) wrote the lyrics. And again, Pears played Aschenback in Britten's adaptation of Mann's *Death in Venice.* That opera received its American premiere here on the stage of the Metropolitan Opera House in October 1974.

Aaron Copland's music marked the nation and the century like perhaps no other composer's. Born in Brooklyn in 1900, he was the youngest of five children. When he was eleven, his older sister began teaching him to play piano, and by the time he was fifteen he had made up his mind to be a composer. In 1920 he went off to study in Paris, and in 1924 he returned to the States and set up a studio in New York, but no students showed up. That fall, though, he played two of his piano compositions at the League of Composers, marking his United States debut: one critic was so impressed with his work that he found a patron who provided Copland with a monthly stipend. (I've been doing a genealogy search on the patron to see if he has a handsome—or even not-so-handsome—grandson.)

Early in his career, Copland began to worry that classical composers were losing their audience. "An entirely new public for music had grown up around the radio and phonograph.

It made no sense to ignore them and to continue writing as if they did not exist. I felt it was worth the effort to see if I couldn't say what I had to say in the simplest possible terms." He began introducing a jazz idiom into his compositions, and then added in other familiar American musical elements: folk songs, cowboy tunes, hymns, and Shaker melodies. So doing, he crafted classical music that remained accessible to the larger public. In addition to creating what he called his "home-spun musical idiom," he also wrote popular books on music appreciation and listening. What's more, he wrote music for plays, dance, and movies (the film version of **Thornton Wilder**'s *Our Town* and the **Henry James**–based *The Heiress*, for which he won an Oscar).

Copland also sponsored a younger generation of composers and was extremely close with colleagues **Leonard Bernstein, Marc Blitzstein, Ned Rorem, Virgil Thomson,** Britten, Barber, and many others. There is a way in which reading through Copland's memoirs is like flipping through a Who's Who of the music world, with the added feature that almost everyone seems to be gay. Rorem said that in the 1940s the music world was dominated by Copland and Thomson. "Aaron had an entourage, so did Virgil; you belonged to one or the other, like Avignon and Rome, take it or leave it." Thomson himself, though, said that it was "Aaron [who] became the patron of American musical youth. . . . Aaron looked at everybody, encouraged them if necessary, discouraged them if necessary."

Perhaps the closest of these relationships was with Leonard Bernstein, who met Copland at a dance concert on the older man's birthday. Bernstein, who had just learned Copland's Piano Variations, said he imagined him as "a sort of patriarch, Moses or Walt Whitman–like figure, with a beard, because that's what the music says." When he met Copland, though, he was shocked: he was "young-looking, smiling . . . with buck teeth and a giggle and a big nose, of a charm not to be described." Copland was equally charmed with Bernstein (then a college junior)—enough to invite him to a birthday party at his loft, where Bernstein played the variations on a dare from Copland. For many years thereafter, Bernstein would bring his compositions to Copland for criticism. "In these sessions," Bernstein later said, "he taught me a tremendous amount about taste, style, and consistency in music. . . . Through his critical analyses of whatever I happened to be working on at the moment, Aaron became the closest thing to a composition teacher I ever had." (You'll be happy to know that since Bernstein had affairs with both men and women, Copland referred to him as PH, for "phony homosexual.")

Copland's loft, by the way, stood smack in the middle of where Lincoln Center now is. It was four flights up, and back in the 1930s and '40s it was a bit of a novelty. "I chose that hideaway," Copland later wrote, "because it was one of the few places in the city where one could make music at any hour of the day or night without jeopardizing the lease. The loft cost twenty-five dollars a month with no heat (we improvised)." As to just how "we" improvised, Copland was rather discreet. He did, though, spend much of his life with the photographer **Victor Kraft.** Interestingly, Kraft appears throughout Copland's two-volume memoir/scrapbook—renting houses for them, encouraging his writing, clearly his domestic partner, yet never really named as such. As Ned Rorem pointed out in one added passage, "Aaron is the most circumspect famous person I have ever known, considering how much he encouraged others to let down their hair."

Cross onto Columbus and follow it uptown before turning right on 67th Street.

5. HOTEL DES ARTISTES • 1 West 67th Street
between Columbus and Central Park West

Home to *Cabaret*'s **Joel Grey,** this landmark building, intended initially for sculptors and painters, has also been a home to the likes of **Noël Coward, Rudolph Valentino** and **Alexander Woollcott.** Valentino, who was born Rodolfo Alfonzo Raffaelo di Valentina d'Antonguolla in Italy in 1895, came to this country when he was a teenager and worked as a gardener, dishwasher, and vaudeville dancer before he made it into films. His appearance in *The Four Horsemen of the Apocalypse* made him a star with a reputation that *The Sheik* and *The Son of the Sheik* only expanded. He became known as "The World's Greatest Lover," earning points both for style and, it is said, for certain physical qualities. (In 1968, the very conservative Mattachine Society suggested in their newsletter that *Eyes of Youth*, a film that preceded *Four Horsemen*, offered "a quick glimpse of his 'virility,' which undoubtedly confirmed the rumors that he was well-endowed.") At the same time, though, Valentino was dismissed and ridiculed in certain circles as being "a pink powder puff," a comment that seems to have haunted him to his death. He did marry, but his first wife, **Jean Acker,** left him, it seems, for a woman. (You can't blame her, but maybe a little jealousy isn't completely inappropriate.) His second wife, the similarly inclined **Natacha Rambova,** published a memoir of Valentino after his death complete with eleven messages "dictated by Rudy directly through the deeply entranced instrument" of Rambova herself.

Follow Central Park West up to 68th Street and turn left.

6. JAMES DEAN'S HOME • 19 West 68th Street
between Central Park West and Columbus Avenue

This was **James Dean**'s permanent home in New York. On the top floor of this building, he had a single twelve-by-twelve room, with a porthole window and a bathroom down the hall. He lived here both before and after going off to Hollywood to film *East of Eden*. One visitor recalled that the room had a shoulder-high shelf that went around it, and on the shelf Dean had empty beer cans, an open peanut butter jar, an album cover of *Romeo and Juliet*, a baseball bat, a hot plate, a bunch of dried leaves stuck in a Maxwell House can, several sheets of music, and a bust of Jimmy himself gazing down upon a new chrome music stand. (Check out the Midtown tour for more dish on Jimmy.)

Follow 68th Street west to Broadway, then turn right, walk up to 72nd, hang a left, and walk a block over to West End.

7. MAE WEST'S HOME • 266 West End Avenue
between 72nd and 73rd Streets

Always a classic, always sexy, **Mae West** had a gift for the smoky turn of phrase, such as "When I'm good, I'm very good, but when I'm bad . . . I'm better." "I never meant 'Come up and see me sometime' to be so sexy," she once said, "but I guess I was thinking about sex all the time." As much a theater performer as a film star, in the 1920s West tangled with the authorities over her creative choices. In 1926, she wrote and starred in a show called *Sex*, which was a big hit—she played a prostitute—but landed her a ten-day stint in jail. Around the same time she staged a play called *The Drag*, which she intended as "a homosexual comedy": the gay son marries the doctor's daughter but falls for the straight man who is in love with the wife; sadly, the son's ex-lover, whom the doctor fails to cure of his "disease" of inversion, kills the son, but the true facts are kept hush-hush and his death is passed off as suicide. (Whew: got it?) In a major headline scandal, West vied with the censors while the show was out of town, and they ultimately succeeded in keeping it from reaching Broadway.

The 1930s took West to Hollywood, where she vamped her way across the screen with a new kind of aggressive female sexuality (new for the movies, that is), often in films she wrote herself. After a twenty-six-year absence, she returned to the big screen in 1970, appearing in the film version of **Gore Vidal**'s *Myra Breckinridge*. **Rex Reed** and Raquel Welch took turns in the transsexual title role, and West played talent agent Leticia Van Allen. In her first scene she evaluates a group of handsome men, including a young Tom Selleck. Asked his height, Selleck tells her he's six feet seven inches, to which West replies, "Let's forget about the six feet and concentrate on the seven inches." In an interview at the time West emphasized (and does this sound like *Sunset Boulevard*, or what?), "I want you to remember that this picture is a return, not a comeback. I've never been away, just busy. I play the role of this fabulous booking agent, Leticia Van Allen. I can tell you that in the course of the picture, I have affairs with all the leading men and I finish up owning everything. My fans would be disappointed otherwise."

Mae's golden rule: "Love thy neighbor—and if he happens to be tall, debonair, and devastating, it will be that much easier." And a thought on womanhood: "Good women are no fun. The only good woman I can recall in history was Betsy Ross. And all she ever made was a flag."

Try the front door: it's a surprisingly beautiful building.

Walk up West End and turn right on 74th Street.

8. CONTINENTAL BATHS • 230 West 74th Street
at the southwest corner of Broadway

"The glory of Ancient Rome recreated with you in mind." So read the slogan for the **Continental Baths,** and what glory! Tucked away here in the bowels of the landmark 1903 Ansonia apartment building—home to such greats as Caruso, Stravinsky, and Toscanini—the Continental Baths were the birthplace of much post-Stonewall celebrity, intrigue, and a fair bit of pleasure. The twenty-four-hour facilities included a sauna, a steam room, a swimming pool, Swedish massage, state rooms, checkers and chess, the Continental Cuisine and Canteen, and the Continental Sun and Sky Club sun roof, as well as a disco, open to men and women both, and three floors of private rooms. Promoter **Don Scotti** described the feeling of checking in, tramping down the maze of halls till you notice "a number on a door, your door! your room! Here you are at last as you rather hurriedly slip out of your everyday costume and get into the towel you've just received. That famous towel, the towel that shook the world, that sensual, vulnerable covering, what physical power in that towel! You take an anxious breath as you safety-pin yourself in for the ultimate trip."

The baths were opened by **Stephen Ostrow** and early in their career were a target for police action. In February 1969, twenty-two patrons were arrested, identified by a towel-clad cop who pointed out the individuals who he alleged either had offered to have sex with him or actually *had* had sex with him! Some life, being a vice cop!

During the 1970s, though, the Continental became a de rigueur stop on anyone's tour of fabulous New York. In

December 1970, a young Barry Manilow started playing his piano in the downstairs lounge, not a hundred feet from the swimming pool. And as Australian-born activist and essayist **Dennis Altman** wrote in 1974, while all the more lavish bath-houses had restaurants and TV rooms, only the Continental provided a full floor show. What's more, "only the Continental has a regular non-gay clientele drawn by the thrill of watching a show surrounded by towel-clad, sex-seeking fags. . . . Many of the queens have changed for the show"— there was a grand marble staircase to descend along from the private floors—"flaunting their Gucci pants and shirts from Bloomingdale's, the gayest of New York's department stores (now featuring the Continental bath towel)."

Indeed, as Altman observed, not only did much of the gay community come here, but soon enough the rest of the world came here to court them. In 1972, Bella Abzug campaigned for Congress here. (She took the stage in a large hat and a floor-length polka-dot gown, saying, "I'm not sure I'm dressed for the occasion," before going on to demand that "people have got to have the freedom to live their lives as they please.") The next year soprano Eleanor Steber gave a black-towel-only concert here, and in 1974 TV personality Pat Collins asked in a live broadcast (with nude men frolicking in the background), "How would you—or I—cope with a man who preferred the baths to us?"

The list of stars who gave it up at the Continental is long and varied—Patti LaBelle, Sarah Vaughan, **Peter Allen, Wayland Flowers,** Freda Payne—but perhaps no performer was more associated with the Continental than the bodacious Divine Miss M, **Bette Midler.** Midler began performing with Manilow in 1972 and, despite her constant complaints about "that goddamn waterfall," met with huge success here that soon led to national fame. (There are those who recall her greatest achievement as the one occasion she convinced the otherwise shy Manilow to strip down to proper bath attire.) Midler remained loyal to her gay beginnings—"Me and those guys just went somewhere else," she said later—and appeared at Gay Pride rallies in Washington Square Park. In an inter-view with *Gay* magazine in the early 1970s, she urged, "For Christ's sake, open your mouths; don't you people get tired of being stepped on?"

The bathhouse closed in the mid-1980s, when AIDS was forcing bathhouse closings across the city. It was called Plato's Retreat by then, however, and had largely gone out of the gay business.

Follow Broadway down to 72nd and head east.

9. ISADORA DUNCAN'S HOME • 115 Central Park West
at the southwest corner of 72nd Street

Born in 1878 in San Francisco, **Isadora Duncan** was one of the most controversial figures in the dance world, leading the way in demanding that interpretive dance be considered a serious art. She believed that ideally, the perfect dance would be a self-containing, self-sustaining expression, not tied to or buoyed by music at all. The rhythm of such a dance would come from the dancer alone, following "the rhythms of some invisible music."

Duncan opened a dance school and lived and toured with her pupils all over the world—landing here in 1915. But it was her personal life that earned her at least as much attention as her dance technique. She had lesbian affairs, two children out of wedlock with two different men (both children died in an automobile accident), and was viewed as an early "free love" advocate. Before she died at the age of forty-nine (strangled by her own enormous tassel-encrusted scarf when it became entangled in a car wheel), she wrote a racy poem to her sometime lover **Mercedes de Acosta.** It rhapsodized in part how her "two sprouting breasts / round and sweet / invite my hungry mouth to eat," and threatened that "my kisses like a swarm of bees / would find their way / between thy knees."

Cross 72nd Street.

10. THE DAKOTA • 1 West 72nd Street
at the northwest corner of Central Park West

When the **Dakota** was built in the 1880s (with a design by Henry Hardenbergh, the architect for the Plaza Hotel) there was little else out here. Indeed, some maintain that the name "Dakota" was a cynical reference to how isolated the building was when it was built. Others, though, suggest it was a boast about the kind of wealth that could be achieved by conquering the frontier. Regardless, it was designed for splendor, with only forty apartments, many having forty-by-twenty-foot drawing rooms. But it's as the place where Rosemary "lost" her baby and where John Lennon was shot that the Dakota has been etched into the national memory.

Who else has lived here?

Judy Holliday, the comedienne, whose career took off when she starred first on Broadway and then on screen (where **George Cukor** directed her) as Billie Dawn, the "dumb blonde" mistress in *Born Yesterday*. Although she married, Holliday (who was born Judith Tuvim) was said to have given her heart to women as often as to men.

William Inge. Though his fame has declined over the years, in the 1950s the playwright had as strong a reputation as **Tennessee Williams.** Born in Independence, Kansas, in 1913, Inge grew up in a house of doting older women—a house he longed to escape. He began his theatrical career as an actor, doing tent shows and performing on the radio. He quickly gave up on acting and taught high-school English and drama instead. In 1946, though, he saw a production of Williams's *Glass Menagerie* and was moved enough to try to write his first play. He was thirty-three. By the time he was thirty-seven, he was being referred to as Broadway's most promising new playwright. His plays—such as *Picnic; Bus Stop; Come Back, Little Sheba;* and *The Dark at the Top of the Stairs*—looked at lonely lives, often overpowered by sexuality. *Picnic* won the Pulitzer, yet Inge himself remained unhappy; he was an alcoholic, repeatedly hospitalized for depression, and seemed always tormented by his homosexuality. When his plays began to fare poorly at the hands of the critics, he fled New York, ending up for a while in Hollywood. At the time, he said, "I just have claustrophobia in New York. . . . I lose my feeling of identification there. It's too big. I was born and grew up with the natural world around me. I feel tense in New York." In Hollywood his screenplay for *Splendor in the Grass* won an Oscar. Nevertheless, a feeling of joy eluded Inge, and, he committed suicide at the age of sixty.

Leonard Bernstein, who gave us "New York, New York," composed a wide range of music, and had a lengthy tenure as conductor of the New York Philharmonic. Born in 1918, Bernstein discovered music at the age of nine or ten when a relative sent an old upright piano to be stored at his family's home. Said Bernstein, "I touched it. It made pretty sounds. Right away I screamed, 'Ma, give me lessons.'" After college, at the suggestion of **Aaron Copland,** among others, he began to study conducting, and in 1943, at the age of twenty-five, he was named assistant conductor of the New York Philharmonic. From his classic understudy debut forward, Bernstein wowed audiences and musicians alike with his combination of musicality and boundless sprightly energy. Recording engineers once decided they had to rerecord the opening bars of a Bruckner symphony because Bernstein had inserted a drum-roll that wasn't in the score. What they thought was drumming, however, was only Bernstein stomping away on the podium to get the orchestra off and running.

Bernstein's energy was at least as much sexual as it was musical. Even stodgy *Time* magazine said of him that "he exudes sex appeal like a leaky electric eel." And that was in 1957! Although Bernstein married and was a father, he had countless affairs with men; though short-lived, such liaisons seemed to be one of the great passions of his life. (He boasted once to **Gore Vidal** that he had slept with all three dancing sailors in his and **Jerome Robbins**'s famous ballet *Fancy Free*.) In the mid-seventies, he and his wife separated and Bernstein publicly set up house with a young man. He told a press conference, "There comes a time in life when a man must be what he really is." Near the end of his life, in 1988, Bernstein spoke to the rumors about him. "Most people do think of me as just another pinko faggot, a bleeding heart, a do-gooder," he said. And then added, "But that's what I am."

Rudolf Nureyev. When Nureyev defected from the Soviet Union's Kirov Ballet and appeared on Western stages, his long hair, hollow cheeks, and passionate intensity left balletgoers breathless. It is said that he lived his life with that same vivacity; choreographing, running companies, dancing well after his physical strength had diminished, he kept himself in the public eye for nearly thirty years. He also actively toured the gay world, signing his own name on gay bathhouse registers around the globe. One biographer notes that while his affairs are much discussed, he had three serious relationships: first, in the 1960s, with **Erik Bruhn,** the Danish dancer, who was perhaps his greatest (if most tortured) love; in the 1970s he lived with **Wallace Potts** for seven years; and at the end of his life, **Robert Tracy** was his lover and caretaker. Nureyev died of AIDS-related illnesses early in 1993.

Walk up Central Park West two blocks.

11. THE SAN REMO • 145 Central Park West
   at 74th Street

Okay, just a touch of pointless dish: Back in 1985 the premotherhood Material Girl tried, with hubby Sean, to buy a pad in this enormous twin-towered co-op building. (Somewhere around a million and a half.) And apparently the co-op board—the last vestige of boss politics—voted her down on the grounds that she drew too much publicity and attention. **Madonna** received only one vote in her favor—from Diane Keaton.

   Other folks who have lived here, but about whom I shall say *nothing:* Barry Manilow, Tony Randall, and Rita Hayworth. Oh, okay—about Rita I'll give you this: she's the one who in the movie *Gilda* taught us the line "If I'd been a ranch, they would've named me 'the Bar Nothing.' " Good work, no?

Take Central Park West up to 77th Street.

12. CENTRAL PARK
   entrance at 77th Street and Central Park West

This may not be the moment you feel like taking a stroll through the high green grass. Heck, it might be winter and pretty barren in there. Central Park will be here for some time, and you can wander in whenever you feel inspired (say, after finishing the Upper East Side tour). Then again, if you feel like taking a nature break, there's enough of gay history here to warrant moving off the sidewalk and onto the footpath. Follow the sidewalk for the 77th Street auto entrance to the overlook at the bottom of the hill.

In 1858, Frederick Law Olmsted and Calvert Vaux joined forces to create for the growing metropolis an escape from the urban jungle: Central Park. Buildings had to be razed, hills leveled, but the hope was to create a place of "pure and wholesome air" that would rejuvenate and restore the poor city dweller. There would be "an antithesis of objects of vision to those of the streets and house, which should act remedially by impressions on the mind and suggestions to the imagination."

As **George Whitmore** pointed out so wonderfully in his novel *Confessions of Danny Slocum*, however, by the time gay liberation roared through town in the seventies those visions, real and imagined, were of a quite different order. About two blocks north and a little east of where you are now lies one of Olmsted and Vaux's sylvan retreats. On a warm day, as Whitmore wrote, this meadow is "brim-full of men: men lounging bare-legged in little short shorts, men lolling bare-chested in teeny bikinis, men rubbing cocoa-butter lotion on each others' broad backs." Even in the 1920s the lawn was nicknamed "the Fruited Plain," and still today the meadow is full.

If you wander around the northern side of the lake, you'll enter an area of rocky climbs and twisted paths that Olmsted and Vaux named the Ramble. The strolling there, over the course of the years, turned more into prowling, though, and by 1976 the local rag *Man Alive!* was noting that the area had "some of the most varied (and beautiful) cruising and hard-core action terrain in the city."

The history of gay men meeting in parks—not just Central Park—is a long one, and true in many parts of the world. There is a charming scene in **Andre Tellier**'s otherwise tragic 1943 novel *Twilight Men* where the young newly arrived European hero is moping and watching ducks in the park one morning (he's already lost his lover, brother, tutor, and uncle) when he is approached by writer Stephen Kent, who seems to have walked the four miles up to the park from his Washington Square apartment. They trade morning chatter and become close for a while. But I'm sorry to tell you, it's just too early a gay novel for things to turn out well for them for very long.

Park cruising remains a complicated part of our history, let alone our present. Some scholars have argued that gay men came to parks, like waterfront districts, out of default—for lack of better options. Or if there were bars to go to, they came here as a way to retain their anonymity. By now, certainly, there are men who, even with all the other options, still find a certain adventure in such outings. The sad truth, though, is that mingling men in parks have been subject to police raids and, after dark, to violence.

Young **Harvey Milk,** long before he roused the nation with his ascendancy as an openly gay politician in San Francisco (or his tragic assassination), was arrested here at the ripe age of seventeen. Milk, who was born in 1930 and grew up out on Long Island, loved to come into the city for cultural outings. During the Second World War, young Milk would ask his mother for money to come to the old Metropolitan Opera House to inhale the rich sounds of his favorite composers. But what with all the excitement in the standing-room galleries, Milk's introduction to opera also became his entree into the gay world. And that brought him, along with countless other men and GIs passing through the city, into this park. At the end of the summer of 1947, on a hot day that found fathers and youngsters shirtless across the park, the gay men in the Ramble, including Milk, were arrested for indecent exposure: they also had their shirts off, but if you were a gay man, that was enough to warrant charges.

Still more frightening, **Dick Button,** Olympic figure-skating champion and sports commentator, was beaten up here along with several other gay men one infamous night. And in 1968, the Mattachine Society newsletter reported that a twenty-nine-year-old had recently stumbled out of the Ramble bushes, fallen to the sidewalk, and died. His throat had been slit and he had been stabbed in the neck. His wallet, though, was not taken: he was not killed for money.

As for happier memories, in September 1980 **Elton John** stood at one end of the park's Great Lawn and 350,000 people filled the rest of it while he sang hit after hit for three hours. And what's more, if you keep wandering across the park and around the lake, you'll find yourself smack in front of the boat lagoon and the Bethesda Fountain. In the hippie days of the 1970s, the fountain was a gathering place for flower children, but you may recognize it as the setting for the last scene in **Tony Kushner's** *Angels in America*. The angel on top, the

Angel of the Waters, was designed by sculptor **Emma Stebbins;** commissioned in 1863, it was the first public sculpture done in New York City by a woman. Stebbins, who lived from 1815 to 1882, was the daughter of a powerful banker and sister to a man who went on to become a congressman, president of the New York Stock Exchange, and, not entirely coincidentally, president of the Central Park Commission.

Stebbins trained as a painter and drawer and got some national recognition in her thirties as a portrait artist. In 1857, though, she went off to Rome, where she discovered two loves that would occupy her for the rest of her life: sculpture and **Charlotte Cushman.** Cushman was an actress. No, strike that. According to one biographical sketch, "there can be little doubt that Charlotte Cushman was the most powerful actress America has produced. . . . Such another dominating figure on our stage is hardly likely to arise until the reign of naturalistic drama is ended." Born in 1816, Cushman became famous for particular roles which she performed again and again: Lady Macbeth, Rosalind in Shakespeare's *As You Like It*, and Queen Katherine in *Henry VIII*. In 1845, she was only the second American actress to strike the London boards, which she did with resounding success, for a time even performing Romeo opposite her sister as Juliet. (The *Times* of London said she was better than any other Romeo of the time.)

Cushman and Stebbins lived principally in Newport, but they frequented New York. For a while they were part of a group of lesbian artists referred to as the "jolly female bachelors." Cushman was forever retiring from the stage and forever returning, two or three years later, with dramatic fanfare. When she did give her absolute last performance in 1874, an ode was read, William Cullen Bryant made a speech and gave her a laurel, and a crowd of 25,000 greeted her outside her hotel with an ovation.

Another of Stebbins's sculptures can be seen in the city, by the way—a portrait of Christopher Columbus out in Brooklyn—but her bust of Cushman is owned by the Handel and Haydn Society of Boston.

All right, grab a lemonade and let's circle out of the park. Follow 77th Street up a few steps, and remember to sneak a peek or two at the American Museum of Natural History as you walk by.

13. PETER ALLEN'S HOME • 6 West 77th Street
between Central Park West and Columbus

If you don't recognize the name, don't tell your friends, but I dare you to pretend that you don't know some of **Peter Allen**'s melodies: "I Honestly Love You" or the theme song from *Arthur*, or better still, "Don't Cry Out Loud" or "I Go to Rio." (On those last two, I bet you can do a full-fledged choreographed rendition.)

Peter Allen's story is a little bit about family. Born in Australia in 1944, Allen was discovered by **Judy Garland,** who saw him performing at the Hong Kong Hilton and hired his group to be the opening act for her show. Judy also, mistakenly enough, encouraged Allen and daughter **Liza Minnelli** to wed, a marriage that was quickly on the rocks—so much for Mama's instincts. In the late 1970s, Allen's solo career began taking off: concert in Central Park, raves from the *New York Times* ("Flashy, campy performer who can suddenly dig deeply"), and sold-out shows at Radio City, where he joined the Rockettes high-kicking through "Rio." Allen died of AIDS-related illnesses in 1992, but before his death he, **Michael Callen,** and Marsha Malamet wrote another song you've probably heard: "Love Don't Need a Reason." It is an AIDS Walk anthem.

Continue heading west on 77th Street and turn right on Columbus.

14. BOY GEORGE'S HOME • 101 West 79th Street
at Columbus Avenue

Basically, I've resisted telling you where all the best queer celebs *now* live. (You have to admire me for that—I mean, discretion isn't exactly my long suit.) But I will let it slip that **Boy George** lived here for a time. The former front man for Culture Club grew up George O'Dowd outside of London and began dressing up when he was fifteen. He got kicked out of school, became a squatter in London (where, get this, his dad would help him out by slipping into his apartment and loading up the cabinets with food!), and worked as a window dresser, makeup artist, and model (for British Airways) before finally entering the music world. There, with his femme-fatale face and his croony sounds, Boy George made it big. When Culture Club received a Grammy award in 1984, Boy George thanked the nation via satellite, adding, "You've got taste, style, and you know a good drag queen when you see one." It was, he later said, meant with irony.

An even greater living legend and an essential figure in our history, **Billie Jean King,** also lived in an apartment near this intersection. Born in 1943, King became a phenomenal tennis player, winning twenty Wimbledon titles, including three—singles, doubles, and mixed doubles—in one year; she was the only woman athlete on *Time* magazine's list of the one hundred most important Americans of the twentieth century; and she beat the former great male champion Bobby Riggs in 1973 in the Houston Astrodome in front of thirty thousand fans and forty million television viewers. With all of that, King almost single-handedly transformed women's tennis from a mere entertainment to an enormous industry and a sport rivaling men's tennis in importance. And though perhaps not always eager to have her personal life made public, she was candid enough in 1981 to tell Barbara Walters that yes, she had had an affair with her personal secretary **Marilyn Barnett.** Indeed, though King's statements—and the surrounding lawsuit—cost her endorsements, her efforts paved the way for the likes of **Martina Navratilova** to stand proud, fifteen years later, as a lesbian, an athlete, and a woman.

Follow Columbus up to 81st Street and then turn right, heading back toward the park.

15. THE BERESFORD · 211 Central Park West
between 81st and 82nd Streets

Although fairly solidly based out in Hollywood for much of his life, **Rock Hudson** kept a six-room apartment in this building for the last several years of his life. (The building was built in 1928–29 by the same fellow who designed Madonna's almost-home, the San Remo.) After his death from AIDS-related illnesses in October 1985, many of Hudson's belongings here were auctioned off, including a silver-plated box with "Dynasty—100th Episode" engraved on it, a rug needle-pointed by the Rock himself, a Steinway, and a footstool from the bathroom that bore the following inscription in lavender: "E.T. stood here, she had to because she couldn't reach the sink. R.H. is a love, and I thank him always—even tho he is one foot taller. Your always friend, Elizabeth." (As in Taylor.)

In an interview late in his career, Rock said, "I wasn't discovered. I knew I wanted to be an actor when I was a little boy. But living in a small town in the Middle West, I didn't say so, because that's just sissy stuff. . . . I once asked my stepfather if I could have drama lessons. The old man said, 'Why?' " When he said he wanted to be an actor, his father hit him. "But," he added, "I think I saw just about every film."

Eventually, young Roy Fitzgerald, as he was known then, set out for Hollywood, and in 1947 he stumbled into the Long Beach gay world. (He'd already had various gay encounters, mostly in the navy, but one dating back to when he was nine and off on a farm.) And it was there, contrary to legend, that his first boyfriend, **Ken Hodge,** and Hodge's friends christened him "Rock." (As for "Hudson," they pulled that out of the phone book.) The magnitude of his success is perhaps conveyed by the simple fact that in the two weeks following the announcement that Hudson had AIDS, he received thirty thousand letters from fans supporting and encouraging him, though his remaining days were brief in number.

A tidbit: Rock loved games. Dictionary, Hearts, Essences, Boccaccio—he couldn't get enough. In Boccaccio, a game that entails trying to guess the identity of a famous person from obscure clues, Rock would sometimes refuse to be told the answer and then call up in the middle of the night still guessing.

Oh, and his taste: blond, blue-eyed, straight-ish . . . fit the bill? Writer **Boze Hadleigh** once asked Rock if people should feel sorry for closeted movie stars. "You mean because they're stuck?" Hudson asked. "To some extent, they're stuck," Hadleigh said, adding, "On the other hand, they live like kings." "*Horny* kings," corrected Hudson.

For the more anthropologically minded: **Margaret Mead** kept a home here as well, from 1966 until her death in 1978. In the 1920s and '30s, the young Mead was part of a New York scene that embraced an enormous degree of sexual liberation. When she went off to study the Samoans (and, as some critics have suggested, project her own opinions about sexuality onto them), she was married, having an affair with a man, and having an affair with a woman. (Busy lady, no?)

The woman was **Ruth Benedict,** a fellow anthropologist, who remained Mead's lover, some say, from 1925 until Benedict's death in 1948. Mead met her at Columbia in 1922. Benedict was a New York–born woman who had returned to school in her mid-thirties after finding herself bored with society life. Having tried out social work, modern dance, and writing detective stories, she encountered the work of Franz Boas, very much the grand old man of anthropology, and soon she became his top graduate student. Influenced by Benedict and Boas, Mead, already in her senior year, decided to devote herself to anthropology (and eventually to Benedict herself). And once their relationship began, both Mead and Benedict went on to examine notions of deviancy and normalcy. "For Ruth Benedict," her biographer notes, "her relationship to Margaret Mead acted as a revelation. It apparently affected her so deeply that from that time forward she became a woman-loving woman."

Benedict separated from her husband in 1931 and went on to pursue work that provided the basis for modern cultural anthropology. (Her book *Patterns of Culture* is seen as the single most influential twentieth-century American anthropological work.) Her writings swept away biology as the primogenitor of experience and replaced it with culture. Mead's own work she once described as a study of the "conditioning of the social personalities of both sexes," which suggests that well before our more recent debates about unalterable differences between the sexes, Mead and Benedict were studying and arguing about the very same questions.

Mead's office, once her career was established, was at the Museum of Natural History (which you peeked at back on Central Park West and 79th Street), a place that seems designed expressly for romantic trysts: just imagine flirting over the dinosaur bones. . . .

Take a few big strides up to 92nd Street.

16. LORENZ HART'S HOME • 320 Central Park West
at 92nd Street

Richard Rodgers and **Lorenz Hart** were one of the great teams to contribute to American musical comedy—*Babes in Arms, The Boys from Syracuse, Pal Joey.* (If you know your show tunes, baby, now's the time!) They met in 1919; Hart was twenty-three and Rodgers was sixteen. (Hart actually grew up down the street from Columbia.) The encounter left Rodgers eagerly chanting to himself, "I have a lyricist, I have a lyricist!"—and left Hart, according to friends, in love. Their early years as collaborators were years of struggle, putting on amateur shows at girls' schools, churches and synagogues. Hart supported himself by doing translations of plays and musicals for the Shuberts. In 1925, though, they finally put together a hit for the Theater Guild, *The Garrick Gaieties*, which ran for 214 performances, and soon the team of Rodgers and Hart took their place in the Broadway firmament.

Hart, who stood not quite five feet tall, was the anxious and disheveled half of the partnership: the one who drank a lot, smoked a lot of cigars, slept late, almost seemed to resist working. (I like him already.) He was forever leaving his hat and coat somewhere and then being rushed into the children's department at Macy's or some such store to replace it. Rodgers described him as the pacer, "walking up and down in back of the audience" on opening nights, "cursing softly if a joke fails to get a laugh and rubbing his hands vehemently if a song goes over well."

Hart spent the last decade of his life here, from the mid-1930s until 1943, living for a time with his mother but still throwing parties that seemed to occur without plan, starting at midnight and going on until dawn. Rodgers said that Hart was prone to "loudly and almost tearfully proclaiming any soirée of his a failure if even one guest has departed sober." More explicitly, though, another fellow remembered that at Hart's parties here in the late 1930s there were lots of actors and, for the time, some pretty outrageous goings-on. "Of course, what was an orgy *then* wouldn't be an orgy *now*. I mean, kissing with the lights on! Shocking! You have to understand, homosexuality in that period was on two levels. To the world at large you were beneath contempt, but *inside*, inside you were a member of the most exclusive club in the world. No ordinary CPA could get into that circle. Larry Hart, Cole Porter, George Cukor. That was *the* world."

Charming, passionate, moody, and nervous, Hart was rarely a happy camper. Details about his love life are mostly speculative, and the speculation runs mostly toward prostitutes. But his anxieties ran deeper than pacing could alleviate, and he became extremely dependent on alcohol, which is what ultimately killed him in 1943. At the same time, he gave us so many outstanding lyrics—"There's a Small Hotel," "The Lady Is a Tramp," "My Funny Valentine." And knowing that he was gay, you might reconsider just what he meant by all those clinging trousers in that loveliest song, "Bewitched (Bothered, and Bewildered)."

Head west on 92nd Street to Broadway.

17. LESBIAN HERSTORY ARCHIVES • 215 West 92nd Street
   at Broadway

In the fall of 1973, a group of women met at the first conference of the Gay Academic Union and decided to form a consciousness-raising group. The women grew closer and began to see a need to collect and preserve the voices of the lesbian community. In 1974, taking over the pantry of historian **Joan Nestle**'s apartment in this building, they began to amass books, magazines, personal papers, manuscripts, news clippings, photos, T-shirts, tapes, and films. For the women involved, such as historian **Judith Schwarz,** the archives were a revelation. Having come of age in the 1950s, Schwarz assumed that there would be no cultural referents to lesbians or lesbian projects. "I did not even search," she later stated, "because I knew we were not a people, just deviant and wanderers, meeting in dark places." The archives challenged that silence, that homelessness. "The roots of the Archives," wrote Schwarz, "lie in the silenced voices, the love letters destroyed, the pronouns changed, the diaries carefully edited, the pictures never taken, the euphemized distortions that patriarchy would let pass. . . . But I have lived through the time of willful deprivation and now it is our time to discover and to cherish and to preserve."

In 1979, the archives was given nonprofit status by the IRS, which was the first such grant given to a group with the word "lesbian" or "gay" in it. The archive has since outgrown its apartment beginnings and is now located in Brooklyn. The collection is vivid, diverse, and extremely engaging, and certainly more than worth a visit.

Follow 92nd Street to West End Avenue and turn right.

18. ADRIENNE RICH'S HOME • 670 West End Avenue
   at 93rd Street

In the 1970s, poet and essayist **Adrienne Rich** kept an apartment here. Born in Baltimore in 1929, Rich went to Radcliffe (the women's half of Harvard back then), and the year of her graduation, **W. H. Auden** chose her collection of poems to receive the Yale Younger Poets Award. Rich married a Harvard economist and had three sons. But in 1966, she started teaching at City College in New York, which brought her into contact with **Alice Walker** and **Audre Lorde,** who became a dear friend. In 1973, her collection *Diving into the Wreck* was given the National Book Award; Rich rejected the prize as an individual honor and then, with Lorde and Walker, accepted it on behalf of "all women whose voices have gone and still go unheard in a patriarchal world."

In her 1980 essay "Compulsory Heterosexuality and Lesbian Existence," Rich offered a profound critique of the suppression of lesbians in feminist thinking and the women's movement. She argued that all relationships between women need to be seen as existing along a "lesbian continuum." Such a perspective, she insisted, would unite a broad community of woman-identified women rather than isolating lesbians. "Woman identification," she wrote, "is a source of energy, a potential springhead of female power, curtailed and contained under the institution of heterosexuality. The denial of reality and visibility to women's passion for women, women's choice of women as allies, life companions, and community, the forcing of such relationships into dissimulation and their disintegration under intense pressure have meant an incalculable loss to the power of all women *to change the social relations of the sexes, to liberate our-selves and each other.*" Unleashing that power remains Rich's long-term goal.

Follow West End up to 100th Street and then turn left.

19. GERTRUDE STEIN'S HOME
- **100th Street and Riverside Drive**

In the winter of 1902, when the modernist writer **Gertrude Stein** was in her late twenties and just back from a European tour with her brother, she stayed for a short time in a wooden apartment building at the end of 100th Street, overlooking the river, known as the White House. She shared it with three friends from Johns Hopkins, where she had gone to school. She had yet to meet **Alice B. Toklas,** who would become her life partner, but she had already had her first lover. And while here, she began a novel (her first) which told of that affair. It was a love triangle in which Stein's roommate was her lover's lover before she was, and, well, you can imagine how things go. The book, *Q.E.D.*, was not published until after Stein's death, and then under the title *Things As They Are.*

Stein was born in 1874 to a wealthy Baltimore family (her brother went on to become an art collector), but she settled in Paris in 1903 and, with Toklas at her side, never looked back: she returned to the States only once, for a lecture tour in 1934. She was an author, critic, and patron of artists—the likes of Picasso and Braque and Matisse. But many a young artist or writer, touring Europe, enjoyed a visit with—or critique from—Stein and Toklas.

Of Alice, whom she met through such a visit in Paris, the wordsmith wrote, "She is very necessary to me . . . My sweetie. She is all to me." She also penned a litany of the marvels of Alice: "I marvel at my baby. I marvel at her beauty. I marvel at her perfection. I marvel at her purity. I marvel at her tenderness. I marvel at her charm." And so forth and so on.

Alice B. Toklas and Gertrude Stein, just before flying from Newark to Chicago, 1934. They were photographed by their dear friend Carl Van Vechten.

You get the idea and can just fill in the rest: industry, humor, intelligence, rapidity, brilliance, sweetness, delicacy, generosity, and cow, as in "I marvel at her cow." Cows, according to Stein-lingo scholars, are orgasms.

Just so you know, it was a mutual affection. When they met, through a friend of Alice's who was studying with Stein, Alice was enraptured. She described Stein—in her brown corduroy suit—as "a golden presence burned by the Tuscan sun and with a golden glint in her warm brown hair." Stein was also wearing a coral brooch that day, and when she talked or laughed (which she did a fair amount) Alice was convinced that "her voice came from this brooch. It was unlike anyone else's voice—deep, full, velvety like a great contralto's, like two voices. She was large and heavy with delicate small hands and a beautifully modeled and unique head." These are the details of modernist love.

Cross Riverside Drive twice and turn left to enter the park at roughly 99th Street.

20. RIVERSIDE PARK • 99th Street and the Hudson River

Riverside Park has been, for at least the whole of the century, a notorious cruising ground, especially for sailors during the World Wars. (Not to mention a place where some of my favorite gay-boys-to-be played their way through childhood.) But as an area where gay men met, it was also a place that shaped their lives. Mind you, even though we now know where some of the gay boîtes of the earlier decades were located, there were no gay bar guides back then, no *Fab!* or *HomoXtra:* for a newcomer it could be difficult to find a way into the scene. The parks, though, afforded easy access. As George Chauncey has reported, one man who moved to New York from Germany in 1927 quickly made his way to the Soldiers and Sailors Monument (down at 89th Street), where, in the bleachers set up for Charles Lindbergh's return from Paris, he met another fellow. The other man was a Harvard graduate who taught ethical culture: they had a relationship that lasted two years, a friendship that lasted much longer, and the new immigrant had a guide to his new world.

A 1920s novel, *Better Angel*, described stepping off along a Riverside Park path to be asked, "Got a match?" And according to Chauncey, the Soldiers and Sailors Monument and Grant's Tomb, up at 122nd Street, were especially popular rendezvous spots. As in Central Park, things here could be tricky: the fellows from **Charles Henri Ford** and **Parker Tyler**'s 1930s novel *The Young and Evil* were more chased out here than cruised. And even at the turn of the century, the police made sweeps through here for men having sex. Nevertheless, even as recently as the 1970s, the gay magazines were talking about how "by day there is cruising all up and down the promenade and some action in the dense bushes at the back of the park and in rest rooms." At night, things got a bit more racy. Take a break, though, and enjoy the view.

When "The Life" Was in Vogue: Touring the Harlem Renaissance

> I can never put on paper the thrill of the underground ride to Harlem. . . . At every station I kept watching for the sign: 135TH STREET. When I saw it, I held my breath. I came out onto the platform with two heavy bags and looked around. It was still early morning and people were going to work. Hundreds of colored people! I wanted to shake hands with them, speak to them. I hadn't seen any colored people for so long—that is, any Negro colored people.
>
> I went up the steps and out into the bright September sunlight. Harlem! I stood there, dropped my bags, took a deep breath and felt happy again.

That absolute thrill belonged to **Langston Hughes,** a brilliant writer who lived on and off in Harlem, but who came into his own during the 1920s and '30s, in the years now called the Harlem Renaissance. His enthusiasm, however, was hardly unique. Whatever you think you know about Harlem, set it aside. Instead, in this tour, we will pursue the wonderful reasons for Hughes's—and many others'—sense of excitement.

Harlem was laid out as European farmland back in the 1630s. But quickly thereafter it also became a residential quarter for the Dutch colony's black residents, largely slaves, and for the next several centuries it retained a sizable black population. Even around the time of the Revolution, Harlem was one-third black, and as the next century wore on, a community of free blacks formed alongside new German and Irish immigrants. At the turn of *this* century, the arrival of the elevated train and the anticipation of the subway inspired a wave of speculation and a construction boom. The expected residents were to be upper-middle-class German Jews and Anglo-Saxons; instead, though, Harlem developed into a newly urbanized black neighborhood.

As that community grew, a uniquely African-American culture began to take shape here, being strongest and most vivid

Langston Hughes, around 1930.

during the Harlem Renaissance of the 1920s and early '30s, a period when the music, clubs, and literature of Harlem were the city's—if not the nation's and the world's—rage. It was a time when black communities were forming in urban centers around the nation, when W. E. B. Du Bois and Marcus Garvey were rallying people's attention, and the NAACP and the Urban League were demanding it.

But at the heart of that culture was a vibrant, acknowledged, and to a degree accepted, gay subculture. And in the music and literature of those years—and the very life of the community—there was a place for homosexuality. Blues giant **Bessie Smith**

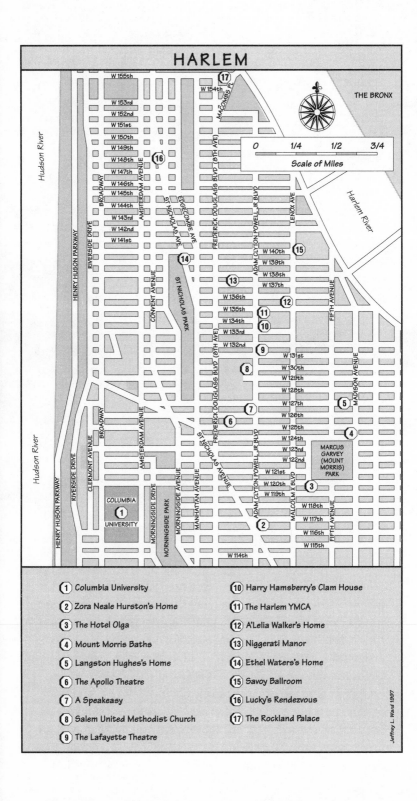

HARLEM

THE BRONX

Hudson River

Harlem River

0   1/4   1/2   3/4
Scale of Miles

W 155th
W 154th
W 153rd
W 152nd
W 151st
W 150th
W 149th
W 148th
W 147th
W 146th
W 145th
W 144th
W 143rd
W 142nd
W 141st
W 140th
W 139th
W 138th
W 137th
W 136th
W 135th
W 134th
W 133rd
W 132nd
W 131st
W 130th
W 129th
W 128th
W 127th
W 126th
W 125th
W 124th
W 123rd
W 122nd
W 121st
W 120th
W 119th
W 118th
W 117th
W 116th
W 115th
W 114th

BROADWAY
RIVERSIDE DRIVE
HENRY HUDSON PARKWAY
AMSTERDAM AVENUE
CONVENT AVENUE
EDGECOMBE AVE
ST NICHOLAS AVE
ST NICHOLAS PARK
FREDERICK DOUGLASS BLVD (8TH AVE)
ADAM CLAYTON POWELL JR BLVD
LENOX AVE
FIFTH AVENUE
MADISON AVENUE
MACOMBS PL
ST NICHOLAS AVENUE
MANHATTAN AVENUE
MORNINGSIDE AVENUE
MORNINGSIDE DRIVE
MORNINGSIDE PARK
CLAREMONT AVENUE
MALCOLM X BLVD

COLUMBIA UNIVERSITY

MARCUS GARVEY (MOUNT MORRIS) PARK

① Columbia University
② Zora Neale Hurston's Home
③ The Hotel Olga
④ Mount Morris Baths
⑤ Langston Hughes's Home
⑥ The Apollo Theatre
⑦ A Speakeasy
⑧ Salem United Methodist Church
⑨ The Lafayette Theatre

⑩ Harry Hamsberry's Clam House
⑪ The Harlem YMCA
⑫ A'Lelia Walker's Home
⑬ Niggerati Manor
⑭ Ethel Waters's Home
⑮ Savoy Ballroom
⑯ Lucky's Rendezvous
⑰ The Rockland Palace

Jeffrey L. Ward 1997

sang about how "there's two things got me puzzled, / There's two things I don't understand, / That's a mannish acting-woman / And a skipping, twistin', woman-acting man." In another song, singer **Ma Rainey** complained of her husband cheating with a fellow named "Miss Kate." And **Langston Hughes, Zora Neale Hurston, Countee Cullen,** and others were writing more and less explicitly a document of gay and sexualized experience.

High on jazz and bootleg liquor, white downtown denizens came up to Harlem for what they felt was a kind of rebel sexuality, each night pouring in to be tourists in a world seemingly full of sexual possibility. *Collier's* magazine called Harlem "a synonym for naughtiness," and nightspots like the Cotton Club offered scandalous and "exotic" black entertainment for white-only audiences. And frequently—at speakeasies with names like the Drool Inn, the Clam House, and the Hot Feet—the exotic was specifically tinged with gay sexuality. Even the city's notorious mayor, Jimmy Walker, would come uptown to watch the drag shows at the big dance halls and rub shoulders with homosexuals.

Nightclubs aside, for those in the know, there were incredible parties to attend as well. **Clinton Moore,** an elegant fellow whose genteel manner belied a wilder disposition, ran what was perhaps the most notorious of the "buffet flats"—one of those party apartments where the gin poured out of milk pitchers and the *full* buffet of life's pleasures was available. Moore had a penchant for celebrities at his parties, and the guest list ran from **Cole Porter** to **Cary Grant.** He also was good at drumming up true entertainment: one performer, **Joey,** was a singing piano player whose *pièce de résistance* was stripping to the bone and then making a lit candle disappear by sitting on it. (Moore, it seems, also ran a more explicit brothel for his ritzy downtown friends, even offering out-calls for Porter when he couldn't leave his apartment.)

Just as compelling were the rent parties, where the cover charge (sometimes a quarter) went to pay that month's rent. Langston Hughes wrote about attending many a Saturday-night rent party in apartments where the host was unknown, but where someone might be playing piano along with a drummer or trumpeter who had wandered in. Fried fish, steaming chitterlings, and "awful bootleg whiskey" were being sold cheap, and "the dancing and singing and impromptu entertaining went on until dawn came in at the windows." What happened at these parties? All things. One 1926 Harlem paper even reported that "one of these rent parties a few weeks ago was the scene of a tragic crime in which one jealous woman cut the throat of another, because the two were rivals for the affections of a third woman."

Into this world were born young poets and writers like **James Baldwin** and **Audre Lorde,** scribes whose words and ambitions would carry them out of Harlem and into the forefront of a new generation still more explicitly exploring sexuality. And they in turn would be followed by a generation of activist Harlemites—including film historian **Vito Russo,** from East Harlem—who would push past exploration to liberation.

Those generations stood on the outrageous, audacious, and thoughtful foundation of the Harlem Renaissance that you are about to discover. You'll see where **Zora Neale Hurston** lived and where **Bessie Smith** and **Ma Rainey** wailed and moaned. You'll walk by where **Countee Cullen** got married, his boyfriend standing up as best man, and where some of the most fabulous drag parties of the century took place. The Harlem Renaissance in those years between the two world wars is certainly only a tiny piece of the living that's taken place up here. By focusing (by and large) on that sliver of Harlem history, this tour leaves out much gay and lesbian life that's gone on here, both before and since. At the same time, though, such a narrow focus exposes how deeply gay something so essential to American and African-American history—and so presumedly *not* gay—actually is.

Now hop on the 1 or 9 train up to 116th Street and let's get going. I'll meet you on campus, inside Columbia's gates.

1. COLUMBIA UNIVERSITY
  • **116th Street between Broadway and Amsterdam Avenue**

The degree to which **Columbia** is rightly considered part of Harlem is a long-standing debate. But even if it's on the geographic periphery, Columbia has been central in shaping a gay life in this city—and not just because most gay people never seem to get up the gumption to start messing around until college. Dating back to pre-Revolutionary days, Columbia educated **Alexander Hamilton** before he went off to break hearts as George Washington's aide-de-camp, as well as poets **Allen Ginsberg** and **Langston Hughes:** they both lived in Hartley Hall, though a few decades apart. It brought anthropologists **Margaret Mead** and **Ruth Benedict** together (more about them on the Upper West Side tour) and trained **Zora Neale Hurston.** It also provided a home for Spanish poet **Federico García Lorca** in 1929 and 1930 when he was living in this country. (Angel Flores, the editor of *Alhambra* and a friend to Lorca, took him one night to Brooklyn to meet **Hart Crane,** who was then polishing up his legendary poem *The Bridge.* Crane was having a party, which was in full swing when Flores and Lorca arrived, and was surrounded by drunken sailors—a favorite milieu. Crane was interested in Spanish culture and eager to talk with Lorca, but couldn't speak the language; for a time Flores translated, and then Crane and Lorca discovered they could both hobble their way through French. Flores realized the two had a great deal in common—say, a shared interest in sailors—and decided to leave. As he departed, he looked back to see Crane again surrounded by a laughing group of sailors and Lorca happily afloat with his own crew.)

Columbia was also the birthplace of the Student Homophile League—the first gay university organization in the country—in April 1967. They started off quietly enough, even considering forming up as a branch of the Mattachine Society. They instead decided to create their own organization, and with the support of the university chaplain (who was later forced out of Columbia), they made a presentation to the administration. The university requested a membership list before approving the group, and the students balked. Eventually, though, they submitted their constitution along with the names of five members (some of whom were campus leaders, such as **Dotson Rader,** who went on to buddy it up with **Tennessee Williams**) to the registrar's office. The constitution consisted of thirteen principles, such as "The homosexual has a fundamental human right to develop and achieve his full potential and dignity as a human being and member of human society." Their ultimate success made all the newspapers, TV, even Paris's *Le Monde.* By 1968, there was also an SHL at

NYU, where one of its founders was **Rita Mae Brown,** author of *Rubyfruit Jungle.*

Walk through the campus and, staying on 116th Street, out to Morningside Park. The stairs at 116th Street (or, if they're closed, at 114th) will get you across the park.

2. ZORA NEALE HURSTON'S HOME
- **1923–1937 Adam Clayton Powell Jr. Boulevard**
between 116th and 117th Streets

Zora Neale Hurston, who would name her fellow literary strivers "the Niggerati" and their white supporters "the Negrotarians," came to New York in 1925 to go to Barnard College. She had grown up in Florida, where her father was a tenant farmer, but from early on Zora was a traveler. "The strangest thing about it," she wrote, "was that once I found the use of my feet, they took to wandering. I always wanted to go." Carted around to aunts and uncles, she ran away (at the age of fourteen) with a Gilbert and Sullivan company—to be an actress's maid. She ended up going to night school in Baltimore, then to Howard University, where, in her sophomore year, she won a fellowship to come to Barnard, the women's half of Columbia. She was the school's first African-American student and ended up studying most eagerly with Franz Boas, the anthropologist who also inspired **Margaret Mead** and **Ruth Benedict.** Boas convinced Hurston to collect African-American folklore, and shortly after graduating, she set out to do just that, first throughout the South, then in the Caribbean. But well before then, she was also publishing short stories and meeting the Harlem literary set. Professor and editor **Alain Locke** (whom you'll meet shortly) included one of her pieces in his anthology *The New Negro.* Over the course of her life, Hurston wrote about the experiences of rural black people and of an open sexuality for women, both in novels and in nonfiction, with works like *Their Eyes Were Watching God, Mules and Men,* and *Moses, Man of the Mountains.*

Entrance to Graham Court, Zora Neale Hurston's home when times were good, as it looks today.

Hurston successfully earned support from the Guggenheim Foundation, from patron Charlotte Mason, as well as from her publications—enough to travel to Haiti, along the Atlantic coast, even to Honduras on a quest for a lost Mayan city—and enough to move in here, the Graham Court Apartments, in 1932. Designed in 1901 for the Astor family, these apartments were considered some of Harlem's most luxurious, with features like butler's pantries, servants' quarters, and marble fireplaces.

And yet Hurston was notoriously uneven with her money, sometimes having it, more often spending it. **Langston Hughes** remembered that one time, on her way to the subway, she was stopped by a blind beggar with a tin cup, asking for a nickel. "I need money worse than you today," Zora said, and took five cents from his cup.

Sadly, in 1948 she was arrested in New York and indicted on a morals charge with two other adults, accused by a ten-year-old of sodomy. Zora had been out of the country, and the indictment was eventually dropped, but the allegations were leaked to the press, and Zora was mortified. She wrote to **Carl Van Vechten,** "All that I have ever tried to do has proved useless. All that I have believed in has failed me. I have resolved to die." Two years later she was back in Florida, working as a maid, although she told a reporter she had plans to start a national magazine for and by domestics. She wrote odds and ends for a local paper and did some substitute teaching until she died in 1960, poor and largely forgotten. She remained passionate to the end, though. One friend recalled going with Zora to a drive-in where the restroom was whites-only. Zora said she was going to use it, but the friend said, "You can't; that's for whites only." She replied, "I'm going," and off she went. "She didn't integrate the restroom," another friend explained. "She commandeered it!"

Hurston was, by the way, a looker: five-six, stylish dresser, with a penchant for hats, though she once caricatured her face as "looking like it had been chopped out of a knot of pine wood with a hatchet on somebody's off day." And a great, if saucy, raconteur: Hughes said of her that she was "a perfect book of entertainment in herself," adding snidely that "she was always getting scholarships and things from wealthy white people, some of whom simply paid her just to sit around and represent the Negro race for them, she did it in such a racy fashion."

One old-girls-network note: **Elizabeth Marbury,** the lesbian politician, theater producer, and agent, was Zora's agent for a time (along with helping our **Wallace Thurman**). The benefits of community.

Walk west to Malcolm X Boulevard, turn left, then walk up to 120th Street and turn right.

3. THE HOTEL OLGA • 42 West 120th Street

Known as "the Proust of Lenox Avenue," **Alain Leroy Locke** was a scholar and schmoozer who, with his academic credentials and his connections to wealthy society matron Charlotte Mason (see the Upper East Side tour), helped carve a place in the world for the emerging African-American artists.

Born in Philadelphia in 1886, Locke was raised largely by his mother (Dad died when he was twelve) and was devoted to her. He was also incredibly smart. (Oh, and a Virgo.) Mom enrolled him first at the new Ethical Culture School in New York and then at the high school there. From high school, he wanted to go straight into Harvard (who wouldn't?), but at Mother's bidding he first did a couple of years at the Philadelphia School of Pedagogy. When he finally arrived at Harvard, he studied philosophy and English, won various awards, and was quickly named Phi Beta Kappa. He was also a cox for the crew team (that's the little guy on the boat who yells "Harder, boys! Pull harder!"), thus meeting the athletic requirement for a Rhodes scholarship to Oxford, which, of course, he won. He was, in fact, the first black man to be a Rhodes scholar. From Oxford he went on to study in Berlin and Vienna before coming back to the States for a teaching post in the Howard University philosophy department, which he soon came to head.

Locke was frequently in Harlem, and when he visited he stayed here at the Olga. In 1925, he edited an anthology, *The New Negro: An Interpretation,* which focused some of the first public attention on the work of Harlem writers and gave their writing a position of respect. It also began to generate a sort of literary community. He pursued **Langston Hughes** to include work in it, and perhaps wooed him in other ways. Langston ducked for a long time, shy about meeting the professor who requested that he send him not only his poetry but a photograph as well. Eventually, though, Locke got writings from **Hughes, Countee Cullen, Wallace Thurman, Bruce Nugent,** and **Zora Neale Hurston.** Two years later he published *Four Negro Poets,* which focused specifically on the works of **Claude McKay,** Jean Toomer, Cullen, and Hughes. Locke also wrote about music and art and the black community. Additionally, Locke's relationship with Mason secured financial support for both Hughes and Hurston. Through these roles, Locke once described himself as "mid-wife to a generation of younger Negro poets, writers, artists." Truly he was.

One other tidbit: Locke is credited with having named New York City "the Big Apple." What do you make of that— the nickname the world uses for this town crafted by a gay man? I, for one, love it.

Head east along the edge of the park to Madison Avenue and turn left.

4. MOUNT MORRIS BATHS • 1944 Madison Avenue
just below 125th Street

The park you just passed, Marcus Garvey Park, used to be called Mount Morris Park. Even before the turn of the century, men were out there cruising—and getting arrested. Just around the corner here were the Mount Morris Baths, the oldest black bathhouse in the country—opened in 1893, and still quite functional. White men were certainly allowed up here, but for years it was the only bathhouse in the city to admit black men; most of the other baths refused them entry until the 1960s. When downtown gay places were underground, unknown, or not open, the Mount Morris was considered the international meeting place for gay black men. It remains one of the only gay bathhouses still in existence from even the Stonewall era, let alone the start of the century.

Head up Madison to 127th Street and turn left.

5. LANGSTON HUGHES'S HOME • **20 East 127th Street**
between Madison and Fifth Avenues

Langston Hughes crashed onto the literary scene in 1926 with his first poetry collection, *The Weary Blues*, and remained prominent and influential well after his death in 1967. Indeed, no name is more commonly associated with the new generation of Harlem writers than his. It was he who declared in 1926, in *The Nation* magazine, "We young Negro artists who create now intend to express our individual dark-skinned selves without fear or shame. If white people are pleased we are glad. It they are not, it doesn't matter. We know we are beautiful. And ugly, too. . . . We build our temples for tomorrow, strong as we know how, and we stand on top of the mountain, free within ourselves."

Hughes's education began at Columbia in 1922, but he quickly dropped out, writing later that the school was too big and "not fun, like being in high school." He finished up college only several years later at Lincoln University in Philadelphia; instead, at the end of his first year at Columbia, at the age of twenty, he moved to Harlem. Though he left often— taken up with travel and working as a sailor—he always returned, and after the Second World War he settled permanently on the top floor of this building. He wrote prolifically, ranging in style from fiction to drama, gospel song-play, history, autobiography, and even opera (the lyrics for Kurt Weill's *Street Scene*). Like **Aaron Copland,** Hughes strove to write with local sounds in his work: his early poems aimed for a kind of blues rhythm, and his later work tried to incorporate bebop. Initially, his poetry was published in *The Crisis* (a journal published by the NAACP and edited by W. E. B. Du Bois himself), but it was **Carl Van Vechten,** the white critic and Harlem aficionado, who helped Hughes get his first books published and became a close friend. For three and a half years he also received financial support (arranged by **Alain Locke**) from Charlotte Mason, who insisted that he call her "Godmother" and write to her several times a week.

During the Depression, Hughes began traveling the country as a kind of wandering minstrel, performing his poetry at public readings. He traveled through the South, across Texas, even reading in Berkeley and San Francisco proper. (Silent-movie idol **Ramon Navarro** attended one of his San Francisco performances, and for many years thereafter they were rumored to be seen here and there together, linked romantically in some way.) The travel bug kept him out in the world for many years, taking him to Moscow, through the belly of the Soviet Union, on to Japan and even China, and then back around through San Francisco, to Mexico, and to Spain in time for the Spanish Civil War. For a while, Hughes was great friends with **Zora Neale Hurston,** but they fought bitterly over a joint project, the play *Mule Bone*, in which each charged the other with stealing his or her work.

Attractive and shy, Hughes was cautious about revealing his emotional attachments, and so while it is certain that he had periods of homosexuality, the full extent is not entirely known. In a fictionalized description of Hughes, later housemate and fellow writer Wallace Thurman described him as "the most close-mouthed and cagey individual . . . when it came to personal matters. He fended off every attempt to probe into his inner self and did this with such an unconscious and naive air that the prober soon came to one of two conclusions: Either [he] had no depth whatsoever, or else he was too deep for plumbing by ordinary mortals." Artist and friend **Bruce Nugent,** who was very open even then, thought that Hughes lacked any "real interest" in the gay life, and one of his biographers concurs. But one Harlemite insisted that "around the streets of Harlem in the 1960s, everyone knew that Langston Hughes was gay. We just took it for granted, as a fact. He was gay, and there was no two ways about it." Another biographer reports that Hughes commented on poet **Countee Cullen**'s wedding that "Countee should never have married for some of the same reasons I should never marry." (Read on to see why.)

Some of Hughes's poems are revealing. One, entitled "Cafe: 3 A.M." describes "detectives from the vice squad" out "spotting fairies." "Degenerates," the narrator quotes some folks as calling them, but then adds, "But God, Nature, / or somebody / made them that way."

Another poem, untitled, was dedicated to "F. S.," who according to one editor was Ferdinand Smith, a merchant seaman from Jamaica who became an activist in Harlem. It read, simply enough,

> *I loved my friend.*
> *He went away from me.*
> *There's nothing more to say.*
> *The poem ends,*
> *Soft as it began,—*
> *I loved my friend.*

(By the way, this block, between Madison and Fifth, has been renamed Langston Hughes Boulevard.)

Turn left on Fifth Avenue and then right on 125th Street. Head west a few blocks along the busy commercial strip.

6. THE APOLLO THEATRE • 253 West 125th Street
between Adam Clayton Powell Jr. and Frederick Douglass Boulevards

Originally a whites-only operation, Hurtig and Seamon's Music Hall came under new ownership in 1934 and reopened as the **Apollo,** with the doors open to all. Performers here have included our own **Alberta Hunter, Johnny Mathis, Little Richard, Bessie Smith,** and **Ethel Waters,** the mysterious Michael Jackson and his brothers, as well as Billie Holiday, Duke Ellington, Count Basie, Miles Davis, Ike and Tina, Diana Ross, and Aretha Franklin. (Bessie was down on her luck by the time she made it here in 1935, and her salary had dropped from $3,500 to $250 a week. Even so, she had to kick and scream to get an advance on her paycheck, rolling on the floor, shouting, "Folks, I'm the star of the show. I'm Bessie Smith, and they won't let me have no money!") And in the 1960s, the Jewel Box Revue—a drag show—became an annual attraction. Actually, in the 1950s and '60s, one of the regular features of the Apollo Amateur Night—every Wednesday—was the group of drag queens who bought a box up in the balcony, right over the stage. One performer remembered that "they had this box and they would stand and tell you, 'You don't look half as good as I do, darling.' So you had better be dressed or when you came on they'd tell you from the box, 'That's some bad crap you're wearing!' " Gladys Knight recalled that "our gay friends would fill that

The young crooning Johnny Mathis, in the late 1950s.

box. On Wednesday night when we came on-stage we felt
their presence. They'd say, 'There's our girl!' or 'Look at
those Pips!' And they would ooh and aah about our costumes.
And I was proud, because they were proud of us."

Stepping away from the Harlem Renaissance, the Apollo
lets us turn for a moment to the much-celebrated (though
rarely as a gay man) **Johnny Mathis,** who performed here in
the late 1950s, and came out publicly in June of 1982. Born at
the end of the Depression in San Francisco's Fillmore district,
Mathis was the son of a former Texas vaudevillian, who
encouraged him to perform and even taught him to sing "My
Blue Heaven," one of his biggest hits. In junior high, Mathis
was popular enough to be the first black student-body president at his school, but he was also a strong athlete and competed in both high school and college. Indeed, he was
considered to be a high-jumper of Olympic quality. In college,
though, he diversified, studying English so that he could be an
English teacher, and singing in local nightclubs. One club
owner was so taken with Mathis's singing that he decided to
push him along; Columbia Records eventually auditioned him

and soon enough brought him to New York to record. For a while he tried to both sing and do sports, but at some point he was forced to choose between the Olympic trials and a recording session: needless to say, singing won out. He sang at the Village Vanguard and the Blue Angel. His first hit was "Wonderful! Wonderful!" and his earliest number-one song was "Chances Are." Curiously, he was one of the first artists to release a greatest-hits album—he'd been too busy to record a new album—and it stayed on the *Billboard* charts for ten years.

Mathis sang at the Apollo in 1957. It was just as his first record was released, and the Apollo managed to sign him to do thirty-one shows for a measly $350 salary. When it actually came time for the shows, the Mathis record was racing up the charts. Nevertheless, the emcee that night later recalled how nervous Mathis was. The Apollo audiences, drag queens and all, can be notoriously tough critics, and Mathis, who it seemed had never performed before an all-black crowd, was worried that they wouldn't like him. Mathis dripped sweat and shook during his first numbers, but, of course, he shone. Buoyed by a successful weekend of performing, and the release of his record, he decided to take a break. He appeared before the boss, claimed he had laryngitis, and walked out on the gig. Two months later, he was back, but his salary had gone up to $1,500.

If you want to poke around the Apollo, it's still open, and some of its history is on display. Otherwise:

Walk a block up Powell Boulevard to 126th Street.

7. A SPEAKEASY • northwest corner of Adam Clayton Powell Jr. Boulevard and 126th Street

During Prohibition days, there was an "open" speakeasy here. That meant it had no doorman—no knocks, no little window, no name-dropping. It catered to "pansies," and artist **Bruce Nugent** said that the large dark hall was usually peopled by "rough trade"—that is, "the kind who fought better than truck drivers and swished better than Mae West."

The speakeasy crowd described in journalist Blair Niles's 1931 novel *Strange Brother* might easily have been seen here—

a group of five young men with carefully coiffed hair: "all had had their eyebrows plucked to a finely penciled line, all had carmined lips, all were powdered and rouged, all had meticulously manicured nails, stained dark red, all had high voices and little trilling laughs, and all expressed themselves in feminine affectations and gestures." Niles's novel recast the life of **Leland Pettit,** a young, white gay man from Milwaukee who was the organist at the East Village's Grace Church. In it, she told the tale of how Mark, the Pettit character, discovered hope and possibility in Harlem. "In Harlem," Mark said, "I found courage and joy and tolerance. I can be myself there. . . . They know all about me and I don't have to lie." Sadly, Harlem didn't turn out to be enough to sustain the young man, who ultimately took his own life (this was, after all, 1931), but his declaration suggests what the possibility of Harlem must have meant to many real-life Marks.

One more tidbit: A big hit in the 1930s—and certainly one you would have heard here—was a song that came straight out of Harlem called "Hold Tight." It was mostly scat singing, with only a few intelligible words, like "seafood" and "chicken and rice." If you knew the lingo, though, you would have known that it was actually a gay song about oral sex. (And that's well before the Village People got the whole nation to sing about young men having fun at the YMCA!) According to my gay dictionary, for instance, sailors were frequently referred to as "seafood," so that if you talked about a place having "good seafood," you weren't necessarily talking about supper.

This speakeasy was hardly unique: there was another gay saloon at 132nd and Fifth Avenue, called Edmond's Cellar, and still another, called the Hot Cha, on the corner of 132nd and Seventh. There **Jimmy Daniels** sang and **Garland Wilson** played piano.

Follow Powell Boulevard up to 129th Street.

8. SALEM UNITED METHODIST CHURCH
- **2190 Adam Clayton Powell Jr. Boulevard**
on the northwest corner of 129th Street

Born Countee Porter in 1903, young **Countee Cullen** was adopted by New York's Reverend Frederick Cullen and went on to become one of the legendary poets of the Harlem era, gaining most attention for his first collection, *Color.* His life-long companion was a schoolteacher named **Harold Jackman;** a friend once called them the "Jonathan and David of the Harlem Renaissance." Jackman, who'd actually been born in London, grew up in Harlem and taught history. He gained a bit of fame when a portrait of him was published in a popular 1925 magazine. Jackman was also a book collector, and it is his collection that forms the heart of the Countee Cullen–Harold Jackman Memorial Collection at Atlanta University. (**Langston Hughes** recounted that the 1920s were the kind of time when "Harold Jackman, a handsome young Harlem school teacher of modest means, could calmly announce one day that he was sailing for the Riviera for a fortnight, to attend Princess Murat's yachting party.")

Cullen lived, for much of his youth, in the building in this photograph. It has been replaced by an expansive housing project, but it stood just two blocks up at 234 West 131st Street. Eventually, though, the family moved into the church parsonage here. And in this sanctuary (peek inside if you like), in 1928, Cullen married Nina Yolande Du Bois, the daughter of W. E. B., in a spectacular ceremony with sixteen brides-maids, Langston Hughes as an usher, and Jackman as his best man: live canaries sang in gilded cages. After the ceremony, Nina returned to her high-school teaching duties in Baltimore and Cullen worked in New York for two more months before he and Jackman set sail for Europe. Nina followed much later—some honeymoon, no? Two years after, the marriage was dissolved. But Cullen lived well, traveling to Europe and Palestine, and for a time, summering in France.

Color was published in 1925, while Cullen was a graduate student at Harvard. Although Hughes eventually came to overshadow him, at the time of its publication Cullen was seen as Harlem's most important younger poet. It seems that when he himself met Hughes, Cullen was rather smitten with him,

The now-demolished home where poet Countee Cullen grew up, photographed in 1932.

sending him an inscribed copy of a somewhat sensual poem, "To a Brown Boy." Cullen, who went on to win support from the Guggenheim Foundation, also taught French and English at Frederick Douglass Junior High School, where one of his pupils was **James Baldwin.** Baldwin reported that he showed Cullen a poem of his once, but that Cullen criticized it as sounding "too much like Langston." Baldwin never tried poetry again.

Cross the boulevard.

9. The Lafayette Theatre
- **2225 Adam Clayton Powell Jr. Boulevard**
between 131st and 132nd Streets

Now the Williams Christian Methodist Episcopal Church, the **Lafayette** was *the* place to see Harlem performers. **Ethel Waters** wrote about making her debut here, at what she called "the Uptown Palace. Those Sunday shows were events. Harlem's dictys got their first gander at my work that evening. They knew performers and they decided that I had a future bigger than my present or my past."

Certainly, the Palace was home for **Bessie Smith.** Bessie, who came to be known as "the Empress of the Blues," started her career in Moses Stokes's traveling company in 1912, home as well to the incomparable singer **Ma Rainey.** Rainey, it has been suggested, introduced Smith to "the life," and within a few years the two women had both joined a second touring show. After being rejected by several recording companies, including Black Swan, where Waters recorded, Smith finally cut a record with Columbia. Her first record—"Down Hearted Blues" together with "Gulf Coast Blues"—was an instant success and quickly established Smith as Columbia's best-selling and most popular artist.

Although Smith married, she also loved her women, reputedly seducing as many of her chorus girls as possible. The *Interstate Tattler,* an East Coast society-and-gossip paper for the African-American world, even published a 1925 column warning a certain Gladys to steer clear of Smith or risk the wrath of Smith's husband.

Bessie was also known to be fearless, once kicking a group of KKK Klansmen out of her traveling show's campsite. In 1929, she starred in the short movie *St. Louis Blues,* and in 1936, hoping to jump-start a slowing career, she took Billie Holiday's spot singing at Connie's Inn, a famous Harlem club. Unfortunately, she died the next year. A car accident in Mississippi left her in a segregated hospital and she did not survive the stay. She was forty-three.

But to talk only about Bessie at the Lafayette is to leave out one beloved Harlem resident, **Mabel Hampton,** who, along with her lover, had danced out at Coney Island before getting a job dancing here. Hampton came to New York from Winston-

Salem in 1920 and was promptly arrested on trumped-up prostitution charges. She spent two years in a reformatory, but soon
enough was out on the town again. "We used to go to parties
every other night," she told **Joan Nestle** of the Lesbian Herstory Archives. "The girls all had the parties." (Near the end of
her life, Hampton became very active with the Archives,
described in the Upper West Side tour.)

And in the audience here could be found a regular entourage
of bisexual (at least) women, including actresses **Beatrice Lillie,
Tallulah Bankhead, Jeanne Eagels** (who was Sadie Thompson in the first version of *Rain*), Ziegfeld dancer **Marilyn
Miller, Lucille Le Sueur** (who later became Joan Crawford),
and married singer **Libby Holman** and her lover **Louisa du
Pont Carpenter Jenny** (of *the* du Ponts). Louisa, for the
record, was very butch, a horsewoman who sailed her own
yacht, died flying her own plane, and preferred bisexual, feminine women. According to one historian, she and Libby visited
Harlem nightly, for a time, dressed in identical men's dark suits
and bowler hats. Quite a crowd, no?

Continue up Powell Boulevard to 133rd Street and turn right.

10. HARRY HANSBERRY'S CLAM HOUSE
  - **146 West 133rd Street**
    between Adam Clayton Powell Jr. Boulevard and Lenox Avenue

This block of Harlem was promoted in the 1920s and '30s as
either "Jungle Alley" (meant to suggest all that exotic primi-
tivism) or "Beale Street," like the Memphis strip. It was a
block packed with nightlife, near the Cotton Club, Connie's
Inn, and Pod and Jerry's. Among the clubs was the **Clam
House,** a narrow, very gay speakeasy run by Harry Hansberry,
which was dense with smoke and the unforgettable music of
growly piano-playing singer **Gladys Bentley.** The building is
now gone, but Bentley was a 250-pound lesbian who played
and sang the night away in white top hat and tails, and developed an international reputation. As Paul Robeson's wife,
Eslanda, told a friend, after hearing Bentley on three nights
you'll "never be the same." **Harold Jackman** wrote to **Coun-**

tee Cullen, "When Gladys sings 'St. James Infirmary,' it makes you weep your heart out."

Langston Hughes wrote about how Bentley played piano and sang from ten at night until first light, "literally all night, without stopping." She slid from one song into the next, playing with what Hughes called "a powerful and continuous underbeat of jungle rhythm. Miss Bentley was an amazing exhibition of musical energy—a large, dark masculine lady, whose feet pounded the floor while her fingers pounded the keyboard—a perfect piece of African sculpture, animated by her own rhythm." Those were also the days of sly double-entendre songs, and, as one contemporary critic put it, "if ever there was a gal who could take a popular ditty and put her own naughty version to it, La Bentley could do it." And not only would Bentley improvise salacious spins on popular songs, she would get her audience to join in. (Bentley recorded eight songs with the OKeh recording company, and a few cuts can still be found on a couple of Rosetta Records albums.)

According to historian **Lillian Faderman,** Bentley appeared in suits both on- and offstage, and was so successful that the first club she worked at changed its name to Barbara's Exclusive Club, taking her then stage name for its own name. She also performed at the Ubangi Club, where her fellow showpeople included a chorus line of drag queens. (They all ended up taking their revue over to the Apollo on occasion.) Bentley eventually moved along to Hollywood, where she performed in a local club and lived out her days.

Although it seems Bentley was bisexual, she kept this a secret from her audience, instead publicizing her *lesbian* identity, including her success in marrying another woman (a white singer) in a New Jersey civil ceremony. According to one recollection, "She seemed to thrive on the fact that her odd habits were the subject of much tongue wagging." Bentley's life was well enough known to appear in Blair Niles's 1931 novel *Strange Brother* (the one about the young gay man finding brief happiness in Harlem), where a journalist not unlike Niles visits a club called the Lobster Pot and finds a Bentleyesque piano player named Sybil. At one point a friend asks, "How's your wife, Sybil? She always used to be here at the Lobster Pot. What's become of her?" "Amy's so jealous,"

Sybil replies. "She makes trouble. Can't stand it if a woman looks at me."

Late in her life, though, Bentley published an essay claiming to have been unhappy as a soul inhabiting "that half-shadow no-man's land which exists between the boundaries of the two sexes." She was living out west and was married, and even published photos of herself making the bed and cooking dinner for her new husband. As she wrote in 1952, "Yes, many strange things have happened to me." (Historian **Eric Garber** has argued convincingly, though, that her essay, which ran in *Ebony* magazine, merely demonstrated the drastic pressures of the McCarthy era and that her recanting was only "a desperate, last-ditch effort to salvage her floundering career.")

*Head up to 135th Street. But as you pass 134th Street, you might enjoy knowing that there was a cellar club there in the early 1930s where one **Gloria Swanson** held court. Ms. Swanson hailed from Chicago, and was actually a Mr. Winston, but here was hostess supreme. According to **Bruce Nugent,** "he reigned regally, entertaining with his 'hail-fellow-well-met' freedom, so perfect a woman that frequently clients came and left never suspecting his true sex." He danced, sang some off-color songs, and posed about in his "net and sequins, velvet-trimmed evening-gown-skirts displaying with professional coyness a length of silk-clad limb," and corsets that pushed his plumpness "into a swelling and well-modeled bosom." He was, according to one historian, the most prominent of gay club hosts, and was embraced by gangsters, prostitutes, and entertainers alike.*

Turn right on 135th Street.

11. THE HARLEM YMCA • 180 West 135th Street
between Adam Clayton Powell Jr. Boulevard and Lenox Avenue

The **Harlem Y** was both first home to **Langston Hughes** on his arrival in Harlem and frequent home for **Claude McKay,** a Jamaica-born writer who came to New York in the early 1910s. McKay, who was born in 1890, initially came to the United States in his early twenties to study agriculture in Kansas. (Mind you, he had already written two books of poetry and had been honored by the Jamaican Institute of Arts and Sciences.) But after two years in Kansas he decided to move to New York (farming can get a little slow, it seems, even for a poet). He continued to write poetry here, but he also began involving himself in political pursuits. He allied himself with Communist and Trotskyist Party people and edited a radical journal called the *Liberator*, but eventually decided to leave the country. He traveled to the new Soviet Union and Germany before settling in France for more than a decade. From there, in 1928, he wrote a novel called *Home to Harlem*. It was the first Harlem novel to be a best-seller, but it showed the seedier side of life there, offering a graphic view of a neighborhood peopled with prostitutes, drug users, and homosexuals. For instance, McKay described how in a bar called the Baltimore, "all round the den, luxuriating under the little colored lights, the dark dandies were loving up their pansies. Feet tickling feet under tables, tantalizing liquor-rich giggling, hands busy above." One dandy even cries out, "Honey gal! Honey gal! What other sweet boy is loving you now? Don't you know your last night's daddy am waiting for you?" It was one of the first novels by an African-American to reach a wide audience, and it excited younger writers like Hughes. At the same time, though, it antagonized Harlem's older intellectuals, like W. E. B. Du Bois, who were striving to craft a "respectable" black community.

McKay was married before he came to Harlem, but his marriage collapsed here. Unlike many of his contemporaries, however, he was very open about his blossoming sexuality. Indeed, even before he came to New York, he had written a poem about the departure of a companion named Bennie. At that time,

> *everything was torn from me.*
> *De fateful day I 'member still*
> *De final breakin' o' my will,*
> *Again de sayin' o' good-bye,*
> *My poor heart's silent wilin' cry;*
> *My life, my soul, my all be'n gone,*
> *And ever since I am alone.*

Walk east on 135th Street to Malcolm X Boulevard and turn left.

12. A'LELIA WALKER'S HOME • 108 West 136th Street
between Adam Clayton Powell Jr. and Malcolm X Boulevards

On the ground now occupied by the Countee Cullen Public Library there once stood the empire of Madame C. J. Walker, a former washerwoman who made millions selling her own hair-straightening process. Her elaborate townhouse sat at number 108 and at 110, the Walker College of Hair Culture. (Down at 202, to keep things in perspective, Marcus Garvey's Urban League had their offices.) Her daughter, **A'Lelia Walker,** involved herself in the literary and performance worlds and gave frequent parties in the townhouse, at one point setting aside one floor as an artists' cafe/hangout.

Herself nearly six feet tall, A'Lelia often wore a jeweled turban and carried a riding crop. Although she married often, she was mostly surrounded by femme-y men and handsome women. Her salons were incredibly well attended, with guests ranging from French princesses and Russian dukes to Harlem intellectuals and New York City socialites. Of these parties, **Langston Hughes** wrote that you had to come early, because A'Lelia sent out far more invitations (hundreds, he claimed) than her home could ever hold, and that those who came late simply stayed out on the street. Those inside found the place "as crowded as the New York subway at the rush hour—entrance, lobby, steps, hallway, and apartment a milling crush of guests, with everybody seeming to enjoy the crowding."

A'Lelia also had more informal parties, which one guest remembers as "funny parties—there were men and women, straight and gay. They were kinds of orgies. Some people had clothes on, some didn't. People would hug and kiss on pillows and do anything they wanted to do." A few guests came just as spectators, it seems, others as players. Either way, though, "you had to be cute and well-dressed to get in." After all, Ms. Walker had *some* standards.

By the way, the building on the corner, the Schomburg Center, is a wonderful resource for Harlem and African-American history and culture. If you have a minute, you might want to go inside and poke around. The entrance is on 135th Street.

Take Malcolm X Boulevard up to 137th Street and make a left.

13. NIGGERATI MANOR • 267 West 137th Street
between Powell and Douglass Boulevards

Here in this parking lot there stood a boardinghouse that eventually came to be home to **Langston Hughes, Wallace Thurman,** and **Bruce Nugent.** (Hughes lived here in the summer of 1926, while he was off from school.) Given its name by **Zora Neale Hurston,** it too was notorious for its wild parties and goings-on.

Artist Bruce Nugent, born Richard Bruce Nugent in 1906, was in many ways the bad boy of the Harlem literati. The most "out" of his friends, Nugent loved to shock with his erotic drawings and suggestive writings. He published both his writing and his illustrations in Locke's *The New Negro, Ebony and Topaz, Challenge,* and the *Crisis.* (He often published under the name Richard Bruce, though, to avoid ruffling his parents' feathers.) In a letter to Hughes, **Carl Van Vechten,** the critic and impresario, described attending an Urban League dinner in the spring of 1927 and being stopped by a fellow who wanted to know "who the 'young man in evening clothes' was. It was Bruce Nugent, of course, with his usual open chest and uncovered ankles. I suppose soon he will be going without trousers." (Read more about Van Vechten in the Midtown tour.)

Wallace Thurman was rather the opposite, an erudite and prolific novelist and playwright with a dark personality, prone toward bitterness, cynicism, and alcohol. As editor of the *Messenger,* he published Hughes's first short stories, paying ten dollars a story. According to Hughes, when Thurman accepted the pieces he "wrote me that they were very bad stories, but better than anything else they could find, so he published them." Hughes described Thurman as the sort "who liked to drink gin, but *didn't* like to drink gin; who liked being a Negro, but felt it a great handicap; who adored bohemianism, but thought it wrong to be a bohemian." Thurman was very successful, though never in a way that seemed to please him: he was a reader for the prominent Macaulay's publishing house, the first black man to hold such a high editorial position. He wrote for Hollywood a bit and had a short story adapted into a play and staged at the Apollo. Thurman also, by the way, lived with a lover, a white man. But it is also known that soon after

Thurman's arrival in New York, he was arrested for having sex with a hairdresser at the 135th Street subway station. Sadly, he died of tuberculosis in the Bellevue charity ward in 1934.

Before his death, though, Thurman wrote a biting roman à clef about his friends called *Infants of the Spring.* The story was set in a house called Niggerati Manor (very few people actually knew the nickname), and no one escaped Thurman's pen. The novel centered on Raymond Taylor, a young black writer (Thurman) who insists that he is going to write "a series of books which will cause talk but won't sell, and will be criticized severely, then forgotten." He falls quickly in love with the white Stephen Jorgenson, and among the coterie surrounding them is continually presumptuous artist Paul (Bruce Nugent) who promptly declares himself a genius and Oscar Wilde "the greatest man that ever lived." **Alain Locke** appears as Dr. A. L. Parkes, described as "a mother hen clucking at her chicks." Zora Neal Hurston appears as Sweetie May Carr, "a short story writer, more noted for her ribald wit and personal effervescence than for any actual literary work." Langston Hughes passes by as a "spotty" poet, published "prematurely," named Tony. And Carl Van Vechten appears, with **Countee Cullen** and **Harold Jackman** in tow. (Jackman gets nailed for having been "a rather timid beau, who imagined himself to be bored with life.") There's a fair amount of liquor, scandal, and bitter violence, as well as a great deal of struggle about the meaning of the Harlem Renaissance itself. All in all, it is a vivid look inside these lives.

For the record, Niggerati Manor was more than just a boardinghouse. It also served as the launching pad for *Fire!!*, a literary journal published by Hughes, Thurman, Nugent, and Hurston along with artist Aaron Douglas. The title was selected, Langston later wrote, with "the idea being that it would burn up a lot of the old, dead conventional Negro-white ideas of the past." Most of the contributions were soundly blasted by the critics, especially Nugent's explicitly homoerotic short story, "Smoke, Lilies, and Jade," and the journal proved hard to sell. According to legend, the bulk of the copies disappeared when the building they were stored in itself caught on fire. The first issue was thus the last.

Head west two blocks to St. Nicholas Avenue and turn right.

14. ETHEL WATERS'S HOME • 580 St. Nicholas Avenue
at 139th Street

Singer and actress **Ethel Waters** didn't start out living up here on Sugar Hill, home for fancy Harlem. No, Sugar Hill was where you lived when you made it. But over the course of her career, Waters came to be considered the first black woman star of stage, screen, and television, and so it was here that she belonged. In fact, the building here was chock full of celebrity tenants and was known, by those in the know, as simply "580." During the 1920s, however, Waters was also well-known in lesbian circles.

Born in 1896, Waters debuted in Baltimore in 1917 and then toured the South in vaudeville, carnivals, and tent shows. Her New York City debut was at the Lincoln Theater, but soon enough she was playing at the Lafayette. Perhaps her most famous song was "His Eye Is on the Sparrow," which she first recorded in 1919; and 1933 found her a big hit on Broadway in Irving Berlin's *As Thousands Cheer.* She also went on to film, appearing in both *Cabin in the Sky* and *Stage Door Canteen* in 1943, for example, and recreating her stage triumph as Berenice in **Carson McCullers**'s *The Member of the Wedding* in 1952.

*Time for something out of the ordinary. These last few stops are a bit of a hike, and not exactly all in one direction. So, though it goes against my grain, I'm going to give you a choice: You can stick with the tour, heading east a few blocks to see where the **Savoy Ballroom** once stood, before circling uptown. Then again, the Savoy photo might just be enough for you; if so, simply head due north eight blocks to where **Lucky's Rendezvous** has changed hands, but drinks and music are still being served. (Mmm, sounds appealing.) Or if you're tuckered out already, maybe you want to wander downtown, find a place to sit and eat, and then read about both these sites, as well as the last one, the **Rockland Palace**. (It too is no longer standing, but it was located up on 155th Street, a bit far for me to insist anyone go, though I'm nothing if not a little pushy.) No pressure— just thought I'd give you some options.*

15. Savoy Ballroom
 • **Northwest corner of Lenox Avenue and 140th Street**

Sadly, the **Savoy,** seen in the picture, is no longer standing. "The Home of Happy Feet" was the site of outrageous dancing and fabulous drag balls. The Lindy Hop and a young Ella Fitzgerald both got started here. And the drag balls gathered thousands to drink, dance, and preen beneath the elegant crystal chandeliers and along the marble staircase. The organizers would obtain a permit for the night that made both the ball and the participants legal, including the highlight of the evening: the competitive squaring-off for the incomparable title of Queen of the Ball. The admission, according to one recollection: a dollar.

Blair Niles described one ball in *Strange Brother,* as did **Charles Henri Ford** and **Parker Tyler** in *The Young and Evil.* There were crowds of people, black and white, who filled the boxes and aisles and stairways while a great orchestra played in the distance. At a certain point, the police themselves cleared the floor and held back the crowd while a long elevated platform was set up for "the parade of the 'fairies.' " And then in came the competitors, in blond wigs and yellow feathers, pink organdy dresses, black picture hats, and red ballet slippers. A spotlight was aimed at them, and in single file they would "mount the platform and slowly walk its length, pausing now and then to strike attitudes, to stiffen into statuesque poses, to drop curtsies or to execute some syncopated phrase." The audience would scream at them, applaud, and they might, in turn, lift their hands off their hips and wave back. In Niles's account, one fellow brought down the house. "He was a slim, very graceful figure in a low-cut, almost backless black velvet gown. He had dazzling shoulders and a pink and white face. His eyes were large and dark, the brows dark too, and the lashes heavily beaded with mascara, in startling contrast to the snow white waves of the wig." The emcee gave out prizes, supposedly according to the amount of applause, but in Ford and Tyler's version "he gave them to those he knew no matter how much they pushed and tore. There were half a dozen running around crying I GOT FIRST PRIZE."

The now-gone Savoy Ballroom, around 1940.

Follow Lenox Avenue up to 145th Street and turn left, returning to St. Nicholas Avenue, and then head right three blocks.

16. LUCKY'S RENDEZVOUS • 773 St. Nicholas Avenue
between 148th and 149th Streets

After the Stock Market crashed in 1929 and the Great Depression rolled its gloomy way across the country, the mood of the nation, let alone its economic health, began to shift. The lights went out on lots of parties, and the spirit of liberality faded. Many of the Harlem clubs—especially those catering to

thinning white audiences—closed. But while the flocks of outsiders may have stopped coming, Harlem didn't simply shut
down and close its doors. Indeed, in the middle of the Second
World War, Lucky Roberts opened a nightclub at this address,
where St. Nick's Pub now operates. Roberts was a pianist and
music teacher (he taught George Gershwin and Fats Waller)
who, before becoming a barman, was one of the city's most
successful society musicians and orchestra leaders. His musicians performed for the Vanderbilts, the Astors, the Wana-
makers, and the Whitneys. By the 1940s, when high society
had fallen from its perch a bit, Roberts was ready for something new, and **Lucky's Rendezvous** became exactly that.
Not only did Lucky's new business attract some of the nation's
greatest entertainers; according to a lengthy 1952 *Ebony* magazine article, it also catered to "boisterous bohemians and
smart sophisticates," attracting a clientele "odd as it is fascinating to newcomers." *Ebony*, without being explicit,
explained that female couples found "an atmosphere of friend-
liness instead of the usual hostility," and "male companions
are commonplace." One photo captured **Langston Hughes**
chatting with a friend, while the caption noted that the place
attracted "more intellectuals, artists—and practitioners of
what playwright **Oscar Wilde** called 'the higher philosophy'—than any other comparable club in Manhattan." In
other words, Lucky's was a vestige of old Harlem, of Harlem
Renaissance Harlem, where it was still okay to be gay.

Lucky told the *Ebony* reporter that "all are welcome here
until they prove themselves objectionable," and coyly declared
himself happy whenever "friendships" were formed in his bar.
"All I insist on is that both parties be willing. Affection and
friendship cannot come through pressure. . . . I don't care
what they do when they get home, just so long as they behave
themselves in here." And as the reporter pointed out, same-
sex hand holding and gooey-eyed "mooning" definitely passed
Lucky's standards.

To walk to the last site, follow St. Nicholas up to 155th Street.

17. THE ROCKLAND PALACE • 280 West 155th Street

Like the Savoy, the **Rockland Palace** stands no more—only a parking lot where it once was. But I tell you, more famous than the balls at the Savoy were those thrown each year by the Hamilton Lodge (a division of the Grand United Order of Odd Fellows) up at the Rockland. The ball dated back to the end of the Civil War and was officially called the Masquerade and Civic Ball, but by the 1920s it had been unofficially renamed the Faggots Ball, and no gathering of gay men and lesbians in the city was larger. It was written up on the first or second pages of the local newspapers (often with photos and costume descriptions). Discreet **Langston Hughes** even wrote about the ball as one of Harlem's "spectacles in color," though he claimed to have attended only once, and that as the guest of **A'Lelia Walker.**

Folks came from across the Eastern Seaboard to attend. Eight hundred came to the 1925 party; eight *thousand* showed up in 1937! Women came as men, men as women; they were mostly black and working-class, but according to George Chauncey, plenty of the upper-middle-class and white folks showed up as well. **Ethel Waters** used to go and brag about the fellows who were wearing her outfits. **Harold Jackman** and **Clinton Moore** were frequently noted in the crowds. One year an alderman served as a judge.

It was a full show. In the language of the day, there were "effeminate men, sissies, 'wolves,' 'ferries,' 'faggots,' the third sex, 'ladies of the night,' and male prostitutes," all gathered for "a grand jamboree of dancing, love making, display, rivalry, drinking and advertisement." And the same kind of competition occurred here as at the Savoy. Mind you, one contemporary commented, the posers "would step out in such finery and with such grace and strolls as to put the world's best mannikins to shame." At the same time, he warned, "the results of this contest have caused many a heart to be broken, many a face to be clawed, and many a friendship to end." This was serious business. (If you haven't seen **Jenny Livingston**'s documentary *Paris Is Burning*, about contemporary drag balls and culture, you have to. But when you do, picture the crowds multiplied tenfold.)

When it wasn't hosting parties, the Rockland was also a showplace for our own treasures like **Bessie Smith, Ma**

Rainey, and Ethel Waters. Rainey was a short, stocky, dark-skinned singer with a voice that seemed to come straight from the earth. These days she carries the title of "Mother of the Blues" and is thought to be the first vaudeville performer to make singing the blues part of her act. Like her protégée Smith, Rainey married but was known to have affairs with women. She also sang revealing songs like the "Prove It on Me Blues." Though different lyrics appear in different volumes, they are mostly variations on:

> *Went out last night with a crowd of my friends,*
> *They must've been women, 'cause I don't like no men. . . .*
> *They say I do it, ain't nobody caught me,*
> *They sure got to prove it on me. . . .*

One version finds the singer looking up from a fight to discover "the gal I was with was gone. / Where she went, I don't know, / I mean to follow everywhere she goes." Her record of the song was advertised with a picture of a large black woman who looked like Rainey and was wearing a man's hat, tie, and jacket. She was talking to two entranced flappers while a cop watched in the distance. The accompanying text read: "What's all this? Scandal? Maybe so, but you wouldn't have thought it of 'Ma' Rainey. But look at that cop watching her! What does it all mean?"

Scandal, for Rainey, wasn't exclusive to promotions. In 1925 she was arrested for hosting a lesbian orgy at her home with women from her chorus. (It seems the neighbors called the cops to complain about the noise.) Reports say that women scrambled for their clothes and dashed out the back door; Rainey, however, fell down a staircase. Accused of running an indecent party, she had to spend the night in jail. But this was, and is, a community, and Bessie Smith bailed her out the following morning.

Pushing Back the Beginning:
Into the Battery

If you have made it through all the tours in this book, you've already seen quite a bit. Your sense of how gay liberation officially began at the end of the 1960s has no doubt improved. At the same time, you've gotten to see that those recent years of liberation represent only a fraction of the gay living that has taken place in this city across much of the last century.

The tour that follows stays mostly down in the Battery, the heart of old New York. It is where the city was first constructed—both the Dutch and the British built their forts down here—and where much of its dynamic municipal and financial energy has remained. It has also been the site of an ongoing challenge and reshaping of how men and women should live together. One constant of that has been the pursuit of affection, intimacy, and desire between people of the same sex. Its meaning and reception have varied with the cultures, but for centuries men and men and women and women have sought each other out on this little piece of land and struggled to redefine how men and women must be.

It is here that we can consider what gay living, gay intimacy, has meant in its broadest context in the American past. To do so, this tour includes significant contemporary sites where the importance of gay life was insisted upon, as at the first major ACT UP demonstration as well as the first protest for excluding gays from the military. But the tour also pushes at the edges of "traditional" gay history. While historians note that the word "homosexual" didn't even exist until late in the nineteenth century, there are records of clear sexual activity between men and

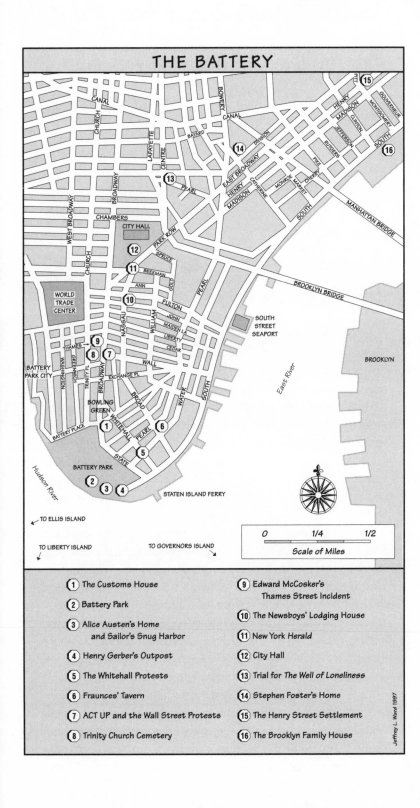

THE BATTERY

1 The Customs House
2 Battery Park
3 Alice Austen's Home and Sailor's Snug Harbor
4 Henry Gerber's Outpost
5 The Whitehall Protests
6 Fraunces' Tavern
7 ACT UP and the Wall Street Protests
8 Trinity Church Cemetery
9 Edward McCosker's Thames Street Incident
10 The Newsboys' Lodging House
11 New York Herald
12 City Hall
13 Trial for *The Well of Loneliness*
14 Stephen Foster's Home
15 The Henry Street Settlement
16 The Brooklyn Family House

Jeffrey L. Ward 1997

men and women and women that date back well before then. Certainly those individuals merit a place in our gay history. At the same time, there are equally clear records of profound intimacy—if not explicit sexuality—between men and men and women and women. This tour suggests that we might include those people in our gay history as well, and begin to think more broadly about the significance of men and women being intimate. To that end, there's a bit of colonial life thrown in here, along with **George Washington** and **Alexander Hamilton.** There's even an encounter with the All-American myth-making master, **Horatio Alger.**

You can take the 1/9 or the 5 train to the end of the line at South Ferry or Bowling Green. Any of these will place you just across Battery Park from the old Customs House, which sits at its northernmost tip.

1. THE CUSTOMS HOUSE (now the National Museum of the American Indian)
corner of Broadway, State Street, and Battery Place

Edward Hyde, Lord Cornbury, may very well be the patron saint of our new gay history. He was named governor of New York just at the start of the eighteenth century, about forty years after Britain took over the area. (If you remember, the place was originally a Dutch colony called New Amsterdam, but the Brits swiped it and renamed it.) Their forts stood here, both the Dutch and the British, where the Beaux-Arts Customs House–turned-museum now rises. Cornbury (we can call him Eddie) arrived in 1702 with good connections—he was a cousin of Queen Anne—but he came at a difficult moment in the colony's history. Tensions between the largely Dutch lower and middle classes and the snooty—and now ruling—British elite were smoldering. As recently as 1688 a German-born militia captain had led a rebellion that ousted the British lieutenant governor, freed various poor debtors from prison, and kicked the wealthy merchants out of public office.

By the time Eddie arrived, the rebellion leaders had been executed, but the smoldering had not died down. Cousin Anne had counseled the new governor to avoid partisanship, but Eddie couldn't resist siding with the elites, who, after all,

*Edward Hyde, Lord Cornbury, captured in one of his swankiest outfits
(and visible in the collection of the New-York Historical Society).*

had more money. Under his watch, everyone who had been a
rebel ally was now removed from office and their legislative
actions largely reversed. Back in power, the English elites
were happy to line Eddie's pockets and oppress the rest,
including those who didn't accept the Anglican Church.

As you can well imagine, none of this boded well for Eddie's
long-term future, and, not surprisingly, his tenure ended after
only six years. But it wasn't *just* his partisan politics that got
Eddie into trouble. (I certainly wouldn't waste your time on
mere colonial politics.) It wasn't even that he wasted the
money he was given, or that he embezzled from the army. It

was that, in addition to all of this, Eddie had a penchant for dressing up in drag. As one historian of the city wrote, "He was loose, careless, extravagant, disreputable; and the most notable thing he did was to dress himself in women's clothes to show how much he looked like Queen Anne, which he frequently did; parading in gaudy attire on the ramparts of the Fort, where the people and the soldiers might see and admire him." A fort rampart, I might remind you, is no nightclub runway. And this isn't even Harlem in the 1920s; this is downtown New York, 1702!

There is an enormous portrait of Eddie, often on display in the New-York Historical Society gallery, which describes him a bit more nastily. (The preceding image is a black-and-white copy; the original, of course, is in color.) The caption engraved on the frame reads: "Among other apish tricks, Lord Cornbury, the half-witted son of Henry Earl of Clarendon, is said to have held his state levees at New York, and received the principal Colonists dressed up in complete female court costume, because, truly, he represented the person of a female sovereign, his cousin German Queen Anne." Sadly, the colonial assemblies of both New York and the Jerseys asked Queen Anne to take Eddie back. Before she acted, he was imprisoned for debt. Fortunately, his father died, making Eddie the new Earl of Clarendon, with enough family fortune to pay off his debts and go home.

I should say that there is nothing to indicate clearly that Eddie was a man-lover: I don't know if his diaries have been scoured, and he did have a wife, whatever that tells you. But as a gender-bending drag queen, well, watch out! Eddie rewrote the script of masculinity. He operated as a powerful political player who was also exploring new ways of being a man, including presenting himself, in clothing, at least, as someone who presumably loved men. He pushed at the very edges of manhood. That, in addition to his great outfits, earns him the position of patron saint. And remember, nearly three hundred years ago a drag queen wasn't just *finally* making it big in Hollywood: honey, she was the governor of all of New York.

Walk around the west side of the building and enter Battery Park, walking down to where the boats leave for the Statue of Liberty.

2. BATTERY PARK

For the moment, I think, it makes sense to sit here in **Battery Park**. See if you can find a clean and comfortable bench . . . perhaps with a view of the Statue of Liberty. If you look just to her right, you can probably make out Ellis Island, not too far in the distance.

Let's get the gossipy stuff out of the way first. Historian **Jonathan Katz** reports that as far back as 1846, according to the *New York Herald*, "revolting and disgraceful acts [were] nightly practiced on the Battery." When **Rudolph Valentino** came to America in 1914, he spent many a night sleeping (at least that I know of) on the benches in this very park. **Noël Coward,** though he didn't sleep here, equally passed many an hour in this park, contemplating his future and whoever else wandered by. And as George Chauncey recently pointed out, the 1930s found these benches filled with youths waiting to meet sailors.

Now, though, I want you to think back further. The exact point where you are sitting hasn't always been here. Indeed, in the last 350 years the width of Manhattan down here has grown by two-thirds, and Battery Park was an early addition. As construction and destruction have occurred—leveling the Dutch fort that used to stand where you just were, or digging the foundation for the World Trade Center—the rubble and soil have been used to widen the island. You can track the expansion by watching the street names. As you move closer to where the water is *today*, you can follow the shifting coastline: Pearl Street (then lined with mother-of-pearl) was followed by Water Street (then at the water's edge), followed by Front Street.

But the action has hardly been limited to the geographic. Try this: Castle Clinton, the roundish brick structure there beside you, which was built as an American fort in the early 1800s, sits on a piece of rock—formerly called Kapsee—that itself used to be an island. Kapsee sat just off the tip of Manhattan and marked the start of the long path that, *thousands* of years ago, connected the tip of Manhattan all the way north to Westchester County. It was a path used by various groups, it seems, to get through the green forests of the island: the Rechgawawanc tribe, which inhabited northern Manhattan;

the Canarsie, who dominated much below 59th Street and over into Brooklyn; the Hackensack, who had a cove in Greenwich Village; and perhaps even an Iroquois or two wandering down from his or her lands upstate.

Historians who have explored the cultures of Native Americans have found that among many of the groups, including the Iroquois, there were long-standing practices of embracing individuals of nontraditional sexualities. Indeed, such people had a unique and identifiable social position, in terms of dress, ritual, and sexual activity. The French coined the term "berdache" to refer to the folks they found in many native tribes who cross-dressed, cross-worked, even cross-spoke—a young man, usually, who became designated a female. The lists of tribes that accepted homosexuals—often in a ritualized way—is large, ranging from the Illinois and Sioux to the Creek, Hopi, and Mohave. One Zuni berdache, named We'Wha, even spent six months in Washington at the end of the nineteenth century visiting with various politicians, including the President, all the while acting as a woman. Many other berdaches, no doubt, passed through here along the Kapsee route.

By the 1620s, with Peter Minuit leading the way, the Dutch had "bought" the island from the Canarsie, and it became the Dutch New Netherlands for nearly forty years. Same-sex intimacies certainly continued, even though the record of it is only a grim one. In the 1600s, officially at least, Holland was not the homo-happy place it is today. Jonathan Katz uncovered a calendar that noted, sadly, the 1646 execution of one **Jan Creoli,** a black man who had had sex with **Manuel Congo,** a ten-year-old boy. Creoli was found guilty of a crime "condemned of God" and was sentenced to be "choked to death and then burnt to ashes." Congo was then carried to the same place, most likely not far from here, tied to a stake with kindling piled around him, and flogged. His punishment, it seems, was intended as a warning. Not fifteen years later a soldier, **Jan Quisthout van der Linde,** was also found guilty of sodomy by the New Netherlands council, for which he was "tied in a sack and cast into the river and drowned until dead." No doubt you can see that river from here. The guilty co-party was an orphan from Amsterdam who was the soldier's indentured servant, **Hendrick Harmensen;** in the court's eyes, Harmensen was an unwilling participant and was therefore sentenced merely to a private whipping and to be sent away.

These are not particularly cheery stories: they are merely the ones for which, because of court and council documents, historians have records. Imaginably, for every Jan or Manuel who got caught, there were ten or a hundred or who knows how many who did not get caught, who wandered along the piers or raced around their homes, laughing and carousing, hundreds of years ago. And probably the same could be said for any decade or any century since.

Walk to the eastern edge of the park, near the Staten Island Ferry building.

3. ALICE AUSTEN'S HOME and SAILORS' SNUG HARBOR
• **Staten Island**

I have two tales of Staten Island to entice you, one of which, a romance, is solidly documented; the other emerges, well, more from speculation. While they're easily enough read from here in the park, the best place to hear them is on the Staten Island ferry. It's one of New York's premier complete attractions, and at fifty cents a pop it's probably the cheapest. If you have an hour, just ride it, over and back. If you have a little more time, you might want to get off and explore.

The first is the story of **Alice Austen,** a woman born in 1866 out on the island. Her father, a Brit, abandoned her and her mother shortly after her birth, so Austen grew up with her mother on her grandparents' beautiful estate, Clear Comfort. (The estate still exists.) At the age of ten she was given her first camera and her uncle taught her to use a darkroom, and Austen quickly became an avid photographer, snapping shots first of her family and home, then of her friends, sailors, and the harbor. Over the course of fifty years, she produced more than seven thousand photographs, spanning from the 1880s until the Great Depression.

Though happily comfortable at the outset, Austen's fortunes grew more tenuous as her family's finances collapsed, especially when the stock market crashed. But she was buoyed in her life by the companionship of **Gertrude Tate,** a woman

Taken in 1891, this early Austen photograph shows Alice and two friends. When Austen saw the photograph some sixty years later, she said, "We look so funny with those mustaches on, I can hardly tell which is which. We did it just for fun. Maybe we were better-looking men than women." Austen is on the left.

she met when she was already in her thirties and with whom she spent the next fifty years of her life.

In 1918, when she was in her forties and Alice her fifties, Gertrude moved into Clear Comfort with her (over the Tate family's objections to her "wrong devotion" to Austen). They lived in shifts, it seems, Alice working in her darkroom into the wee hours (it was next to Gertrude's room), then making Gertrude breakfast and carrying it to her on a tray. To support them, Gertrude taught dance and deportment, and as things got rougher, they sold off family furniture and even tried opening a restaurant. Eventually, though, in 1945, they were foreclosed upon and evicted. They shared an apartment together for a bit, but finally their money was gone and Alice ended up in the poorhouse and Gertrude with relatives.

The year before Alice's death, a historian uncovered first her photos and then her, and tried to get her some money. Success and fame smiled briefly down: several of her photographs were published in places like *Life* magazine, and Alice was interviewed on television and ultimately was able to go into a private nursing home. Nevertheless, she died a pauper. Sadly, Gertrude hardly fared so well, and when she died several years later, her family could not afford to bury her next to Alice, although this was her wish.

Now for something more nebulous: the story of the **Sailors' Snug Harbor** off on Staten Island. Sailors are without question a kind of gay icon. I, for one, am a great fan of Fleet Week, when the city swarms with boys in white uniforms. But sailors have been more than mere icons of gay life; they've also been participants. Certainly there is a long history of wayward sailors in port for the night or the week hooking up with local men. The tradition of intimacy probably runs deeper, though.

This story starts off not far from here back in the early 1800s—1801 to be exact—when one **Robert Richard Randall** is approaching his final days. Randall is quite wealthy, having inherited the fortune of his father—Cap'n Tom, a sailor and privateer. Now to some, the historical record might seem thin: to me, it speaks volumes. Robert is dying, and although he has friends he gives some gifts to, *he has no family to inherit his wealth*. (First clue.) He speaks to his attorney, **Alexander Hamilton** (about whom you'll read more in a moment), who happens to be there *at his bedside*. (Is that where you meet with your attorney, let alone Hamilton? Check two.) Three: when Hamilton asks where his money came from, Randall explains that he inherited it from Dad, who earned it at sea. "He was a seaman, and a good one," he states. "He had money, so he never suffered when he was worn out. But," he adds, perhaps misty-eyed, "all are not like that." And then I picture him taking a big breath, grasping Hamilton's arm, and staring him in the eye as he tells him his final wish and reveals his true love: "I want to make a place for the others. I want it to be a snug harbor for tired sailors." (Jackpot.)

Beats me, kids, if it could be any sweeter or more explicit than that. Explain it away: a man with a fortune who has managed to stay unmarried his whole life—not an easy thing to do back then—no illegitimate children, even—decides that his favorite people are sailors. Yes, of course, this was a charitable gentleman. And certainly it was the wealthy who established many of the finest charities. But at the very least, we have to recognize that this was a man who intimately cared about other men. For my money, I would bet this was hardly the first time Randall made a sailor snug. But regardless of what happened between Randall and various sailors in the years before his death, for this man, being charitable and nurturing meant taking care of men. That is essential. This was a man who, in some way, loved other men.

Randall's will stated that the charity should be set up on twenty-one acres near Washington Square, but his bratty family (cousins, I assume) contested the will for three decades. By then it was clear that Washington Square was too developed and too residential for a sailors' camp. Instead, the trustees bought 131 acres out on Staten Island and built the home for the sailors out there. It opened in 1833 and operated until the 1960s, serving as a place for sailors to rest and recreate (they were often only in their thirties and forties) and worry about their souls. There were two thousand of them at times, living off in their little village—certainly somebody's idea of paradise. While parts of the complex have been lost, what remains was granted landmark status not so long ago: you can visit it and decide for yourself.

Shift your gaze to the island to the left of the Statue of Liberty, Governor's Island.

4. HENRY GERBER'S OUTPOST • Governor's Island

Born in 1892, **Henry Gerber** came to this country from Bavaria when he was twenty-one. He settled in Chicago, but the following year he enlisted to fight in the First World War and eventually was returned to his home country as part of the

American occupying force from 1920 to 1923. While there he discovered Germany's ongoing homosexual-emancipation movement. When he came back to the States, he decided to try to do the same work here, and the following year he formed the Society for Human Rights in Chicago.

Seven men sat on the society's board. The charter made no mention of homosexuals, stating simply that the society strove to "promote and to protect the interests of people who by reasons of mental and physical abnormalities are abused and hindered in the legal pursuit of happiness which is guaranteed them by the Declaration of Independence." Cloaked within so broad a declaration, however, is the first known effort in this country to recognize gay rights or organize for gay liberation. Gerber et al. even published two issues of a magazine called *Friendship and Freedom.*

Within a year, however, one member—who the others did not know was married—was seen having sex with a man by the fellow's wife. Soon enough, Gerber and two other co-founders were arrested and written up in the paper under the headline "Strange Sex Cult Exposed." The case was dismissed since the police had no warrant for the arrests. But the publicity cost Gerber his job, and, as he later wrote, "that definitely meant the end of the Society for Human Rights."

Out of work, Gerber eventually re-enlisted, and he ended up serving for much of the 1930s right ahead of you on Governor's Island. A round red-brick fort, which was the East Battery, an early American defense point, now houses the U.S. Coast Guard. While stationed there, Gerber wrote frequent essays criticizing novels and medical literature about homosexuality. Some of his writing appeared in a mimeographed journal (for which he was the circulation manager) called *Chanticleer.* He dismissed *The Well of Loneliness* as "anti-homosexual propaganda" and blasted one Dr. W. Beran Wolfe's theories about homosexuality and neurosis. "After all," he wrote, "it is highly futile for Dr. Wolfe to worry about neurotic homosexuals when the world itself, led and ruled by the strong heterosexual 'normal' men, is in such chaotic condition, and knows not where to turn. It is quite possible that if called upon, the homosexuals in this country would put up the money to send Dr. Wolfe to Washington to examine these great big 'normal' men, who guide the destinies of millions, to find their 'neurosis' and to cure it."

In addition, Gerber published another mimeographed newsletter, called *Contacts*, for people who were looking for pen pals. He ran his own ad there which described him as "an avowed atheist" who was "immune to the alleged charms of the female sex, but do not 'hate' women; consider them necessary in the scheme of things." He also portrayed himself as "truly civilized and self-sufficient, but always welcome people of like mind . . . who can share the simple pleasures of discussion, music and travel." Gerber died in Washington, D.C., in 1972 in a military home, having lived long enough to see gay liberation finally begin to work its way across this country.

Time to leave the park. Cross under the ferry terminal ramp and walk diagonally across the square to the corner of Water and Whitehall.

5. THE WHITEHALL PROTESTS • 39 Whitehall Street
between Pearl and Water Streets

Over the last fifty years, governmental anxiety about same-sex intimacy has become such a staple of our nation's political culture that we almost expect the "controversy" that surrounds any policy discussion about lesbians and gay men. Certainly the recent struggles over gays in the military and same-sex marriages indicate that the likelihood of official outrage has hardly diminished. What those conflicts also demonstrate, however, is that hostile governmental actions have more and more been met with stronger and louder gay community reactions. And that change has been a long time coming. In fact, the first public battle in the fight over the military occurred here well over thirty years ago, where the army used to maintain a recruitment center (before the New York Health & Racquet Club took over), and where **Randy Wicker** decided to resist.

Randy Wicker was not his given name; that was Charles Hayden Jr. But when Charles Senior understood what Charles Junior was becoming, he asked that he use a different name. And a new name was only the first of many things he took on himself. Wicker arrived in New York as a young man in 1958 and quickly became his own one-man gay liberation band. He signed up with the Mattachine Society and began going around to bars leafleting for people to come to Mattachine meetings. The response he received was underwhelming, and what's more, Wicker felt increasingly disappointed with the conservative tone at Mattachine. Working in the world of advertising and magazines, he quickly started his own organization, the Homosexual League of New York, and began to use it to obtain media coverage on homosexuality. His first major success came in 1962 on New York's radio station WBAI. He spoke on a program there as the first self-identified gay person to speak on the radio. He also organized a two-hour radio program with eight gay men speaking for and about themselves.

And then in 1964, at this site, Wicker organized the first-ever gay picket in front of what was then the Whitehall Military Induction Center to protest the army's more than twenty years of actively seeking out and discharging gay men and women. Wicker's organizing efforts brought together a picket line of seven, including Wicker's lover, **Peter,** the children's book writer **Nancy Garden,** and **Craig Rodwell,** the eventual founder of the Oscar Wilde Memorial Bookshop. The protest was just the kind of thing Mattachine people hated. Rodwell, who was fairly active in Mattachine at the time, was told, "You can't do that! Mattachine will lose its incorporation. Our charter forbids any kind of political activity—you'll ruin us if you do anything militant like that!" What's more, as historian **Martin Duberman** has pointed out, a gay rights draft-board protest in 1964 was a dangerous undertaking. "There seemed a fair chance that they would be summarily arrested, carted off to jail and possibly beaten."

Instead, they merely picketed and tried to hand out leaflets. It was a Saturday and it was rainy and the streets were fairly empty. There was a sergeant stationed outside the entrance, but he merely shot them occasional dirty looks. And when the day was over, the seven were ecstatic. As Duberman later wrote, "They had done something different and daring, made a beginning. And they believed bigger and better actions would soon follow." And they did. By the end of the following year, there had been protests in front of Independence Hall in

Philadelphia, the United Nations Building, and the White House. Nevertheless, the struggle to welcome gay men and women into the military remains incomplete today.

Turn right on Pearl Street and follow it east two small blocks.

6. FRAUNCES' TAVERN • 54 Pearl Street
at Broad Street

Back in the late 1700s, the Queen's Head Tavern was run for twenty-three years by a man named Fraunces, Samuel Fraunces. It was a place destined for history and historic gatherings: the founding of the New York Chamber of Commerce, meetings of the Sons of Liberty, plottings for New York's own little Tea Party. And when New York was the nation's capital, in the 1790s, the War, Treasury, and Foreign Affairs Departments all took their turns being housed here.

Much of that history can be pursued in the museum inside. Especially in light of the Whitehall protests, though, I want to tell you instead about the 1783 farewell that George Washington gave to his troops at the end of the Revolutionary battles. Washington had been extremely close to his soldiers, and he referred to the closest coterie of young men as his "family." He and Martha had no children of their own, by the way, only hers from a previous marriage.

On a drizzly December afternoon, the week after the Evacuation, forty-four of Washington's great military leaders, as well as the governor of New York, gathered in the tavern for what was to be a farewell celebration. Sentiment ran heavy that day, however, and I defer to Colonel Benjamin Tallmadge, who was in attendance, to fill you in:

> When his Excellency entered the room his emotion, too strong to be concealed, seemed to be reciprocated by every officer present. After partaking of a slight refreshment in almost breathless silence, the General filled his glass with wine, and turning to the officers, said: "With a heart full of love and gratitude I now take leave of you. I most devoutly wish that your latter days may be as prosperous and happy as your former ones

Fraunces' Tavern (as reconstructed) today, where Washington bade farewell to his "family."

have been glorious and honorable." After the officers had taken a glass of wine, the General added: "I cannot come to each of you, but shall feel obliged if each of you will come and take me by the hand." [He was nothing if not discreet.] General Knox, being nearest to him, turned to the Commander-in-Chief, who, suffused in tears, was incapable of utterance, but grasped his hand, when they embraced each other in silence. In the same affectionate manner every officer in the room marched up to, kissed, and parted with his General-in-Chief. Such a scene of sorrow and weeping I had never before witnessed, and hope I may never be called upon to witness again. Not a word was uttered to break the silence that prevailed, or to interrupt the tenderness.

And while it seemingly broke his heart to do it, according to one calculation the Father of Our Country that day wept over and kissed fourteen generals, New York's Governor Clinton, a number of colonels and majors, and a young lieutenant. From here, he walked down to the wharf and shipped off to Martha and Mount Vernon.

What does it mean? Does it mean that George Washington was gay or somehow *identified* as homosexual? Probably not. Does it mean that if you passed him on the street in a snug pair of colonial britches he might give you the eye? Well, now, that's a whole different story. At the very least, it means he loved the young men he surrounded himself with: they were his intimates and they sustained him deeply. The controversy surrounding gays in the military is a direct result of the nation's failure to remember this piece of our past.

But Washington's life points to another layer of complexity. It suggests that being a married man (not to mention a war hero and the President), on the one hand, and being intimate—physically and emotionally—with men, on the other, have not always been the contradictory things we treat them as today. Washington probably loved both his wife and his men, even if in different ways. But rather than simply ticking him off as bisexual, we might do better to reconsider the narrow categories we have for understanding and describing sexuality and intimacy. Certainly a life like Washington's seems to exceed their capacity. Such an effort would not only radically alter our considerations of what a gay past might have been like, it might also expand our expectations of a gay future as well.

Follow Broad Street up several blocks to Wall Street and turn left. When you do, the Stock Exchange will be on your left and Federal Hall, where Washington was inaugurated as President, will be on your right.

7. ACT UP and the WALL STREET PROTEST
- **Wall Street and Broadway**

No contemporary situation has more painfully demonstrated the failure of the nation to remember its essential gay past than the poorly fought battle against AIDS—waged for so long as if it really didn't matter, as if "those people" were not part of the country's identity. **ACT UP,** the **AIDS Coalition to Unleash Power,** was founded out of that pain, and for those who remember its formation, the memory is still visceral.

Nora Ephron, the humorist and novelist, had been scheduled for a usual writer's talk at the Lesbian and Gay Community Center one Tuesday night in March 1987, but she canceled. The organizers replaced her with another writer—**Larry Kramer.** But as **Avram Finkelstein,** who attended that meeting, recalled, Kramer hardly spoke about writing that night. His topic was AIDS, and he made two-thirds of the room stand up and then, turning to those still seated, declared, "For the rest of you, everyone on this side will be dead." You can imagine the sensation. "What are we going to do?" he demanded. "People are dying! We should be storming the Bastille!" The group agreed to meet again that coming Thursday and they decided that each person would invite ten other people. On Thursday, a list of demands about experimental drugs and congressional oversight was prepared and proposals were made for action: fill the sky with black balloons, blockade the Midtown Tunnel, make the Gay Pride Parade into the Gay Rage Parade. At the end of the night, the top three proposals focused on the coming March on Washington, a demonstration at the Supreme Court, and an action on Wall Street. ACT UP had begun.

The Wall Street demonstration occurred first, on March 24, only two weeks after Kramer's call to arms. Protesters, Finkelstein among them, began coming to this corner at 6:15 in the morning in order to block traffic. Officially, the action ran from 7:00 to 9:30, and several hundred people participated, sitting in the intersection and stopping traffic. To Finkelstein, the crowd felt small, insignificant in size. "But," he remembered, "almost everyone stopped and looked at the demonstration. It really interrupted business as usual." Seated in the center of the United States financial community, ACT UP wanted attention focused on the pharmaceutical companies, especially Burroughs Wellcome, the manufacturer of AZT, and their extraordinary profiteering. They also hung Frank Young, the Food and Drug Administration commissioner, in effigy from a lamppost.

Finkelstein, who was also central to the development of the "Silence = Death" pink triangle icon, remembered thinking that "people might be resentful, that it was a strategy that might backfire. Instead, people seemed startled, sympathetic, not hostile." And for the protesters, like Finkelstein, "there was a tremendous sense of conviction. There was a real resonant sense of connection that I'd never experienced before." This was not simple demonstration theatrics: "people were truly dying."

Seventeen people were arrested that day, but following the demonstration the FDA announced that it would shorten the drug-approval process by two years. By the end of their first year, ACT UP had thousands of members in New York and more than seventy chapters across the country and the world. There were a slew of committees: actions, media, issues, outreach, zaps, prisons, and fund-raising. And on March 24, 1988, ACT UP returned here. More than one hundred activists were arrested, but there was major media coverage, and somehow the notion and necessity of AIDS activism gained a certain credibility. The next year, after a series of demonstrations that included an effort to shut down the Food and Drug Administration in Washington, ACT UP took the protest up the street to City Hall, where more than three thousand protesters converged; and that September, seven ACT UP members went into the New York Stock Exchange itself to disrupt trading. Outraged at the still-high price of AZT and the high profits of Burroughs Wellcome, they chained themselves to the VIP balcony. When the opening bell rang, they drowned out its sound with foghorns and unfurled a banner above the floor demanding "Sell Wellcome!" Four days later, Burroughs Wellcome lowered the price of AZT by 20 percent.

The crisis that is AIDS horrifyingly—shockingly—continues. Despite recent hope-inspiring treatment developments, the rates of infection, even among the seemingly well-informed gay community, demand our attention and action. No one has led that cause and inspired that fight any more powerfully than ACT UP.

Turn around and step into the cemetery.

8. Trinity Church Cemetery
at the intersection of Wall Street and Broadway

Stepping into a cemetery after reading about ACT UP may feel all too appropriate, but this cemetery carries us back a couple of centuries before AIDS. Head for the tall pyramid-like stone on the southern edge and reflect on the name **Alexander Hamilton.** Now there's a name out of history class: Hamilton, a young revolutionary who fought beside **George Washington,** first on the battlefield and then in creating the new national government. Born in the West Indian colony of Nevis, in 1757, he lived much of his early life with various relatives who eventually sent him off to New York to be educated, studying at what is now Columbia College. But as the Revolution loomed on the horizon, education ceased, and Hamilton began speaking out in support of the rebellion and writing with vigor. He joined Washington in fighting for Long Island and in fortifying Harlem, and Washington made him his secretary and aide-de-camp. He also argued with the intellectuals in favor of democratic representative government, and after the war he lobbied for a stronger federal government. He served briefly in the Continental Congress and later in the New York State legislature. He wrote fast and furious on behalf of the Constitution and later worked out the financing of the new nation as the secretary of the treasury. He also became a popular businessman's lawyer and kept an office at 58 Wall Street.

Enough résumé! Hamilton also had reddish hair and deep blue eyes, and though he stood only five feet seven, he was full of quick energy. (Hey, I hear Tom Cruise is five-seven.) Hamilton additionally lived at a time when men were perhaps more expressive, emotional, and passionate with each other than they are today. Hamilton's passions apparently exceeded the norm, though, most of all for another revolutionary fighter, **John Laurens.** Laurens was born in 1754 to a wealthy South Carolina family and sent off to be schooled in England and Switzerland. There he married, but three months into his marriage, he came back across the ocean to fight in the Revolution. He too became an aide to Washington, part of the close male circle surrounding the general that he referred to as his "family," and at one point he fought a duel to defend Washington's honor from

Alexander Hamilton's grave at Trinity Church.

"constant personal abuse." Laurens was elected to the South Carolina assembly but left his post to fight off a British invasion; he did not succeed and was taken prisoner.

The exact extent of Hamilton and Laurens's relationship is hard to know. One historian has referred to it as a "romantic friendship," a term that has almost exclusively been used to describe women's intimacy. It suggests that they cared deeply about each other, and were intimate, but not necessarily physically so. What remains from between these men is a series of passionate letters written during the Revolutionary years. And while they offer no unquestionable revelations about bedtime activities, they do speak of true romantic love, of a loving relationship.

By 1779, when Laurens left the assembly to take up the defense of South Carolina, Hamilton was twenty-two and Laurens twenty-five. Hamilton wrote to him at that moment that he wished it was in his power to "convince you that I love you. I shall only tell you that 'till you bade us Adieu, I hardly knew the value you had taught my heart to set upon you." Hamilton then wrote a long, rambunctious passage suggesting that Laurens hunt him up a wife in South Carolina, especially one with a large fortune. He further prompted that Laurens might take out an ad in the papers to do so: "To excite their emulation," he noted, "it will be necessary for you to give an account of the lover—his *size*, make, quality of mind and *body*, achievements, expectations, fortune, &c. In drawing my picture, you will no doubt be civil to your friend; mind you do justice to the length of my nose and don't forget that I—" The original letter, not surprisingly, has been mutilated precisely at that point, though the mind needn't wander too far to imagine what came next. (What were you guessing?) Historian Jonathan Katz has suggested that the mutilation is the product of an "editorial" decision by a Hamilton descendant who deleted this whole section in the publication of Hamilton's letters. Regardless, in the next paragraph Hamilton recants his request, saying "I have plagues enough without desiring to add to the number that *greatest of all*"—i.e., a wife.

Once Laurens was taken captive, Hamilton lobbied hard for him to be exchanged for a British prisoner, but it seems Washington and the others objected. "I am the only one in the family," he wrote, "who think you can be exchanged with any propriety, on the score of your relation to the Commander in Chief. We all love you sincerely; but I have more of the infirmities of human nature, than the others, and suspect my self of being byassed [biased] by my partiality for you."

A few months later, mind you, Hamilton did get engaged to be married—plainly, in those years one thing didn't necessarily rule out the other. As Hamilton wrote his friend, "In spite of Schuyler's [his fiancée's] black eyes, I have still a part for the public and another for you; so your impatience to have me married is misplaced; a strange cure by the way, as if after matrimony I was to be less devoted than I am now." Sadly, though, the fun of balancing those public and private selves was never played out. When Laurens was twenty-eight, he was shot down in a final skirmish with the British. Several years, political intrigues, and scandals later, Hamilton was also gunned down, killed in his infamous duel with Aaron Burr. (Hamilton fired into the air, Burr directly at Hamilton.) He lies buried here.

Walk back out of the cemetery, turn left on Broadway, and then make a quick left on Thames Street.

9. EDWARD MCCOSKER'S THAMES STREET INCIDENT
somewhere on Thames between Broadway and Church

If you don't recognize the name of **Edward McCosker,** don't worry: you're off the hook. Here's the story. About midnight one Valentine's Day, Thomas Carey was standing around the block on Cedar Street taking a whiz. McCosker, who was a cop, came over to take a gander and, it seems, in some way or another, convinced Carey to walk around the block with him toward Thames and Church Street, near where you are now.

While McCosker later denied it, Carey said that once there, McCosker "took hold" of him "by the privates and at the same time requested" that Carey "feel his privates." Carey said he got angry, called McCosker names, including "pretty policeman" or words to that effect, and a shouting match ensued. Carey challenged McCosker to fight him without his club, and McCosker threatened to take him down to the station house. Neither happened. Two other police officers intervened, the men were separated, and Carey was sent home. A few days later, though, administrative charges were leveled against McCosker, with the additional charge that he had groped an unsuspecting fellow on the corner of Washington and Rector Streets the previous month. It was the mayor's call, and the mayor decided that McCosker should be dismissed from the force. He was.

The year was 1846.

Head back out of Thames Street, crossing Broadway and continuing on Cedar Street to Nassau. Turn left.

10. The Newsboys' Lodging House
   • **Southwest corner of Fulton and Nassau Streets**

Brace yourself. What we're about to discuss here is big, as in "a **Horatio Alger** story," as in "a rags-to-riches story," as in one of the centerpieces of American mythology. According to a couple of literati, "Alger is to America what Homer was to the Greeks." This is Americana in the highest. Got the picture?

Okay, here we go. Horatio Alger was a writer, true. He wrote a series of stories about young fellows—street urchins—doing well for themselves, pulling themselves up by their bootstraps with the help of good fortune: also true. But before that, Alger, who was born on Friday the thirteenth of January, 1832, was a man at sea with his life, a man who wanted to be a writer but struggled to become a minister, like his father, and then buckled (or unbuckled, as the case may be) before his love of young men.

In 1859 Alger met presumably his first great love, a young Bostonian named **Joseph Dean,** who lived with his mother and sister. Dean was sixteen when they met, Alger nearly twenty-eight. In the fall of 1862, Dean suited up in the Massachusetts military to fight in the Civil War, and Alger wrote a poem called "He Has Gone, and I Have Sent Him." It was written, it would seem, from a woman's perspective, but speaks much more for Alger, with passages like:

> *He has gone, and I have sent him!*
>   *Could I keep him at my side*
> *While the brave old ship that bears us*
>   *Plunges in the perilous tide?*
>
> *Nay, I blush but at the question.*

Things did not pick up for Alger; his writing was hardly brilliant. (It's a telling poem, not a great one.) And so, at the end of 1864, he took a position as minister of the First Unitarian Church in Brewster, Massachusetts. His fortunes did not improve. Within a year and a half, rumors of "evil deeds" began to circulate. One congregant alleged that he had committed some "unnatural crime" with a boy, whose poor sister sat "waiting in the carriage, in the cold, [during] this diabolical transaction." A committee of three church members was formed to investigate. Their report stated, "We learn from John Clark and Thomas S. Crocker that Horatio Alger Jr. has been practicing on them at different times deeds that are too revolting to relate." The committee confronted Alger, and within twenty-four hours he left town. Eager for Alger never to work again, the Brewster church dispatched a statement to the American Unitarian Association headquarters, charging Alger with "the abominable and revolting crime of unnatural familiarity with boys."

Alger's ministerial career, needless to say, was finished. He went home to his family in Natick, Massachusetts, and then on to New York, to make a determined effort to become a writer; some would claim he also tried to expiate his sins. Whether or not he succeeded at the latter, he maintained a strong interest in street boys and the homeless youths who roamed the city. He visited them at the YMCA and the poor-houses. His sister once commented that "nothing delighted him more than to get a lot of boys between the ages of 12 and 16 years in the room with him, and while they were cutting up and playing about he would sit down and write letters or a paragraph of a story."

The strongest ties that Alger developed were to the **Newsboys' Lodging House** on the top floor of this building. He was rather a regular here. The Newsboys' was founded by Charles Loring Brace, a Unitarian minister himself, and served as a "street boys' hotel." Alger wrote articles about the Lodging House, urging readers to donate books and money. "How cheap is virtue; how costly is crime," he wrote. "For one a little money and care discreetly bestowed at the outset; for the other untold suffering, and losses, and expenses for courts and jails, and a ruined man at the end."

And of course, Alger wrote both for and about his boys in stories that were first serialized in the press, then published in book form. Most famously, he told the tale that became *Ragged Dick, or Street Life in New York*, the most celebrated of his street urchins turned hero and success. Despite the recollection of these stories as tales of self-reliance, more often than not the route from rags to riches was cleared by some caring older man. Calling them tales of self-made men erases that intimacy. Now, far be it from me to praise a pedophile. More striking, though, is the nation's wholehearted yet whitewashed embrace of Alger. For beneath a layer or two of the original American myth of success lie two undiscussed narratives: that of older men aiding their younger intimates, and that of Alger basking in the love of his boys.

Wander up Nassau slowly two blocks to Beekman Street, and turn left onto Park Row.

11. The *New York Herald*
  • **the northeast corner of Beekman and Park Row**

This neck of the woods, along Nassau Street and Park Row, was for much of the nineteenth century, Newspaper Central. It was a stone's throw from City Hall and became a journalist's haven. The *New York Times* built three buildings down here, and the Associated Press was birthed in the area. **Walt Whitman** spent much of his life shuttling between here and Brooklyn, working variously for at least eight papers. Mind you, in 1893 the city had nineteen daily papers plus dozens of foreign journals.

A curious tidbit, though: In April of 1905, the *New York Herald*, whose offices stood not far from this intersection, ran two ads, later clipped by a German anthropologist. He recognized them as early gay personals; they're not exactly 550-BOYS material, but they're intriguing nonetheless.

"SIR—" said the first. "Would you appreciate faithful, genteel companionship: refined, trustworthy gentleman. Address CONVERSATION, 270 Herald."

The second read: "FRIENDSHIP CLUB: CORRESPONDENCE EVERYWHERE: PARTICULARS FREE. BOX 24. CLEVELAND, OHIO."

Ah, yes, the old friendship club. Card-carrying member myself.

Cross Park Row to the City Hall side.

12. City Hall • **Park Row and Broadway**

Two City Hall protests, among many, to recall: The more recent brought ACT UP here with three thousand protesters in March 1989. At the time it was the largest AIDS demonstration in the world. Their goal had been to take over City Hall, but they failed; instead, the crowd they gathered all but blockaded the Brooklyn Bridge. Two hundred were arrested, but within two months then-mayor Ed Koch had fashioned a new city policy for housing people with AIDS.

Back in the early 1970s, though, the Gay Activists Alliance made City Hall a regular part of their stomping grounds. In an early City Hall zap (as they called their actions), sixty or seventy GAA members came down here to insist that the city council majority leader introduce a gay rights bill to the council. Not only was he unwilling, he wouldn't meet GAA; so they came to the steps of City Hall to demand it. About a dozen activists went inside, some chaining themselves to desks. Another fifty stayed outside, picketing, not making a move to enter the building. Nevertheless, the police tried to disperse them, and suddenly people were running everywhere. GAA president **Jim Owles** and his lover, **Arnie Kantrowitz,** sat on the top step, "only to have our grips ripped forcibly from the banister by unyielding policemen's hands," Kantrowitz recalled. The men were flung to the bottom of the steps. Kantrowitz ran, chased by a mounted policeman until he hid behind a parked car. Owles charged back up the steps and was caught and arrested. All told, nine people were arrested, and it would be another decade before the city would pass any gay rights legislation.

Walk north along Centre Street to Foley Square at Pearl Street. Cross the boulevard to the front of the Foley Court House.

13. TRIAL FOR *THE WELL OF LONELINESS*
  • **the northeast corner of Pearl and Centre Streets**

Radclyffe Hall's *The Well of Loneliness* was published in England in 1928, one of the first English-language novels by a lesbian to speak seriously about lesbian life; it gained quick notoriety when it was banned over the protests of figures like George Bernard Shaw and H. G. Wells. Alfred Knopf, who published many of the Harlem Renaissance writers, obtained the rights to publish it in the States and actually had it typeset.

After legal counseling, however, Knopf decided not to go forward. Instead, Donald Friede of Covici-Friede published it in December 1928.

Within a month, over twenty thousand copies were sold, but in mid-January, hundreds more were impounded and the publisher arraigned on obscenity charges. The prosecutor objected to no particular scene in the novel, but rather to its overall concept. Before the court could try the publisher, a judge first read the novel and officially deemed it obscene. The judge, Hyman Bushel, did not dispute that the book had "literary merit." Nevertheless, his opinion continued, "the unnatural and depraved relationships portrayed are sought to be idealized and extolled. The characters in the book who indulge in these vices are described in attractive terms, and it is maintained throughout that they be accepted on the same plane as persons normally constituted, and that their perverse and inverted love is as worthy as the affection between normal beings and should be considered just as sacred by society." If the lesbians had been held up to shame or seemed apologetic, he clearly might have approved of the work. Instead, he determined that the book "is calculated to deprave and corrupt minds open to its immoral influences and who might come in contact with it." The book was obscene, he insisted, and Friede had been charged rightly.

Friede, though, took the case further, and it promptly arrived at the Court of Special Sessions. (The building, which stood on Centre Street up a block, has been demolished, but the courthouse here gives you some of the flavor.) There a panel of three judges disagreed with Bushel, and while agreeing that the novel dealt with "a delicate social problem," they decreed that it was not in violation of the law. The charges were dropped. And *The Well of Loneliness*, of which Henry Gerber was so critical, went on into the world.

Follow Centre Street up to Pearl, head right to Park Row, and then left until Park Row meets Bowery.

14. STEPHEN FOSTER'S HOME • 15 Bowery
now Confucius Plaza, between Pell and Division Streets

Right now you stand at the bottom of the Bowery. (It travels north, past the domed building on the left.) There's more about the neighborhood in the East Village tour, but suffice it to say that a century or so ago the Bowery was *it*. It wasn't fancy or elegant: it wasn't about that. No, it was about getting down and dirty and racy in a way only a nineteenth-century New Yorker could. Even Jimmy Durante, who started his career playing piano well after the Bowery's prime, wrote that "the first place I worked in was a Bowery joint run for the boys with five finger-marks on the hip. You know, the la-de-la lads who are that way about each other." Durante was only fourteen, and he said he had never heard that there were such things as "mixed-singles champions. Of course, they looked and sounded funny to me, but you learn to keep your opinions to yourself on the Bowery if you don't want to run into trouble. After all, I was hired to play the piano, and not to try to find out what the dump was doing."

One fellow who came to live (and die) on the Bowery back in its heyday was **Stephen Foster.** If you're into American musical lore, you know his name; if not, you probably only know his songs: songs like "Oh! Susanna," "Camptown Races," and "Jeanie with the Light Brown Hair." Destined to be an American legend, Foster was born in Pittsburgh on July 4, 1826—the same day that both Thomas Jefferson and John Adams died—into a wealthy and seriously American family (Grandpa fought in the Revolution, Dad in the War of 1812). Young Stephen's gift was music: he could pluck out a melody on the guitar by the time he was two (so they say) and could play the flute at the age of seven with no instruction—a regular child prodigy. But his family wanted an earner instead, and so they sent him off to Cincinnati to keep his brother's books, an endeavor he didn't enjoy. At age twenty-four he also married, which seems to have made him no happier. The family eventually realized that publishing his songs could prove profitable, and so he was allowed to invest himself more fully in that—although he had no copyright protection on the more than two hundred poems and melodies he wrote, so the income was far less than it could have been.

Regardless, at age thirty-four Stephen gave up on wife and family and business, and he and **George Cooper** (scribe of "Sweet Genevieve") decided to head off to New York City together. They came to the Bowery, to be exact, and Foster took a room in a building long since gone, at number 15. Once here, he wrote prolifically, one year putting out forty-eight songs. Eleanor Early, a student of New York lore, described Foster as "a handsome man with dark unhappy eyes and a weak, sweet mouth. He wore a flowing black tie which was then the mark of a poet, and tragedy became him as mourning became Electra. He was drinking heavily, and if people had heard then of mother fixations, they might have remarked upon his new songs, 'Oh, Tell Me of My Mother' and 'Farewell, Mother Dear, Farewell, Sweet Mother.' "

Whom, besides Cooper, Foster was fixated on, I do not know. But one day when Cooper came here to fetch his friend from his room, he found Foster naked on the floor, unconscious in a pool of blood: according to the story, true or not, he had fallen and cut his throat on a crockery bowl. Cooper took him to Bellevue Hospital, where a doctor stitched him up with ordinary thread and sent him home; after crying for three days, Foster died. Cooper, hardly in the money, bought a simple coffin to send him back to his family in Pittsburgh. But when the railroad officials found out that the coffin was Foster's, they simply refused to accept Cooper's money. Instead they ordered a special car and covered the coffin with roses. By the time the train reached Pittsburgh, a brass band was out at the station playing "Swanee River," one of Foster's songs. And when the coffin was lifted out onto the platform, the band played another:

> *Beautiful dreamer, wake unto me,*
> *Starlight and dewdrop are waiting for thee.*
> *Sounds of the rude world heard in the day,*
> *Lulled by the moonlight have all passed away.*

Cross Division onto Catherine Street, turn left on Henry, and keep walking till you reach Montgomery.

15. THE HENRY STREET SETTLEMENT • 265 Henry Street
at Montgomery Street

Lillian Wald was born in Cincinnati and grew up in Rochester in the years following the Civil War. Her education, which consisted largely of training for motherhood and marriage, left her dissatisfied. Rochester, though, was a center of American feminism: the National Woman Suffrage Association met there, and **Susan B. Anthony** was tried there for attempting to vote. As a young woman, Wald met Anthony, along with abolitionist leader Frederick Douglass. She also discovered nursing, a new career at the time, populated by a community of women activists fighting to raise nurses from the status of maids to that of professionals.

Early in the 1890s, Wald heard about an immigrant school on the Lower East Side—a largely immigrant and poor neighborhood—and asked to teach a course there in home nursing. When one student fell ill, the student's child came and asked Wald to visit her. "That morning's experience," she later wrote, "was my baptism of fire. That day I left the laboratory and the college. What I had seen had shown me where my path lay." In the fall of 1893 Wald and friend Mary Brewster moved to the Lower East Side, and settled in this building. Their idea was that charity should not be a matter of rich or middle-class women merely visiting poor neighborhoods. Instead, they tried to live among the poor families, working with them and for them. Wald, who was practical-minded (and had an old girls' network that included working women, settlement workers, labor organizers, and revolutionaries), came to see the task as one of reshaping attitudes and publicizing the life and experience of the poor.

The world that Wald created—and that was created at similar settlement houses across the country—was, as even the most conservative historians note, distinctly "a women's world." Comparable to Washington's "family," the settlement house was populated by women who lived and worked and played hard together. As one scholar put it, Wald "could say about many women, as she did about Mrs. **Belle Moskowitz,** that they were 'more than friends.' " (**Eleanor Roosevelt,** you'll be interested to know, worked in a Lower East Side settlement house before getting married.) This was a place where women loved women and, even leaving sexual activity aside, women's primary commitments were to each other. As **Mabel Kittredge,** a resident of Henry Street early on, wrote, "I am getting altogether too close to you—Lady Wald—or is it your life and all those doors that you have pushed open for me— half open—dear—just half open—and then I come up here and grow hungry for more."

Turn left on Montgomery and walk the last few blocks to the river. If there's an open gate ahead of you, walk right to the water's edge; if not, head right on South Street two blocks to Jefferson, where the view will open up.

16. THE BROOKLYN FAMILY HOUSE

seen from the corner of South Street and Montgomery or Jefferson Street

If you actually want to walk to Brooklyn, you can easily stroll back down to the Brooklyn Bridge and walk across. From here, though, you can have a view.

It would be silly to think that we can take care of Brooklyn in a paragraph or two. (Although far be it from me not to try something just because it's silly.) The gay life of Brooklyn— from **Walt Whitman**'s daily ferry rides across this murky river to the large lesbian community that's grown up there in more recent years—is itself enormous. But I do want you to hear a little bit about a house that used to stand along what is now the edge of the Brooklyn Bridge (that's the second bridge you see looking downtown, toward the harbor).

Seven Middagh Street. The house, which you can see in this photograph, was flattened some years back to make way for a new on-ramp to the Brooklyn–Queens Expressway, but it stood steps from the river docks. It was a group home that must have sparkled with literary life as well as hung heavy with poetic malaise. Officially its tenants included poet **W. H. Auden,** novelists **Jane** and **Paul Bowles,** writer **Thomas Mann**'s son **Golo,** and stage designer Oliver Smith. Once writer **Carson McCullers** wised up and left her husband—and the Bowleses left the house—she joined up. The fabulous Gypsy Rose Lee found them a cook, and the range of visitors, long-term and short-, went from author **Christopher Isherwood,** to composer **Benjamin Britten** and his lover, the singer **Peter Pears,** composers **Aaron Copland** and **Leonard Bernstein,** and writers **Anaïs Nin** and Richard Wright. It was a place where gay community, and even more, gay family, were fashioned.

Each of the people who lived in the house is worth a full biography, and many of them show up elsewhere in this slim volume. But to try two more: the Bowleses, Jane and Paul, two writers who married despite the fact that their own sexual proclivities were otherwise and for whom making a family was purely a deliberate act of will. Born in 1917, Jane had been partially crippled by bad knee surgery when she was a teen and called herself "Crippie, the Kike Dyke." One of her biographers described her as possessing "a mystique of sexual promiscuity" that far exceeded the reality. "The power of her personality captured and heightened other people's hidden fantasies. . . . Almost any woman she knew and a great many she did not know were identified in terms of this mystique as one of her lovers."

Writing was a struggle for Jane. When she was nineteen, she wrote a friend, "I get nauseous at the thought of putting a pen to paper—for any purpose, literary or otherwise," and added, "This incapacity of mine to 'act' is spreading. I stare at my corset for hours now before I put it on." Her most famous tale, the novel *Two Serious Ladies*, was written at the rate of one line a day. (She also had a play on Broadway in 1953 called *In the Summer House*.)

Paul Bowles was born in New York in 1910, a son of old New England stock. Initially he pursued a career as a composer, studying with both **Aaron Copland** and **Virgil Thomson.** When he was twenty and in Paris, he met **Gertrude Stein** and **Alice B. Toklas,** after corresponding with them. Amused, Stein said, "I was sure from your letters that you were an elderly gentleman of at least seventy-five." To which Toklas added, "A highly eccentric elderly gentleman."

Paul once explained that as he and Jane became friends, they "used to spin fancies about how amusing it would be to get married and horrify everyone, above all, our respective families. From fantasy to actuality is often a much shorter distance than one imagines." The Bowleses traveled together often, both settling for a time in Tangier. There Jane fell in love with an illiterate Moroccan peasant woman known as Cherifa, whom she described as being "like a public monument . . . like a woman who sold coal under a certain tree in the Grand Socco or the man who sold spells and potions in the church courtyard." Loving Cherifa only made Jane more miserable. She drank a lot, took many pills, had high blood pressure and strokes, and died in a sanitarium in Malaga at the age of fifty-six. But Paul still lives in Tangier, in a three-room apartment with no telephone.

Above all, though, the wonderful thing about the Middagh Street house—and indeed, even, about the Bowleses' marriage—is the eagerness and willingness to fashion family where traditions would suggest otherwise. Carson McCullers, who wrote a fair amount about her life in Brooklyn, suggested that "comparing the Brooklyn that I know with Manhattan is like comparing a comfortable and complacent duenna to her more brilliant and neurotic sister." Brooklyn was a place of traditions, and the house, she wrote in *Vogue* in 1941, was in "a real neighborhood. I buy my coal from the man who lives next-door. And I am very curious about the old lady living on my right," a stingy rich woman who seemed to have "a mania for picking up stray, starving dogs." Indeed, it was the acceptance of individuality that seemed most striking to McCullers. And when one local described another as "just about the dirtiest woman in Brooklyn," McCullers quickly pointed out that she did not do so with malice. "Rather," she noted, "there was in it a quality of wondering pride. That is one of the things I love best about Brooklyn. Every one is not expected to be exactly like every one else." Certainly that was the beauty of it.

The Middagh Street house was furnished with what Paul Bowles described as "19th Century American Ugly" and ran, according to him, under Auden's direction: "He was exceptionally adept at getting the necessary money out of us when it was due." A cook and a maid tended their needs, and when meals were served, Auden, who sat at the head of the table, would announce, "We've got a roast and two vegetables, salad and savory, and there will be no political discussion." Auden tolerated no bickering at supper, and, according to Bowles, "he had enough of the don about him to keep us all in order." Papa Auden and the Five Little Poets.

It begins to sound like family, doesn't it? Ultimately, that might be the most useful way to think about gay and lesbian living—as forging a variety of intimate and familial ties, even when not sexual ones. Such a conception links the importance and magnitude of Hamilton's feelings for Laurens, Washington's bonds to his comrades, and Wald's ties to her coworkers. And the imperative of recognizing such a vibrant community is as visible in ACT UP's protest as in Randy Wicker's picket.

From here you might want to wander down to the Brooklyn Bridge and cross over into the next borough. Even if you don't, you might wish, for a moment, to imagine yourself there, looking back over your shoulder at the island of Manhattan. The poet **Hart Crane** tried to capture the view in a letter to his mother. "At twilight on a foggy evening, such as it was at this time," he wrote, "it is beyond description. Gradually the lights in the enormously tall buildings begin to flicker through the mist. There was a great cloud enveloping the top of the Woolworth tower, while below, in the river, were streaming reflections of myriad lights, continually being crossed by the twinkling mast and deck lights of little tugs scudding along, freight rafts, and occasional liners starting outward. Look far to your left toward Staten Island and there is the Statue of Liberty, with that remarkable lamp of hers that makes her seen for miles. And up at the right Brooklyn Bridge, the most superb piece of construction in the modern world, I'm sure, with strings of light crossing it like glowing worms as the L's and surface cars pass each other going and coming. It is particularly fine," he said, "to feel the greatest city in the world from enough distance, as I do here, to see its larger proportions."

A Final Thought

Before his death, **Vito Russo,** the activist, writer, and film historian, spoke in an interview with **Eric Marcus** about the tradition of gay history and the imperative of leaving a record, a legacy. He believed, he said, that after he died his book, *The Celluloid Closet*, would "be on a shelf someplace and that some sixteen-year-old kid who's going to be a gay activist will read my work and carry the ball from there. That'll happen. It happened with me. Harry Hay passed the ball to Mattachine, and Mattachine passed the ball to us. We've already started passing it on. There are young people in ACT UP who don't remember the *Cruising* demonstrations because they were kids. Now they're teenagers. They'll be here to fight over the more radical issues, like whether gay people have the right to adopt children, get married, teach in the public schools, and be open about being gay. And they'll be fighting those battles long after you and I are gone."

Each of us stands somewhere in that line: from Hay to Mattachine to Daughters of Bilitis to GLF to GAA to GMHC to ACT UP to Queer Nation and beyond. Each of us is a recipient of the dream, the hope, that has been passed along. But it is a dream that comes encumbered.

One: Know where it came from, and be buoyed by that past. Know that twenty years before today's kiss-in and thirty years before this afternoon's civil rights trial and one hundred years before tonight's drag ball, somebody else, not so different from you, was kissing and fighting and dancing and loving. Take strength in that.

Two: Carry the dream to a place none of us have ever been, have ever even imagined, so that when you pass it along, the dream is larger, the hope stronger, the possibility more real. And remember that the footsteps you leave will mark the path for someone else.

Three: Step out and enjoy the gift.

For Further Reading

The work in this book relies heavily on the efforts of other gay
and lesbian historians, archivists, and scholars. Much that is in
here, they found out first, and you may wish to hunt down
their more elaborate and detailed writings. I encourage you to
do so. You might begin with these: Arthur Bell's *Dancing the
Gay Lib Blues*; George Chauncey's *Gay New York*; John
D'Emilio's *Sexual Politics, Sexual Communities*; Martin Duberman's *Stonewall*, as well as his personal memoirs of the 1950s,
1960s, and 1970s; Martin Duberman, George Chauncey, and
Martha Vicinus's collection of essays, *Hidden from History*
(which includes, among other things, some of Eric Garber's
work on the Harlem Renaissance); Lillian Faderman's *Odd
Girls and Twilight Lovers*; Arnie Kantrowitz's *Under the Rainbow*; Jonathan Ned Katz's *Gay American History*; Eric Marcus's
Out in History; and Leigh Rutledge's *Book of Gay Lists*.

You might also want to look at some of the novels mentioned here, especially: Ann Bannon's *I Am a Woman*; James
Baldwin's *Giovanni's Room* and *Another Country*; Caleb Carr's
The Alienist; Andrew Holleran's *Nights in Aruba* and *Dancer
from the Dance*; John Rechy's *City of Night*; and George Whitmore's *Confessions of Danny Slocum*.

Illustration and Quotation Credits

All of the contemporary photographs reproduced in this book were taken by Mark Woods in 1996.

Use of the historical photographs was generously granted through the courtesy of the following organizations: The Schlesinger Library, Radcliffe College: 75, left and right; DC Moore Gallery: 51 (photo by George Platt Lynes); permission of Harcourt Brace & Company: 85 (photo by Sarony, from *Oscar Wilde Discovers America* by Lloyd Lewis and Henry Justin Smith, 1936, by Harcourt Brace & Company and renewed 1964 by Kathryn Lewis and Harold P. Smith); Ellen Shumsky/ Image Works: 20–21, 114; *Los Angeles Times* Archive, Special Collections, University Research Library, University of California at Los Angeles: 38; National Archive of the United States: 98; New York City Municipal Archives: 72, 317; courtesy of the New-York Historical Society, New York City: 286; The New York Public Library, Astor, Lenox and Tilden Foundations: Henry W. and Albert A. Berg Collection: 102, 247 (photo by Carl Van Vechten, courtesy estate executor, Joseph Solomon), International Gay Information Center Archives, Manuscripts and Archives Division: 135 (photo by Rich Wandel), Photographs and Prints Division, Schomburg Center for the Study of Black Culture: 251, 264, United States History, Local History and Genealogy Division: xiv–xv, 63, 129, 145, 268, 279; and the Staten Island Historical Society: 291 (photo by Alice Austen).

Quotation permission was also granted for "Foolish Man Blues," by Bessie Smith, © 1927 (renewed by Frank Music Corp.). All rights reserved. Reprinted by permission. "I Am What I Am," music and lyrics by Jerry Herman, © 1983 Jerry Herman. All rights controlled by Jerryco Music Co. Used by permission. Selections from *The Big Sea* © 1940, 1986, by Langston Hughes, and from *The Collected Poems of Langston Hughes*, edited by Arnold Rampersad, © 1994, Alfred Knopf, Inc. Selections from *W. H. Auden: Selected Poems* by W. H. Auden, edited by Edward Mendelson, © 1976, Random House, Inc. Passages from John Rechy's *City of Night*, 1963 by Grove/Atlantic, Inc.

Index

Asterisked page numbers denote tour sites particularly identified with the subject. *Italic* page numbers refer to photographs and maps.